The International Criminal Court and the Prosecution of Sitting Heads of State

Mattia Cacciatori

The International Criminal Court and the Prosecution of Sitting Heads of State

Democracy, Enforcement, and Symbolism of a Revolutionary Practice in International Politics

palgrave
macmillan

Mattia Cacciatori
Dept. of Pols, Languages & Int. Studies
University of Bath
Bath, UK

ISBN 978-3-031-54645-7 ISBN 978-3-031-54646-4 (eBook)
https://doi.org/10.1007/978-3-031-54646-4

This Palgrave Macmillan imprint is published by the registered company Springer Nature Switzerland AG.
The registered company address is: Gewerbestrasse 11, 6330 Cham, Switzerland

Paper in this product is recyclable.

Contents

Abbreviations

ARLPI	Acholi Religious Leaders' Peace Initiative (Uganda)
AU	African Union
BIA(s)	Bilateral Immunity Agreement(s)
CAR	Central African Republic
CPA	Comprehensive Peace Agreement (Sudan)
DRC	Democratic Republic of Congo
ECCC	Extraordinary Chambers in the Courts of Cambodia
ECK	Election Commission of Kenya
EU	European Union
FRONASA	Front for National Salvation (Uganda)
HAC	Humanitarian Aid Commission (Sudan)
HRW	Human Rights' Watch
ICC	International Criminal Court
ICJ	International Court of Justice
ICTR	International Criminal Tribunal for Rwanda
ICTY	International Criminal Tribunal for Former Yugoslavia
IO(s)	International Organization(s)
IR	International Relations
IRC	International Rescue Committee
ISIS	Islamic State for Iraq and Syria
JEM	Justice and Equality Movement (Sudan)
LRA	Lord's Resistance Army (Uganda)
MSF	Medicines Sans Frontiers
NATO	North Atlantic Treaty Organization
NCP	National Congress Party
NFSL	National Front for the Salvation of Libya
NGO(s)	Non-Governmental Organization(s)

NIF	National Islamic Front (Sudan)
NRA	National Resistance Army (Uganda)
NTC	National Transitional Council (Libya)
ODM	Orange Democratic Movement (Kenya)
OTP	Office of the Prosecutor
P-5	Permanent Members of the UNSC
PBOA	Public Benefits Organizations Act (Kenya)
PNU	Party of National Unity (Kenya)
PRA	Popular Resistance Army (Uganda)
R2P	Responsibility to Protect
RLP	Refugee Law Project
SC-SL	Special Court for Sierra Leone
SHoS	Sitting Head(s) of State
SLA	Sudan Liberation Army
SPLA	Sudan People Liberation Army
SPLM	Sudan People Liberation Movement
UK	United Kingdom
UN	United Nations
UNAMID	United Nations African Union Mission in Darfur
UNLF	Ugandan National Liberation Front
UNSC	United Nations' Security Council
UNSG	United Nations' Secretary General
UPDF	Uganda's People Defence Force
US	United States

List of Boxes

CHAPTER 1

Introduction: The Politics of Prosecuting Sitting Heads of State

It is the task of theologians to establish the limits of justice and injustice regarding the intrinsic goodness or wickedness of an act; it is the task of the observer of public life to establish the relationships of political justice and injustice, that is, of what is useful or harmful to society.
—Cesare Beccaria, On Crimes and Punishment *(1764)*

The hope that punishment will come for those who stain themselves with the most heinous crimes conceivable by humankind is so morally compelling, that writing a book about the political complexities that this pursuit entails is challenging. This is even truer when the alleged perpetrators are those in charge of ruling a country, or Sitting Head(s) of State (SHoS). After all, the notion that the law is equal for all is one of the main constitutive dogmas of democratic politics and is well-engrained in the conceptual architecture of modern statehood. In contemporary times, the dilemma of what to do with these powerful criminals has persisted since, at least, WWII. While the questions that relate to this idea have remained largely the same since, the institutional framework that underpins this practice has changed dramatically since the early 2000s. This has sparked a revived interest in the conceptual, theoretical, and policy issues relating thereto. It is no coincidence (and perhaps somehow worrying) that, in 2015, the most popular book borrowed from the United Nations (UN) library (the

M. Cacciatori, *The International Criminal Court and the Prosecution of Sitting Heads of State*,
https://doi.org/10.1007/978-3-031-54646-4_1

Dag Hammarskjold) was "Immunity of Heads of State and State Officials for International Crimes" by Ramona Pedretti.[1]

As a result of the establishment of the International Criminal Court (ICC) in 2002, the idea of prosecuting SHoS for genocide, war crimes, gross human rights violations, and the crime of aggression (since 2010)[2] was institutionalised internationally and permanently. Art.27 of the Rome Statute, the Treaty that underpinned the creation of the ICC, reads as follows

1. This Statute shall apply equally to all persons without any distinction based on official capacity. In particular, official capacity as a Head of State or Government, a member of a government or parliament, an elected representative or a government official shall in no case exempt a person from criminal responsibility under this Statute, nor shall it, in and of itself, constitute a ground for reduction of sentence.
2. Immunities or special procedural rules which may attach to the official capacity of a person, whether under national or international law, shall not bar the Court from exercising its jurisdiction over such a person.[3]

While the legal and institutional provisions seem to be clear,[4] the practice of prosecuting SHoS remains under scrutiny because, as every other international organisation (IO) the ICC requires state cooperation to function in most cases. This has raised numerous questions about the effective independence of the Court, its objectivity, and its politicisation. Many explanations have been forwarded across the discipline of international relations (IR) as to why states cooperate with IOs, as will be shown in the remainder of this Chapter. But the idea of asking SHoS to cooperate

[1] Alison Flood, 'Most-Browsed Book in the UN Library in 2015? A Primer on War-Crime Immunity', the Guardian, January 8, 2016, http://www.theguardian.com/books/2016/jan/08/un-library-united-nations-most-2015-war-crime-immunity-heads-of-state-officials-international-pedretti.

[2] Patrick S. Wegner, *The International Criminal Court in Ongoing Intrastate Conflicts: Navigating the Peace-Justice Divide* (Cambridge University Press, 2015).

[3] Mahnoush H. Arsanjani, 'The Rome Statute of the International Criminal Court', *The American Journal of International Law* 93, no. 1 (1 January 1999): Art.27.

[4] Although it will be shown later in the book how several states challenged even the legal provisions that concern SHoS prosecutions.

with an institution tasked specifically with their prosecution sounds, *prima facie*, impracticable, delusional, and irrational at best. And yet, the ICC has been directly involved in this practice in several situations: the issuing of the arrest warrants for Omar al Bashir in Sudan, Muammar Gaddafi in Libya, and Vladimir Putin in Russia, the summons to appear for Uhuru Kenyatta in Kenya, along with murky negotiations with Ugandan President Yoweri Museveni and the Syrian quagmire involving Bashar al Assad. So far, the ICC has been unsuccessful in this domain. Al Bashir has evaded prosecution for a decade, before being deposed by an internal *coup d'etat*; Gaddafi was killed before he could witness trial; and Uhuru Kenyatta enjoyed a boost in popularity that culminated with his election as President of Kenya and coincided with the ICC operations. Meanwhile Russia and China vetoed the resolution to refer Assad to the Court and, in Russia, prospects of seeing Putin behind bars seem extremely slim. The book explores these cases and also investigates the dynamics that the ICC's involvement in Uganda entailed, because Uganda is generally understood as a situation in which (at least initially) the Court and the sitting government cooperated following the Prosecutor's decision not to investigate the Ugandan President. *What is important, from a political perspective, is to ask what are the main political challenges that the ICC faces when it attempts at prosecuting SHoS. In addition to this, it is also necessary to question what effects such attempts contributed to producing, both for the countries that hosted the investigations and internationally.* These are the main objectives of the book, which are often lost in discussions of peremptory norms and moral imperatives. The political challenges that this book aims at discussing are essentially three, and are encapsulated in three paradoxes that underpin the analysis offered here. These are: the democracy paradox, the enforcement of justice paradox, and the symbolism paradox. The conceptual architecture that stems from these instances is explored in Chap. 2 of this project.

Before starting to venture on the contents of the book, it is important to introduce three caveats to ease the understanding of its intentions. First, the book relates specifically to the practice of prosecuting SHoS, it doesn't examine the ICC in its entirety as an institution. It may very well be that the ICC is effective in some domains that this book doesn't explore, but this is beyond the scope of the research proposed here. Second, the book is not a legal text. As such, explorations of the legal debates that surround the practice of prosecuting SHoS, despite being introduced in this Chapter and referenced throughout the work, are largely left to legal scholars. When the book discusses legal implications, these are always related to the politicisation of the legal ground by states, policy-makers, and institutions, to highlight how politics has deeply shaped even the legal dimension of the practice under scrutiny. Third, and final, every case presented in the book would deserve a single research project. And in fact, several manuscripts that deal with specific cases have been produced in the last 15 years and are often referenced throughout the Chapters. The book only focuses on those aspects of these cases that are considered as particularly relevant to debate the political implications of the practice of prosecuting SHoS.

This Chapter is organised in seven main parts. After this brief introduction, it focuses on exploring the legal perspectives on the practice of prosecuting SHoS, and what the Rome Statute specifically postulates in relation to it. In section 3 the Chapter reviews the debate around the politicisation of SHoS prosecutions, to justify the idea that the main challenges that the practice faces are in fact political in nature. In the fourth section the Chapter introduces the peace and/or justice debate, which underpins many of the debates around the legitimacy, efficacy, and desirability of SHoS prosecutions. In section 5 the Chapter unpacks the saliency of the justice versus order debate—mainly focusing on the revolutionary nature of the practice as *de facto* challenging two of the most established norms in international politics: sovereignty and non-intervention. Section 6 provides a structure of the book.

Accountability and Immunities for SHoS: The Legal Perspective

There seems to be a general acceptance that perpetrators of the most serious international crimes will be subject to investigation independently from their position, or where those crimes are committed.[5] Under customary international law, however, there are two types of immunities for government officials that can be considered as potential impediments for prosecutions: functional or diplomatic immunities (*rationae materiae*), and personal immunities (*rationae personae*). Both these immunities shield

[5] Joanne Foakes, 'Immunity for International Crimes?', *Developments in the Law on Prosecuting Heads of State in Foreign Courts*, 2011, 2.

government officials from jurisdiction in foreign national tribunals and,[6] as Foakes noted, "[…] both types [of immunity] are based on notions as to the independence and equality of states and the resulting view that no state should claim jurisdiction over another. Both belong to the state, not the individual, and can be waived by the state should it choose to do so".[7]

In general terms, these provisions must be related to the ability of the officials to exercise their governmental duties without being subject to another state's jurisdiction, to secure the peaceful conduct of inter-state cooperation. Functional or diplomatic immunities have three main characteristics. They:

1. protect officials indefinitely for conduct committed as part of their official duties in their official capacity,
2. apply even after the official has abdicated his or her official position with that government, so even former officials can invoke functional immunity, however
3. The immunity attaches only to acts committed while the person served in his or her official capacity.[8]

It is commonly accepted however that these three characteristics don't shield perpetrators from prosecution in case of international crimes such as genocide, crimes against humanity, gross human rights violations, and the crime of aggression.[9] This is because such acts can never be considered as being part of governmental duties towards citizens.

Personal immunities, on the other hand, concern only a small group of senior government officials including SHoS, Heads of Government, Foreign Ministers, and diplomats. This kind of immunity is an extensive provision that is generalisable enough to cover both public and private

[6] Dapo Akande and Sangeeta Shah, 'Immunities of State Officials, International Crimes, and Foreign Domestic Courts', *European Journal of International Law* 21, no. 4 (2010): 815–16.

[7] Foakes, 'Immunity for International Crimes?', 4.

[8] Iverson, 'Jen, Head of State Immunity Is Not the Same as State Immunity: A Response to the African Union's Position on Article 98 of the ICC Statute', 2012 EJIL: Talk!, accessed 30 November 2015, http://www.ejiltalk.org/head-of-state-immunity-is-not-the-same-as-state-immunity-a-response-to-the-african-unions-position-on-article-98-of-the-icc-statute/.

[9] Salvatore Zappalà, 'Do Heads of State in Office Enjoy Immunity from Jurisdiction for International Crimes? The Ghaddafi Case before the French Cour de Cassation', *European Journal of International Law* 12, no. 3 (2001): 601.

acts, and includes immunity from criminal prosecution. Personal immunities attach to these official status or offices, and shield individuals for acts conducted as part of their official duties, as well as any other private acts.[10] The rationale for personal immunity

> [...] is to prevent a foreign State from exercising and even abusing jurisdiction over another State's high-ranking official, to facilitate the smooth conduct of foreign relations and cooperation between States, and to allow the sending State to function properly under the leadership of its senior representatives.[11]

According to the International Court of Justice (ICJ), personal immunity is enjoyed by "Heads of State, heads of government, foreign ministers and, possibly, a limited category of other very high-ranking state representatives". However, unlike functional immunity, it is still contested whether personal immunities cover high-ranked officials even for the most serious crimes in the international arena. While still debated, it is undeniable that a norm in favour of the erosion of the idea of personal immunity is emerging in international jurisprudence, especially when these individuals are facing international tribunals. In fact, a plethora of international tribunals emerged in the 1990s as a response to what Samantha Power described as the "Age of Genocide".[12] The norm underpinning SHoS prosecutions, has emerged in international jurisprudence, for instance, in the arrest warrant case at the ICJ, the Charles Taylor case before the Special Court for Sierra Leone (SC-SL), the Augusto Pinochet case before the British House of Lords, the statuses of the International Criminal Tribunal for Former Yugoslavia (ICTY) and the International Criminal Tribunal for Rwanda (ICTR) and, as will be shown in the next section, in the Rome Statute of the ICC. It must be noted that all these expressions of international law are purpose-built for the prosecution of crimes that are often committed by state officials in pursuance of state policy. As such, Sukhija noted that "[...][t]his recent trend in international criminal prosecutions of Heads

[10] Akande and Shah, 'Immunities of State Officials, International Crimes, and Foreign Domestic Courts', 409.

[11] Iverson, 'Head of State Immunity Is Not the Same as State Immunity'.

[12] Samantha Power, *A Problem from Hell: America and the Age of Genocide* (Perseus Books Group, 2013).

of State shows that derogation from norms requiring personal immunities is permitted for international crimes in international courts".[13]

The major differences between the two immunities relate to their applicability and rationales. If personal immunity is more linked to the notions of "dignity and majesty of sovereigns" and their equation with the state itself when it comes to external relations, functional or diplomatic immunities apply to all former officials of any rank and is based on the idea that an individual should not be held responsible for acts that belong to the state. In short, despite its historical evolution, the idea that all individuals allegedly responsible for international crimes such as genocide, war crimes, gross human rights violations, and the crime of aggression should be held accountable doesn't seem to contrast with personal or functional immunities. This understanding is based on the idea that these crimes are of such magnitude that independently from the position of the alleged perpetrators and from domestic jurisprudence, should be contained via prosecution.

The Rome Statute on the Prosecution of SHoS

The scope of the ICC, according to the preamble of the Rome Statute is to put an end to impunity for the perpetrators of the most serious crimes of concern to the international community *in toto*.[14] Such crimes, as defined by Art. 5 of the Statute, are genocide, war crimes, and crimes against humanity. Since 2010, for the states that ratified the Kampala Amendment, the ICC also has jurisdiction on the crime of aggression. To unpack the scope of the Court it is crucial to familiarise with two provisions of international jurisprudence known as *jus cogens* and *obligatio erga omnes*. While deeply intertwined, "*jus cogens* refers to the legal status of certain international crimes, and *obligatio erga omnes* pertains to the legal implications arising out of a certain crime's characterization as *jus cogens*".[15] More specifically, the term *jus cogens* is used in international law to encapsulate the idea of crimes of such magnitude that they need to be addressed, regardless of where or by whom they were committed.[16] So everybody should be aware of the norms that regulate the definitions and procedures

[13] Iverson, 'Head of State Immunity Is Not the Same as State Immunity'.

[14] Rome Statute of the International Criminal Court (last amended 2010), 17 July 1998.

[15] M. Cherif Bassiouni, 'International Crimes: "Jus Cogens" and "Obligatio Erga Omnes"', *Law and Contemporary Problems*, 1996, 63.

[16] Larry May, 'Le Norme Dello Jus Cogens e Il Diritto Penale Internazionale', *Ars Interpretandi*, 2001, 223–24.

to cope with such crimes. This should also mean that every actor in the international arena considers them as binding. According to such interpretations these norms are not necessarily consensual, and for this reason they hold a universal value.[17] Because of the gravity, magnitude, and universality of the crimes it was designed to cover, *jus cogens* addresses violations considered *erga omnes*, or concerning the entirety of the international arena, by not making any distinction among perpetrators. Bassiouni noted how

> [...] legal obligations which arise from the higher status of such crimes include the duty to prosecute or extradite, the non-applicability of any immunities up to and including Heads of State, the non-applicability of 'obedience to superior orders (save as mitigation for sentence), the universal application of such obligations whether in time of peace or war, their non-derogation under 'states of emergency', and universal jurisdiction over perpetrators of such crimes.[18]

For this reason, and for states that ratified the Rome Statute or when the United Nations' Security Council (UNSC) refers a situation to the Court, the ICC holds personal jurisdiction over every person over the age of 18, regardless of their status, of the domestic immunities they might benefit of, or their official capacities. This consequently means that every SHoS, member of the government, military official, and civilian is subject to the jurisdiction of the ICC.

While Art.27 of the Rome Statute, mentioned earlier, seems to clarify that legally the Court can prosecute SHoS, there exists a tension with another article of the Statute, Art. 98(1), which postulates that:

1. The Court may not proceed with a request for surrender or assistance which would require the requested State to act inconsistently with its obligations under international law with respect to the State or diplomatic immunity of a person or property of a third State, unless the Court can first obtain the cooperation of that third State for the waiver of the immunity.
2. The Court may not proceed with a request for surrender which would require the requested State to act inconsistently with its obli-

[17] Jerzy Sztucki, *Jus Cogens and the Vienna Convention on the Law of Treaties: A Critical Appraisal* (Springer-Verlag, 1974).

[18] Bassiouni, 'International Crimes', 63.

gations under international agreements pursuant to which the consent of a sending State is required to surrender a person of that State to the Court.[19]

Two interpretations can be advanced to minimise the tensions between Art.27 and Art.98 of the Rome Statute. First, if the investigation of the ICC was triggered by a referral of the UNSC, the state under investigation should be treated as a state party to the Rome Statute.[20] This should reduce the potential for states to invoke their non-membership to the Rome Statute as a justification for committing the crimes covered by the ICC. The second interpretation is that, when Art. 98 seems to grant "state and diplomatic immunity" this doesn't include absolute personal immunity because

1. customary international law no longer accords Heads of State absolute immunities even before international tribunals; or
2. customary international law norms regarding accountability for international crimes trump customary norms to provide personal immunities.[21]

Despite various interpretations of the relationship between Art.27 and Art.98, two things are evident: first, the ICC advances the idea of a normative shift aimed at formalising the rejection of any kind of immunity for the gravest crimes in international politics. Second, the tensions between Art.27 and Art.98 are likely to be exploited by those states who are reluctant to cooperate with the ICC. In light of this last consideration, questioning the political nature of the ICC is even more crucial.

Prosecuting SHoS: Law or Politics?

Before proceeding any further, it is necessary to clarify that international law, as a concept and a *praxis*, is treated in the book as a constant bargain between the international community, states, perpetrators, and victims. This view is sustained by the absence of an organ that can enforce

[19] Arsanjani, 'The Rome Statute of the International Criminal Court', Art.98.

[20] Iverson, 'Head of State Immunity Is Not the Same as State Immunity'.

[21] Dapo Akande, 'A Single Comment—International Criminal Court Forum', 2014, accessed 2 July 2015, http://iccforum.com/forum/permalink/93/4084.

international law on states, that is a world government.[22] This means that the enforcement of international laws and standards is always subject to political calculations by both abiding and non-abiding states. So that the decision to invoke international law in specific contexts and not others is subjugated to political demands, just as much as cooperation with institutions of international law is subdued to similar dynamics. Precisely because of this permanent condition of bargaining, one of the most obstinate criticisms that has been moved towards international law is that it only prosecutes the losing side of conflicts – or that the institutions tasked with its implementation are puppets in the hands of powerful states. This idea, encapsulated in the term "Victor's Justice", has underpinned several IR approaches to the operations of international tribunals. Evidently, the belief that the international community can effectively hold accountable SHoS is designed to challenge this conception. However, it is important to remember that Victor's Justice, before being an ideological standpoint, can be considered as an operational necessity. This is the reason why the Rome Statute deals extensively with the notion of sovereign statehood, and it does so in the following terms. First, the Statute postulates that the Court can intervene only in those situations when states are unwilling or unable to investigate or prosecute the crimes which fall under the jurisdiction of the ICC. Domestic inability to prosecute crimes is characterised by "[a] total or substantial collapse or unavailability of its national judicial system, the state is unable to obtain the accused or the necessary evidence and testimony or otherwise unable to carry out its proceedings".

The fact that the Statute differentiates inability from unwillingness presupposes that the former applies to those states that are willing to prosecute but practically unable to do so. Matters get much thornier when the ICC must deal with unwilling states. Art. 17 of the Statute identifies three kinds of unwillingness: the first is that the investigation was designed to shield the person concerned from criminal responsibility for the crimes covered by the Rome Statute. The second is that "there has been an unjustified delay in the proceedings which in the circumstances is inconsistent with an intent to bring the person concerned to justice", and the third

[22] See for instance Gerry Simpson, 'Juridical Investigations: Martin Wight as International Lawyer', *British Influences on International Law, 1915–2015*, 14 July 2016, 484–96.

regards partiality and bias of the proceedings.[23] It seems plausible to speculate that when the Court attempts at prosecuting a SHoS, this is not going to be enthusiastic about it. This consideration sustains the idea that in the absence of a legitimate coercive power to enforce legal provisions even when states are reluctant to cooperate, international law is not law. It is politics. This is particularly evident when we look at the exercise of jurisdictional competence, as defined especially by Articles 12–14 of the Rome Statute. This jurisdiction is limited by certain preconditions, in which a situation: (1) Is referred to the Prosecutor by a state party to the treaty, (2) Is referred to the Prosecutor by the UNSC or, (3) Is under an investigation initiated by the Prosecutor *proprio motu*.[24]

Ideally the first trigger was set up in order for states to signal the existence of a humanitarian problem in *another* state. Because authoritarian regimes are not likely to publicly broadcast their criminal activities, this mechanism was placed to act as a "red-light" for humanitarian crises. The second mechanism through which the ICC can initiate an investigation is through a referral by the UNSC. This mechanism allows the Court to investigate humanitarian crises even on the grounds of non-parties to the Rome Statute. The existence of this "trigger" underlines the fact that, while the ICC does not have universal jurisdiction, there are mechanisms that can generate jurisdiction over states that are not part of the ICC. Investigations *proprio motu*, on the other hand, happen when a state party to the ICC comes under scrutiny, and the Office of the Prosecutor (OTP) believes there is enough evidence to commence an investigation even without any sort of referral.

The mechanisms above signal that Court's actions are heavily politicisable from the very beginning. As for states' referrals, states started referring themselves, in a process that has been later described as "self-referral". Most ICC investigations have initiated in this manner. The political problem posed by these self-referrals is that they are likely to be motivated by the desire to expose the crimes of non-governmental actors. In fact, prosecuting just one side of a conflict (as happened in Uganda), legitimises the sitting government by *de facto* proclaiming its innocence. As for UNSC

[23] Lijun Yang, 'On the Principle of Complementarity in the Rome Statute of the International Criminal Court', *Chinese Journal of International Law* 4, no. 1 (June 1, 2005): 121–22.

[24] See Rome Statute of the International Criminal Court, Art. 13; cfr. Jordan J. Paust, *The Reach of ICC Jurisdiction Over Non-Signatory Nationals*, SSRN Scholarly Paper (Rochester, NY: Social Science Research Network, 2000), 1–2.

referrals, because of the ways in which decisions are made within the Council, this mechanism is interwoven with the international climate that underpins international politics. So that the volatility of relationships among the P-5 directly affects the Court and its possibility of intervention. At the diametrical sides of this spectrum lie the warrant of arrest released for Gaddafi following UN resolution 1970 and the Russian and Chinese vetoes to refer Syria to the Court. Finally, investigations *proprio motu* bear questions related to selection bias, and equanimity in the selection of cases, as happened in Kenya. These trigger mechanisms are closely related with the three paradoxes that the book introduces in Chap. 2, and that will constitute the conceptual underpinning of the empirical analysis offered in Chaps. 3, 4, and 5. The starting point is to acknowledge the fact that political dynamics shape both the Court's ability to initiate an investigation and its capability to following it through. Given these political starting points, considering prosecutions of SHoS as a political matter more than a legal one is both difficult and necessary: difficult because it forces commentators to move beyond questions of legal enforcement to doubt the morality and legitimacy of the practice. Necessary because if commentators and policy-makers continue to treat prosecutions of SHoS as ontologically compelling, the political complexities that characterise them, and the undesired consequences that they might contribute to produce, are likely to be always buried by discussions of abstract moral imperatives.

Prosecuting SHoS: Peace and/or Justice?

By claiming that international law is not disentangled from international politics, the question should be what happens when the ICC attempts at doing the impossible – prosecuting a SHoS. Approaching this question from a political standpoint requires going back to the peace and/or justice dilemma. This has shaped the discourse on the mechanisms and policies that societies should redress gross human rights violations[25] and, broadly speaking, is underpinned by two schools of thought: pragmatism and legalism. The case against ICC's prosecutions of SHoS is rooted deeply in the pragmatist wing of the pragmatist-legalist dichotomy, which argues that prosecutions should not take place in fragile contexts. Pragmatist

[25] Linda Marie Keller, 'The False Dichotomy of Peace versus Justice and the International Criminal Court', *Hague Justice Journal* 3, no. 1 (2008): 25.

arguments forcefully emerged after the Third Wave of Democratisation in South America and Eastern Europe,[26] which were infused with the idea that punishment for gross human rights violation should be postponed during situations of delicate political transformations.[27] These experiences were characterised by the promulgation of amnesty laws, which aimed to minimise the divisive impact of trials and for the establishment of several truth-telling mechanisms to uncover the details of the atrocities.[28]

The major line of justification for these prosecutorial *vacuums* has been synthesised by the idea that "[...] justice, in its prosecutorial acceptation, could be more pursuable in a later stage of the transitional process, when institutions are stronger".[29] Despite attempts to quantitatively argue in favour of forgive and forget approaches,[30] pragmatist strategies have been often perceived as "state-sponsored repression of the past"[31] and not being able to fulfil the aim of producing solid democracies.[32] The emergence of contemporary pragmatist views preceded the creation of the ICC by at least 20 years, but remains relevant due to the inherently divisive nature of the manifestations of international criminal justice, such as international tribunals. These manifestations, of which the ICC has been considered the institutional zenith,[33] are criticised by pragmatists for being an expansion

[26] Samuel P. Huntington, *The Third Wave: Democratization in the Late 20th Century* (University of Oklahoma Press, 2012).

[27] Luc Huyse, 'Justice after Transition: On the Choices Successor Elites Make in Dealing with the Past', *Law & Social Inquiry* 20, no. 1 (1995): 53–56.

[28] See for instance Louise Mallinder, 'Global Comparison of Amnesty Laws', SSRN Scholarly Paper (Rochester, NY: Social Science Research Network, 1 August 2009), http://papers.ssrn.com/abstract=1586831.

[29] Leslie Vinjamuri and Jack Snyder, 'Advocacy and Scholarship in the Study of International War Crime Tribunals and Transitional Justice', *Annual Review of Political Science* 7, no. 1 (June 2004): 345–46.

[30] See for instance Peter McCold in Heather Strang and John Braithwaite, *Restorative Justice and Civil Society* (Cambridge University Press, 2001), 157–67.

[31] Guillermo O'Donnell and Philippe C. Schmitter, *Tentative Conclusions about Uncertain Democracies, Volume 4, Transitions from Authoritarian Rule* (Baltimore: Johns Hopkins University Press, 1986).

[32] Mark Arenhövel, 'Democratisation and Transitional Justice', *Democratisation* 15, no. 3 (2008): 570–71.

[33] Thomas W Smith, 'Moral Hazard and Humanitarian Law: The International Criminal Court and the Limits of Legalism', *International Politics* 39, no. 2 (June 1, 2002): 175–76; John M. Czarnetzky and Ronald J. Rychlak, 'Empire of Law: Legalism and the International Criminal Court, An', *Notre Dame L. Rev.* 79 (2003): 55.

of Westernised justice which is alien to local realities and because they favour an international "sense of justice achieved" over the needs of the societies directly affected by the gross human rights violations.[34]

Diametrically opposed to the pragmatist approach legalism has, since the mid-1990s, potently argued against the creation of impunity gaps for gross human rights violations.[35] The main tenet advanced by legalists can be summarised in the idea that there is no peace and no reconciliation without punitive justice.[36] Legalist literature has theorised that the prosecution of perpetrators of gross human rights violations can redeem the suffering of victims. Furthermore, according to this strand of literature, punitive justice can have a significant effect on both preventing and deterring future reiterations of violations, and serve as an educational example of rule of law for societies in transition to democracies, authoritarian regimes, and failed states.[37] This approach manifested in the proliferation of the UN-sponsored *ad-hoc* tribunals in the mid-1990s, such as the ICTY, the ICTR, the SC-SL, and the Extraordinary Chambers in the Courts of Cambodia (ECCC).[38] The legalist approach has not been immune to criticism, which developed from the assumption that the practices of such tribunals reduce the complexity of reckoning with a past of gross human rights violations to a mere transaction between international society and the offender, characterising the victims as mere recipients of their prosecutorial efforts.[39]

One of the issues that emerges potently from the dissection of this dichotomy is that both pragmatists and legalists end up focusing on the challenges and unintended effects of prosecutions in the international

[34] Charles Chernor Jalloh, 'Africa and the International Criminal Court: Collision Course or Cooperation', *North Carolina Central Law Review* 34 (2012 [2011]): 210–11.

[35] Geneviève Parent, 'Reconciliation and Justice after Genocide: A Theoretical Exploration,' *Genocide Studies and Prevention* 5, no. 3 (December 1, 2010): 282.

[36] Parent, 'Reconciliation and Justice after Genocide', 283.

[37] Vinjamuri and Snyder, 'Advocacy and Scholarship in the Study of International War Crime Tribunals and Transitional Justice'; Cécile Aptel, 'Prosecutorial Discretion at the ICC and Victims' Right to Remedy Narrowing the Impunity Gap,' *Journal of International Criminal Justice* 10, no. 5 (December 1, 2012): 1357–1375; Clark, 'Hybridity, Holism, and Traditional Justice,' 765.

[38] Cesare Romano, 'Proliferation of International Judicial Bodies: The Pieces of the Puzzle, The', *NYUJ Int'l L. & Pol.* 31 (1998): 710.

[39] Charles Villa-Vicencio, 'The Reek of Cruelty and the Quest for Healing: Where Retributive and Restorative Justice Meet', *Journal of Law and Religion* 14, no. 1 (January 1, 1999): 166.

arena. However, while pragmatists can be considered as mainly focusing on the domestic outcomes of redressing gross violations,[40] legalists seem to be more concerned on the symbolic value of prosecuting individuals for those crimes for the broader international community.[41] Despite this marked distinction, it is clear that both approaches do not simply refer to the effectiveness of prosecuting criminals, but rather include a multiplicity of discourses about democracy, deterrence, norm promotion, and interventionism. As it will be shown in the remainder of the book, questions about the prioritisation of peace over justice, or justice over peace, are not limited to the academic sphere of the debate but seem to inform the approach of policy-makers to the thorny cases presented in the next Chapters. These will be recurring themes of debate among political elites when they attempt to justify either the necessity of prosecuting a SHoS to establish the rule of law, or the urgency of postponing (and even abandoning) the idea of a criminal proceeding to create the preconditions for peace. As such, the peace and/or justice debate continues to be a crucial point of reference for the practice of prosecuting SHoS.

Prosecuting SHoS: International Justice and/or Order?

The justice versus order debate can essentially be considered as an elevation of the peace and/or justice dilemma, mainly treated as an intra-state issue, to the international level. The starting point of this discussion is that the ICC has been described as shaping the course of domestic policy formation,[42] influencing the construction or de-construction of international norms,[43] and altering the *status quo* of the international arena

[40] James D. Meernik, Angela Nichols, and Kimi L. King, 'The Impact of International Tribunals and Domestic Trials on Peace and Human Rights after Civil War', *International Studies Perspectives* 11, no. 4 (2010): 309.

[41] Sim B. Sitkin and Robert J. Bies, *The Legalistic Organization* (Sage Publications, 1994), 83.

[42] Michael A. Newton, 'Comparative Complementarity: Domestic Jurisdiction Consistent with the Rome Statute of the International Criminal Court', *Military Law Review* 167 (2001): 23–24.

[43] Judith Kelley, 'Who Keeps International Commitments and Why? The International Criminal Court and Bilateral Nonsurrender Agreements', *American Political Science Review* 101, no. 03 (2007): 575–76.

towards a more interventionist understanding thereof.[44] Order and justice can be considered as desired dichotomic outcomes of different normative understandings of international politics. What norms are and how they influence intra-state behaviour has been subject to widespread debate in IR. From Richard Morris' assumption that "[n]orms are generally accepted, sanctioned prescriptions for, or prohibitions against, others' behavior, belief, or feeling"[45] to Robin Williams' idea that "[n]orms [...] are rules of conduct; they specify what should and should not be done by various actors"[46] the debate is still ongoing. However, there seems to be a general agreement on the definition (that this book shares) of norms as "standards of appropriate behaviour for actors with a given identity".[47] This study will elucidate how the addition of identity is crucial in understanding both Western pushes for accountability, and the resistance that non-Western actors are manifesting towards the norms underpinning the ICC.

The fact that the Court has the potential to influence norm formation and erosion seems to be a shared assumption among those who supported its creation. Antonio Cassese, in the wake of the establishment of the ICC, wrote that "[...]the International Criminal Court is destined to flesh out and bring into effect those peremptory norms of international law which safeguard such fundamental values as human dignity, the respect for life and limb of innocent persons, and the protection of ethnic, religious or racial groups".[48] There is little doubt that the ICC's prosecution of SHoS challenges concepts which have traditionally been associated with state sovereignty, such as the administration of punitive justice. In this sense, the ICC can be perceived as pushing the boundaries of international politics by attempting to erode the two interrelated normative pillars that Hedley Bull described as the most fundamental: sovereignty and

[44] Steven C. Roach, *Governance, Order, and the International Criminal Court: Between Realpolitik and a Cosmopolitan Court: Between Realpolitik and a Cosmopolitan Court* (OUP Oxford, 2009), 4.

[45] Richard T. Morris, 'A Typology of Norms', *American Sociological Review* 21, no. 5 (1956): 610.

[46] Robin M. Williams, 'Social Order and Social Conflict', *Proceedings of the American Philosophical Society* 114, no. 3 (1970): 24.

[47] Martha Finnemore and Kathryn Sikkink, "International Norm Dynamics and Political Change," *International Organization* 52, no. 04 (1998): 891.

[48] Antonio Cassese, 'A Big Step Forward for International Justice', *Crimes of War Project Magazine*, 2003, 8.

non-intervention.[49] These norms essentially establish "a doctrinal mechanism to express the outer limits of permissible influence that one state may properly exert upon another".[50] They, in other terms, reassert the notion that states are, and are likely to continue to be, the most important actors in international politics. Questions about what is permissible, and when the international community may infringe the sovereign statehood of a state, are crucial for understanding the practice of prosecuting SHoS, and these are necessarily related to the dichotomy between order and justice.

Certain authors, broadly described as "pluralists", like Bull, Robert Jackson, and James Mayall, have postulated that states should act as functional instruments to limit and curtail the spread of excessive disorder in the ontological condition of systemic anarchy,[51] an approach that emphasises the saliency of sovereignty as the benchmark for "the cultivation of political difference and distinctness".[52] These scholars contend that the promotion of universal values, on which no clear consensus has been reached among states, can jeopardise and hamper efforts to achieve a stable, peaceful, and diverse international community.[53] This conceptualisation of international politics implies that certain kinds humanitarian intervention constitute a violation of the basic principles of order in international politics, especially when they encompass the international use of force.[54] The reasoning behind this prioritises the need for order in ontological conditions of ethical diversity and anarchy, which might be undermined in the pursuance of universal ideals and norms.[55] It seems only natural that SHoS prosecutions by the ICC are likely to be perceived as actions that risk destabilising order at the international level by claiming

[49] Hedley Bull, 'The Anarchical Society: A Study of World Order', *World Politics*, 1977, 238.

[50] Richard A. Falk, 'United States and the Doctrine of Nonintervention in the Internal Affairs of Independent States, The', *Howard LJ* 5 (1959): 159.

[51] On this see for instance: Bull, "The Anarchical Society," 13; Jackson, *The Global Covenant*, chap. 1; James Mayall, *Nationalism and International Society* (Cambridge University Press, 1990), chaps. 1–2.

[52] Barry Buzan, 'The English School: An Underexploited Resource in IR', *Review of International Studies* 27, no. 03 (July 2001): 478.

[53] Bull, 'The Anarchical Society', 152–53.

[54] Nicholas J. Wheeler, *Saving Strangers: Humanitarian Intervention in International Society: Humanitarian Intervention in International Society* (Oxford University Press, 2000), 11.

[55] Bull, 'The Anarchical Society', 153.

that SHoS can be prosecuted by an international actor, despite the fact that the Court only acts on states that ratified the Rome Statute or through an UNSC referral. This is even truer for those instances in which the ICC acts in cooperation with international military interventions.

Other scholars, sometimes described as "solidarists", argue that derogations of the principles of sovereignty and non-intervention can be justified in exceptional, mainly humanitarian, circumstances. Barry Buzan noted how there is a "[…]possibility of shared moral norms underpinning a more expansive and almost inevitably, more interventionist, understanding of international order".[56] If for pluralists the prioritisation of order over justice seems like a *condicio sine qua non* for the existence of an interdependent international community, solidarists have directed their efforts at finding some common ground between sovereignty and more interventionist practices to safeguard human rights across the globe. The defining character of the solidarist view of international politics is one in which "[s]tates accept not only a moral responsibility to protect the security of their own citizens, but also the wider one of guardianship of human rights everywhere".[57] As a testament of how revolutionary such an idea is, Linklater labelled such propositions as pure assaults on the Westphalian order.[58]

There seems to be a tendency among solidarists to consider the ICC as an expression of the institutionalisation of the enforcement of human rights law and, therefore, as a manifestation of solidarism in international politics.[59] The debate between these schools of thought continues to influence political discussions about the viability and legitimacy of ICC interventions, and questions about order and justice at the international level lie at the heart of many of the debates that emerge from the dissection of the cases presented in this book. In other terms, if states perceive the necessity of maintaining order despite calls for justice, they are likely to

[56] Barry Buzan, *From International to World Society?: English School Theory and the Social Structure of Globalisation* (Cambridge University Press, 2004), 478.

[57] Wheeler, *Saving Strangers*, 12.

[58] Andrew Linklater, 'Men and Citizens in International Relations', *Review of International Studies* 7, no. 01 (1981): 34–35.

[59] John Williams, 'Pluralism, Solidarism and the Emergence of World Society in English School Theory', *International Relations* 19, no. 1 (2005): 19–20; Jason Ralph, 'International Society, the International Criminal Court and American Foreign Policy', *Review of International Studies* 31, no. 01 (2005): 275.

antagonise ICC prosecutions of SHoS. If, on the other hand, they perceive the necessity of prioritising justice, then they would be willing to sacrifice order to achieve it. However, if the debate between those support and those who antagonise the legitimacy of SHoS prosecutions is still ongoing, this must mean that there is currently no consensus on the norm or the means for its enforcement. This, in turn, renders the Court and its operations against SHoS rhetorical spaces for these two views to clash.

A final consideration emerges from the speculation on the consequences of attempting to enforce norms that some perceive to be universal but seem to pertain only to a group of states in international society, usually Western ones. In this book, it will be shown, how SHoS prosecutions by the ICC have attracted considerable non-Western resistance and this has manifested in events that can be read as a prolongation of the "third-world revolts against the West".[60] According to Bull, these unfolded in three moments: the first was characterised by an anti-colonial struggle for independence and sovereign equality between the 1940s and the 1960s; the second, from the 1970s through the 1980s, can be characterised as a struggle for liberation from racial inequalities and economic discrimination; and the third was a cultural liberation to reaffirm traditional and indigenous cultures in the third world.[61] Despite their diverse political contexts, these three waves of contestation had the common feature of challenging a sense of self-assurance expressed by Western powers.[62] Bull's specific proposition of a potential revolt against the West has been widely overlooked in contemporary discussions on the significance of resistance claims for international politics (with some notable exceptions, like Jason Ralph). Ralph himself outlined five characteristics which define third-world revolts against the West:

> ...a psychological awakening in the non-Western world, a weakening of the will on the part of the Western powers to maintain their position of dominance, or to at least accept the costs necessary to do so, the rise of new powers such as the Soviet Union, a more general equilibrium of power, and a

[60] Hedley Bull and Adam Watson, *The Expansion of International Society* (Oxford University Press, USA, 1984).

[61] Bull and Watson, *The Expansion of International Society.*

[62] Bull and Watson, *The Expansion of International Society*, 261.

> transformation of the legal and moral climate of international relations, which was influenced by the majorities of votes held by third world states.[63]

In contingency with the considerations above, this book finds that the patterns of resistance towards the practice of prosecuting SHoS can be read in the context of the revolt against the West. This is not to dismiss claims that certain states are resisting the practice because of selfish considerations, but rather to reinforce the idea that if a group of states perceives a certain practice to be in opposition to their collective interests, then this must be taken seriously. As such, even though the cases presented in the book aim at outlining various political implications that the prosecutions of SHoS entailed, this project shouldn't be read as a solidarist attack to those who are opposing the prosecutions. But rather as a step towards the identification of the problematics that the practice poses, and the meaning that these have for the future composition of international politics.

Structure of the Book

After this introduction, the book proceeds in five Chapters. These delve into the situations in which the ICC has become involved, directly or indirectly, with the idea of prosecuting a SHoS. The book is underpinned by a conceptual framework that highlights the existence of three paradoxes that, it is argued, greatly influence the ICC in the delivery of this mandate. These constitute the political tribulations that the Court has to deal with especially when prosecuting SHoS and are: the democracy paradox, the enforcement of justice paradox, and the symbolism paradox. While for pragmatic purposes these three shape the remainder of the book, in the sense that the six cases that this book explores are grouped in couples to highlight the implications of these three paradoxes, it is necessary to acknowledge the fact that they often overlap. So when the book discusses the democracy paradox, it is very possible to find in the same situations also traits of the symbolism paradox, and so forth. The cases in this book include two situations in which the Court decided not to, or wasn't able to, prosecute SHoS. These are Uganda and Syria. The book then explores all the cases in which the ICC did investigate a SHoS: Sudan, Kenya,

[63] Jason Ralph, 'Another Revolt Against the West?', 2013, *E-International Relations* (blog), accessed 16 November 2015, http://www.e-ir.info/2013/05/13/another-revolt-against-the-west/.

Libya, and Russia. Of these six situations, one was a self-referral (Uganda), two were UNSC referrals (Sudan and Libya), one was a *proprio motu* investigation (Kenya), and one was a referral by 39 state parties to the Rome Statute (Russia). So, the book offers a full spectrum of cases that unpack various political implications that the ICC has faced in relation to SHoS prosecutions.

Chapter 2 is dedicated to the conceptual architecture of the book and explores the three paradoxes mentioned above as the fundamental ideational limit to the idea that the ICC can effectively prosecute SHoS. Chapter 3 highlights the existence of the democracy paradox, or the idea that while the ICC should influence democratic transitions in the countries that host its investigations, governments under scrutiny are able to exploit the Court's actions to solidify their (often) authoritarian power and avoid international prosecution. This notion is explored in the Chapter by referring to the situations in Uganda and Kenya. In Uganda, the then Prosecutor of the Court Luis Moreno-Ocampo decided to focus solely on the Lord's Resistance Army (LRA) for gross human rights violations that plagued the country since the mid-1980s. The fact that the Prosecutor decided to investigate only the LRA fuelled accusations that the ICC had *de facto* shielded the Museveni government from prosecution and, in this sense, played a pivotal role in legitimising the government. The Chapter then outlines the evolution of the Kenyatta case in Kenya – which remains the only situation in which a SHoS appeared voluntarily in front of the ICC. The situation in Kenya is also fundamental because Kenyatta wasn't the President of Kenya when the ICC opened the investigation, but the Court's actions seemingly played a crucial role in his election. Further to this, the Chapter explores the emergence of authoritarian practices that the Kenyatta government adopted to silence those actors that cooperated with the ICC to ensure that Kenyatta faced trial.

Chapter 4 outlines the dynamics of the enforcement of justice paradox by introducing the Libyan and Syrian cases that are perceived, in this book, as a cornerstone in the practice of prosecuting SHoS since the birth of the ICC. The enforcement of justice paradox contends that while the ICC should be more effective in encouraging domestic authorities to abandon their criminal intents when coupled with the threat of international punitive measures, the presence of such a threat can make governments even less likely to engage cooperatively with the Court. This, in turn, can encourage authoritarian governments to use any instrument at their disposal to cling to power and avoid international condemnation, making them more likely to continue their criminal activities. The Libyan situation is crucial for the understanding of this dynamic, as it is one in which the ICC was formally coupled with the Responsibility to Protect (R2P) norm to militarily intervene against President Muammar Gaddafi. In this sense, the Chapter investigates the legitimising role that the ICC can play for the taboo practice of regime change, and how coercive measures influence the course of SHoS prosecutions. Further to this, the Chapter provides with an investigation into the discussion occurred within the UNSC to refer Syria to the ICC in relation to the alleged crimes committed by Syrian President Bashar al Assad against Syrian civilians. While this is not a situation in which the ICC was formally allowed to open an investigation against a SHoS, this case is fundamental to understand the changing relationship between members of the UNSC and the ICC, which seems to be reflecting the complexities of great power politics especially when the ICC is coupled with international punitive measures against sovereign states.

Chapter 5 introduces the existence of the symbolism paradox, which can be summarised as the idea that while the ICC can be perceived as a global beacon for the promotion of universal human rights, it can also be depicted and understood as an expression of Westernised, and even neo-colonial, interventionism. This notion creates the space for domestic and regional agencies to develop symbolically against the Court. The Chapter, to unpack this notion, introduces the Al Bashir case in Sudan, the longest to-date proceeding against a SHoS, and the recent situation against Vladimir Putin in Russia. The Sudanese investigation is a cornerstone to understand current resistance to the practice of prosecuting SHoS because it seems to be intimately linked with the strong resurgence of anti-imperial diplomacy in Africa. The focus on the very recent issuing of the arrest warrant for Russian President Vladimir Putin aims at indicating a certain degree of inconsistency in the emergence of humanitarian narratives in the West. This suggests that Western support for the Court is extremely selective and, as such, allegations of prosecutorial bias are still undermining the legitimacy of the institution. Further to this, the Chapter also considers the future for the relationship between the UNSC and the ICC after the Russian investigation. In Chap. 6, after reviewing the main findings of the project, the book discusses the prospects of the practice of prosecuting SHoS, what they mean for the ICC, and what they tell us about current international politics.

References

Akande, Dapo, and Sangeeta Shah. 'Immunities of State Officials, International Crimes, and Foreign Domestic Courts'. *European Journal of International Law* 21, no. 4 (2010): 815–52.

Aptel, Cécile. 'Prosecutorial Discretion at the ICC and Victims' Right to Remedy Narrowing the Impunity Gap'. *Journal of International Criminal Justice* 10, no. 5 (2012): 1357–75.

Arenhövel, Mark. 'Democratization and Transitional Justice'. *Democratization* 15, no. 3 (2008): 570–87.

Arsanjani, Mahnoush H. 'The Rome Statute of the International Criminal Court'. *The American Journal of International Law* 93, no. 1 (1 January 1999): 22–43.

Bassiouni, M. Cherif. '"International Crimes": "Jus Cogens" and "Obligatio Erga Omnes"'. *Law and Contemporary Problems*, 1996, 63–74.

Bull, Hedley. 'The Anarchical Society: A Study of World Order'. *World Politics*, 1977.

Bull, Hedley, and Adam Watson. *The Expansion of International Society.* Oxford University Press, USA, 1984.

Buzan, Barry. *From International to World Society?: English School Theory and the Social Structure of Globalisation.* Cambridge University Press, 2004.

———. 'The English School: An Underexploited Resource in IR'. *Review of International Studies* 27, no. 03 (July 2001): 471–88.

Cassese, Antonio. 'A Big Step Forward for International Justice'. *Crimes of War Project Magazine*, 2003.

Clark, Phil. 'Hybridity, Holism, and Traditional Justice: The Case of the Gacaca Courts in Post-Genocide Rwanda'. *George Washington International Law Review* 39 (2007): 765.

Czarnetzky, John M., and Ronald J. Rychlak. 'Empire of Law: Legalism and the International Criminal Court, An'. *Notre Dame L. Rev.* 79 (2003): 55.

Dapo Akande. 'A Single Comment - International Criminal Court Forum', 2014. Accessed 2 July 2015. http://iccforum.com/forum/permalink/93/4084.

Falk, Richard A. 'United States and the Doctrine of Nonintervention in the Internal Affairs of Independent States, The'. *Howard LJ* 5 (1959): 163.

Finnemore, Martha, and Kathryn Sikkink. 'International Norm Dynamics and Political Change'. *International Organization* 52, no. 04 (1998): 887–917.

Flood, Alison. 'Most-Browsed Book in the UN Library in 2015? A Primer on War-Crime Immunity'. *The Guardian*, 8 January 2016. http://www.theguardian.com/books/2016/jan/08/un-library-united-nations-most-2015-war-crime-immunity-heads-of-state-officials-international-pedretti.

Foakes, Joanne. 'Immunity for International Crimes?' *Developments in the Law on Prosecuting Heads of State in Foreign Courts [Online]*, 2011. http://www.operationspaix.net/DATA/DOCUMENT/6610~v~Immunity_for_

International_Crimes__Developments_in_the_Law_on_Prosecuting_Heads_of_State_in_Foreign_Courts.pdf.

Huntington, Samuel P. *The Third Wave: Democratization in the Late 20th Century*. University of Oklahoma Press, 2012.

Huyse, Luc. 'Justice after Transition: On the Choices Successor Elites Make in Dealing with the Past'. *Law & Social Inquiry* 20, no. 1 (1995): 51–78.

Iverson, Jens. 'Head of State Immunity Is Not the Same as State Immunity: A Response to the African Union's Position on Article 98 of the ICC Statute'. *EJIL: Talk!*, 2012. Accessed 30 November 2015. http://www.ejiltalk.org/head-of-state-immunity-is-not-the-same-as-state-immunity-a-response-to-the-african-unions-position-on-article-98-of-the-icc-statute/.

Jackson, Robert H. *The Global Covenant: Human Conduct in a World of States*. Oxford University Press, 2000.

Jalloh, Charles Chernor. 'Africa and the International Criminal Court: Collision Course or Cooperation'. *North Carolina Central Law Review* 34 (2012 2011): 203.

Kelley, Judith. 'Who Keeps International Commitments and Why? The International Criminal Court and Bilateral Nonsurrender Agreements'. *American Political Science Review* 101, no. 03 (2007): 573–89.

Linda Marie Keller. 'The False Dichotomy of Peace versus Justice and the International Criminal Court'. *Hague Justice Journal* 3, no. 1 (2008): 24.

Linklater, Andrew. 'Men and Citizens in International Relations'. *Review of International Studies* 7, no. 01 (1981): 23–37.

Mallinder, Louise. 'Global Comparison of Amnesty Laws'. SSRN Scholarly Paper. Rochester, NY: Social Science Research Network, 1 August 2009. http://papers.ssrn.com/abstract=1586831.

May, Larry. 'Le Norme Dello Jus Cogens e Il Diritto Penale Internazionale'. *Ars Interpretandi*, 2001, 223–48.

Mayall, James. *Nationalism and International Society*. Cambridge University Press, 1990.

Meernik, James D., Angela Nichols, and Kimi L. King. 'The Impact of International Tribunals and Domestic Trials on Peace and Human Rights after Civil War'. *International Studies Perspectives* 11, no. 4 (2010): 309–34.

Morris, Richard T. 'A Typology of Norms'. *American Sociological Review* 21, no. 5 (1956): 610–13.

Newton, Michael A. 'Comparative Complementarity: Domestic Jurisdiction Consistent with the Rome Statute of the International Criminal Court'. *Military Law Review* 167 (2001): 20.

O'Donnell, Guillermo, and Philippe C. Schmitter. *Tentative Conclusions about Uncertain Democracies, Volume 4, Transitions from Authoritarian Rule*. Baltimore: Johns Hopkins University Press, 1986.

Parent, Geneviève. 'Reconciliation and Justice after Genocide: A Theoretical Exploration'. *Genocide Studies and Prevention* 5, no. 3 (1 December 2010): 277–92.

Paust, Jordan J. 'The Reach of ICC Jurisdiction Over Non-Signatory Nationals'. SSRN Scholarly Paper. Rochester, NY: Social Science Research Network, 2000. http://papers.ssrn.com/abstract=2446632.

Power, Samantha. *A Problem from Hell: America and the Age of Genocide*. Perseus Books Group, 2013.

Ralph, Jason. 'International Society, the International Criminal Court and American Foreign Policy'. *Review of International Studies* 31, no. 01 (2005): 27–44.

Ralph, Jason. 'Another Revolt Against the West?'. *E-International Relations*, 2013. Accessed 16 November 2015. http://www.e-ir.info/2013/05/13/another-revolt-against-the-west/.

Roach, Steven C. *Governance, Order, and the International Criminal Court: Between Realpolitik and a Cosmopolitan Court: Between Realpolitik and a Cosmopolitan Court*. OUP Oxford, 2009.

Romano, Cesare. 'Proliferation of International Judicial Bodies: The Pieces of the Puzzle, The'. *NYUJ Int'l L. & Pol.* 31 (1998): 709.

Simpson, Gerry. 'Juridical Investigations: Martin Wight as International Lawyer'. *British Influences on International Law, 1915–2015*, 14 July 2016, 484–96.

Sitkin, Sim B., and Robert J. Bies. *The Legalistic Organization*. Sage Publications, 1994.

Smith, Thomas W. 'Moral Hazard and Humanitarian Law: The International Criminal Court and the Limits of Legalism'. *International Politics* 39, no. 2 (1 June 2002): 175–92.

Strang, Heather, and John Braithwaite. *Restorative Justice and Civil Society*. Cambridge University Press, 2001.

Sztucki, Jerzy. *Jus Cogens and the Vienna Convention on the Law of Treaties: A Critical Appraisal*. Springer-Verlag, 1974. http://www.sidalc.net/cgi-bin/wxis.exe/?IsisScript=FARN.xis&method=post&formato=2&cantidad=1&expresion=mfn=000096.

Villa-Vicencio, Charles. 'The Reek of Cruelty and the Quest for Healing: Where Retributive and Restorative Justice Meet'. *Journal of Law and Religion* 14, no. 1 (1 January 1999): 165–87.

Vinjamuri, Leslie, and Jack Snyder. 'Advocacy and Scholarship in the Study of International War Crime Tribunals and Transitional Justice'. *Annual Review of Political Science* 7, no. 1 (June 2004): 345–62.

Wegner, Patrick S. *The International Criminal Court in Ongoing Intrastate Conflicts: Navigating the Peace-Justice Divide*. Cambridge University Press, 2015.

Wheeler, Nicholas J. *Saving Strangers: Humanitarian Intervention in International Society: Humanitarian Intervention in International Society*. Oxford University Press, 2000.

Williams, John. 'Pluralism, Solidarism and the Emergence of World Society in English School Theory'. *International Relations* 19, no. 1 (2005): 19–38.

Williams, Robin M. 'Social Order and Social Conflict'. *Proceedings of the American Philosophical Society* 114, no. 3 (1970): 217–25.
Yang, Lijun. 'On the Principle of Complementarity in the Rome Statute of the International Criminal Court'. *Chinese Journal of International Law* 4, no. 1 (1 June 2005): 121–32.
Zappalà, Salvatore. 'Do Heads of State in Office Enjoy Immunity from Jurisdiction for International Crimes? The Ghaddafi Case before the French Cour de Cassation'. *European Journal of International Law* 12, no. 3 (2001): 595–612.

CHAPTER 2

Three Paradoxes for Sitting Heads of State Prosecutions: Promoting Democracy, Enforcing Justice, and Dual Symbolisms

There are two main reasons why writing this book is important. The first one is that prosecuting SHoS is a revolutionary practice that can effectively alter conventional understandings of international politics. This is the main conceptual reason why this book focuses on this specific practice. International politics has indeed a florid tradition of international prosecutions, and even prosecutions of former Heads of State. But prosecuting SHoS is something that seemingly contradicts the power-structure of the international arena. As outlined in Chap. 1 this is because the current architecture of international relations continues to be determined by notions of state sovereignty and non-intervention reminiscent of the Westphalian order. So, having an international organisation that contends that SHoS can be internationally prosecuted when they violate international law can be understood as an assault to a system that has been in place for, at least, four centuries. The second reason is that, so far, the ICC has failed in this effort. Understanding these proceedings, and their shortcomings, helps not only in questioning the viability of the practice per se, but should also aid in the understanding of those systemic traits that characterise international relations and how these interplay with the ICC in its endeavours.

As already noted, despite being a legal institution, the ICC was created and operates in a political world where domestic preferences are shaped by

M. Cacciatori, *The International Criminal Court and the Prosecution of Sitting Heads of State*,
https://doi.org/10.1007/978-3-031-54646-4_2

political opportunism and international support is vitally linked to global shifts in the balance of power, among other reasons. This is the background that gives birth to three paradoxes that, this book argues, lie at the conceptual heart to explain the difficulties of the Court in delivering on the mandate of prosecuting SHoS. These three paradoxes, unpacked in the following pages, are: the democracy paradox, the enforcement of justice paradox, and the symbolism paradox. Until these are resolved, despite international proclaims, the ICC will continue to be ineffective at least in this area of performance. It is in this sense that the book departs from a considerable body of current scholarship, which will be reviewed in each analytical Chapter. In addition to this, the existence of these paradoxes suggests that efforts to hold SHoS accountable can have unintended consequences both for the countries that host the investigations and globally—and this should be considered not only when launching these investigations, but also in their assessment both from an academic and a policy-making standpoint.

The ICC and the Democracy Paradox

The first component of the theoretical framework that this book introduces and utilises concerns the relationship between actions of the ICC and the promotion of democracy in countries that host the investigations. While the relationship between the ICC and democracy is a complex and multifaceted subject that has garnered significant attention since the inception of the Court, there is little doubt that among the many secondary objectives of the Court, beyond putting criminals behind bars, promoting democracy is a pivotal one. In fact, many argued that the ICC's role in promoting accountability, justice, and the rule of law, is intrinsically related to the promotion of democratic governance.[1] This notion stems not only from the idea that democratic states are less likely to commit the crimes covered by the Rome Statute, but also by considering the fact that the ICC is underpinned by democratic values that should permeate the contexts in which the Court operates.[2] The topic is particularly salient

[1] Jamie Mayerfeld, 'The Democratic Legacy of the International Criminal Court', *The Fletcher Forum of World Affairs* 28, no. 2 (2004): 147–56; Leslie Vinjamuri, 'Deterrence, Democracy, and the Pursuit of International Justice', *Ethics & International Affairs* 24, no. 2 (2010): 191–211.

[2] Marlies Glasius, 'Do International Criminal Courts Require Democratic Legitimacy?', *European Journal of International Law* 23, no. 1 (1 February 2012): 43–66.

considering that there are obvious concerns that lie at the nexus between the promotion of global human rights and states' sovereignty.[3] In other terms, the fact that the ICC has the potential to supersede national sovereignty when these crimes occur, is often considered as a controversial point when examining the potential of the Court's democratic promotion. Scholars have in fact highlighted that exogenous impositions of law are not necessarily conducive to the spread of democratic values, particularly in fragile or conflict-affected contexts.[4]

From this perspective, some examined how the ICC influences democratic governance within states under scrutiny, considering its impact on domestic political dynamics, regime stability, civil society engagement, and government accountability.[5] This strand of research seems to suggest that ICC prosecutions can contribute to democratic consolidation by challenging impunity and fostering a culture of accountability, two fundamental values of any democratic state.[6] However, the fact that the Rome Statute emphasises the idea of complementarity between the ICC and domestic

[3] Markus Benzing, 'The Complementarity Regime of the International Criminal Court: International Criminal Justice between State Sovereignty and the Fight against Impunity', *Max Planck Yearbook of United Nations Law Online* 7, no. 1 (1 January 2003): 591–632; Christa-Gaye Kerr, 'Sovereign Immunity, the AU, and the ICC: Legitimacy Undermined', *Michigan Journal of International Law* 41 (2020): 195; David A. Nill, 'National Sovereignty: Must It Be Sacrificed to the International Criminal Court?', *BYU Journal of Public Law* 14 (2000 1999): 119.

[4] Tom Buitelaar and Gisela Hirschmann, 'Criminal Accountability at What Cost? Norm Conflict, UN Peace Operations and the International Criminal Court', *European Journal of International Relations* 27, no. 2 (1 June 2021): 548–71; Michael P. Donnelly, 'Democracy and Sovereignty vs International Human Rights: Reconciling the Irreconcilable?', *The International Journal of Human Rights* 24, no. 10 (25 November 2020): 1429–50.

[5] Terrence L. Chapman and Stephen Chaudoin, 'Public Reactions to International Legal Institutions: The International Criminal Court in a Developing Democracy', *The Journal of Politics* 82, no. 4 (October 2020): 1305–20; Marlies Glasius, 'Does the Involvement of Global Civil Society Make International Decision-Making More Democratic? The Case of the International Criminal Court', *Journal of Civil Society* 4, no. 1 (1 June 2008): 43–60.

[6] Kjersti Lohne, 'Penal Humanitarianism beyond the Nation State: An Analysis of International Criminal Justice', *Theoretical Criminology* 24, no. 2 (1 May 2020): 145–62; Darryl Robinson, 'Serving the Interests of Justice: Amnesties, Truth Commissions and the International Criminal Court', *European Journal of International Law* 14, no. 3 (1 June 2003): 481–505.

institutions carries some implications that question the effective ability of the Court to sustain democracy in authoritarian contexts. The ICC's reliance on state cooperation and UNSC referrals has, in fact, raised fundamental questions about its impartiality and effectiveness in delivering on its mandate.[7] This is reflected in certain procedural traits of the Court, such as the manner in which certain investigations are launched and others are not, or the fact that in some instances only one part of a conflict is investigated. Such matters have been perceived as potentially exacerbating domestic political tensions and, consequently, hinder democratisation efforts.[8] Moreover, the ICC's own democratic legitimacy has been subject to scrutiny. Scholars have debated the Court's authority and accountability mechanisms in relation to democratic principles.[9] To this end, some highlighted that the ICC should uphold democratic norms such as transparency, participation, and representation in its decision-making processes. Others, on the other hand, contend that the ICC's legitimacy derives from its adherence to universal human rights principles rather than democratic standards.[10]

The above literature has found florid empirical application that has enriched the discourse. African states, for instance, have raised concerns about the ICC's alleged bias and neo-colonial tendencies, leading to

[7] Valerie Oosterveld, 'The Cooperation of States with the International Criminal Court', *Fordham International Law Journal* 25 (2002 2001): 767; Rod Rastan, 'Testing Co-Operation: The International Criminal Court and National Authorities', *Leiden Journal of International Law* 21, no. 2 (June 2008): 431–56.

[8] S. J. Tilden, 'Africa's Conflict with the International Criminal Court: The African Court of Justice and Human and Peoples' Right as an Alternative to the ICC', *Tulane Journal of International and Comparative Law* 27 (2019 2018): 201.

[9] Kamari M. Clarke, Abel S. Knottnerus, and Eefje de Volder, *Africa and the ICC* (Cambridge University Press, 2016).

[10] Nicole Deitelhoff and Lisbeth Zimmermann, 'Norms under Challenge: Unpacking the Dynamics of Norm Robustness', *Journal of Global Security Studies* 4, no. 1 (1 January 2019): 2–17; Beth A Simmons and Hyeran Jo, 'Measuring Norms and Normative Contestation: The Case of International Criminal Law', *Journal of Global Security Studies* 4, no. 1 (1 January 2019): 18–36; Armin von Bogdandy and Ingo Venzke, 'In Whose Name? An Investigation of International Courts' Public Authority and Its Democratic Justification', *European Journal of International Law* 23, no. 1 (1 February 2012): 7–41.

withdrawals and calls for reform.[11] This, of course, is particularly relevant when discussing ICC prosecutions of SHoS. In fact, when the ICC initiates investigations into SHoS, it must confront the reality that its operations occur within contexts where information is often subjected to governmental censorship and manipulation. Consequently, governments can portray the Court as an external aggressor targeting the sitting regime, effectively rallying popular support against both international adversaries and the ICC itself. Paradoxically, instead of catalysing democratic transformation, ICC interventions may inadvertently reinforce domestic authoritarian practices.

For this reason, the considerations above hint at a paradox with profound implications, serving as one of the foundational premises of this book and set to be empirically explored in Chap. 3. This paradox stems from the complex interplay between the ICC being potentially depicted and perceived as an external entity meddling in internal affairs and the imperative for the Court to promote democratic values, particularly the rule of law, through its actions. This tension can manifest in various forms, from governments supporting the ICC when it is useful to legitimise their ruling, to individuals antagonising ICC actions to galvanise domestic support and retain or access power.

The crux of this first paradox can be summarised as follows: on one hand, the actions of the ICC ostensibly aim to bolster democracy by upholding the rule of law. This, among ideational and normative pushes, is also for very practical reasons. The Court's ultimate aim has to be the minimisation of the spread of the crimes covered by the Rome Statute, and democracies are less likely to commit those than authoritarian governments. Also, it is much easier for the Court to cooperate with a democracy than it is to engage in diplomatic dialogue with authoritarian states. However, in practice, regimes under ICC scrutiny can exploit these actions to solidify their, often authoritarian, power. This dynamic gains further significance when considering historical precedents, as only deposed SHoS

[11] Lucrecia García Iommi, 'Whose Justice? The ICC "Africa Problem"', *International Relations* 34, no. 1 (1 March 2020): 105–29; Makau W. Mutua, 'The International Criminal Court in Africa: Challenges and Opportunities', SSRN Scholarly Paper (Rochester, NY: Social Science Research Network, 1 September 2010); Lea Schneider, 'The International Criminal Court (ICC)—A Postcolonial Tool for Western States to Control Africa?', *Journal of International Criminal Law (JICL)* 1, no. 1 (2020): 90–109.

have been subject to international prosecution. As a result, SHoS may perceive relinquishing power as the sole pathway to potential prosecution, incentivising them to cling to power even more staunchly.

The ICC and the Enforcement of Justice Paradox

The second conceptual plexus that underpins this book is related to the efficacy of the ICC in enforcing domestic compliance with its rulings when non-compliant SHoS are indicted. This is both particularly complex given the status of the alleged criminal, and crucial for the Court to be perceived as a credible actor in international politics. Unfortunately, the enforcement ability of the ICC resides at the complex nexus of coercive action and government cooperation, yielding a multifaceted interplay with significant implications. While the Rome Statute underscores the pivotal role of governmental cooperation for the ICC, as highlighted in Chap. 1, it also empowers the Court to act in cases where states are unwilling to prosecute perpetrators themselves. This has opened a space for debate which has evolved around the idea that the ICC necessitates of some form of enforcement and coercive power to be considered a credible threat by domestic authorities.

The presence of coercive measures, or the threat of punishment, would in theory shape the preferences of national actors encouraging them to avoid the perpetration of crimes covered by the Rome Statute.[12] This idea has been central to academic discourse since at least 1998, which has often suggested that it is precisely the lack of such coercive measures which could greatly undermine the credibility of the Court as an

[12] Hirad Abtahi and Steven Arrigg Koh, 'The Emerging Enforcement Practice of the International Criminal Court', *Cornell International Law Journal* 45 (2013): 1; Jacob Katz Cogan, 'International Criminal Courts and Fair Trials: Difficulties and Prospects', *Yale Journal of International Law* 27 (2002): 111; Yvonne M. Dutton, 'Explaining State Commitment to the International Criminal Court: Strong Enforcement Mechanisms as a Credible Threat', *Washington University Global Studies Law Review* 10 (2011): 477; Caroline Fehl, 'Explaining the International Criminal Court: A "Practice Test" for Rationalist and Constructivist Approaches', *European Journal of International Relations* 10, no. 3 (1 September 2004): 357–94.

international actor.[13] However, it is important to underscore that certain strands of research highlighted that the Court's ability to encourage compliance with international norms lies more in processes of entrenched socialisation,[14] or that the legitimacy of the ICC is determined not only by its threats, but is also (and perhaps mostly) shaped by ideational and cultural factors.[15]

Recent research indicates that the threat of punishment for wrongdoers, including but not limited to economic sanctions or military interventions, is often thought to be quintessential in the formation of positive policy-making preferences for governments under scrutiny.[16] However, scholars caution against over-reliance on such punitive threats due to the ability of governments under scrutiny to manipulate such threats to

[13] Antonio Franceschet, 'The International Criminal Court's Provisional Authority to Coerce', *Ethics & International Affairs* 26, no. 1 (April 2012): 93–101; Philippe Kirsch, 'The Role of the International Criminal Court in Enforcing International Criminal Law', *American University International Law Review* 22 (2007 2006): 539; Jamie Mayerfeld, 'Who Shall Be Judge?: The United States, the International Criminal Court, and the Global Enforcement of Human Rights', *Human Rights Quarterly* 25, no. 1 (2003): 93–129; Mary Margaret Penrose, 'Lest We Fail: The Importance of Enforcement in International Criminal Law', *American University of International Law Review* 15 (2000 1999): 321.

[14] Michael J. Gilligan, 'Is Enforcement Necessary for Effectiveness? A Model of the International Criminal Regime', *International Organization* 60, no. 4 (October 2006): 935–67.

[15] Nicole Deitelhoff, 'What's in a Name? Contestation and Backlash against International Norms and Institutions', *The British Journal of Politics and International Relations* 22, no. 4 (1 November 2020): 715–27; Lucrecia García Iommi, 'Al-Bashir Didn't Start the Fire. Diversity, Low Contestedness, and the Adoption of the Rome Statute of the International Criminal Court', *Cambridge Review of International Affairs* 34, no. 1 (2 September 2020): 105–36; Sara L. Ochs, 'Propaganda Warfare on the International Criminal Court', *Michigan Journal of International Law* 42 (2021 2020): 581.

[16] Geoff Dancy, 'Searching for Deterrence at the International Criminal Court', in *Strengthening the Validity of International Criminal Tribunals* (Brill Nijhoff, 2018), 43–73; Beth A. Simmons and Allison Danner, 'Credible Commitments and the International Criminal Court', *International Organization* 64, no. 2 (April 2010): 225–56.

retaliate against the Court by questioning its legitimacy.[17] Governments, in fact, seem to constantly exhibit reluctance to cooperate with the ICC when faced with the threat of punitive measures, often citing concerns about sovereignty, political stability, and perceived bias within the Court's proceedings.[18] Moreover, powerful states may strategically undermine the ICC by withdrawing support or influencing others to resist its jurisdiction, leaving the Court unable to execute its rulings.[19]

While this second paradox is already almost evident, it is important to highlight that in this picture the UNSC plays a crucial, but not unique, part. In fact, the UNSC remains the only international body that can authorise ICC action in cases where the state under scrutiny is not a signatory member of the Rome Statute. While the Council wields leverage through the ability of referring situations to the Court, and also often plays a central role in the authorisation of international sanctions against international wrongdoers, its politicisation and the veto mechanism are often thought as hindering decisive action. Recent studies have explored reforms to enhance UNSC effectiveness in supporting the ICC's mandate while

[17] Gwen P. Barnes, 'The International Criminal Court's Ineffective Enforcement Mechanisms: The Indictment of President Omar Al Bashir', *Fordham International Law Journal* 34 (2011 2010): 1584; Mikkel Jarle Christensen, 'The Borderlands between Punitive and Non-Punitive Transitional Justice: Distinct Elites and Diverging Patterns of Import/Export', *International Journal of Transitional Justice* 14, no. 3 (1 November 2020): 464–82; Joe Oloka-Onyango, 'Unpacking the African Backlash to the International Criminal Court (ICC): The Case of Uganda and Kenya', *Strathmore Law Journal* 4 (2020): 41; Maartje Weerdesteijn and Barbora Holá, '"Tool in the R2P Toolbox"? Analysing the Role of the International Criminal Court in the Three Pillars of the Responsibility to Protect', *Criminal Law Forum* 31, no. 3 (1 September 2020): 377–414.

[18] Alexander Beresford and Daniel Wand, 'Understanding Bricolage in Norm Development: South Africa, the International Criminal Court, and the Contested Politics of Transitional Justice', *Review of International Studies* 46, no. 4 (October 2020): 534–54; Courtney Hillebrecht, 'International Criminal Accountability and the Domestic Politics of Resistance: Case Studies from Kenya and Lebanon', *Law & Society Review* 54, no. 2 (2020): 453–86.

[19] Adam Bower, 'Contesting the International Criminal Court: Bashir, Kenyatta, and the Status of the Nonimpunity Norm in World Politics', *Journal of Global Security Studies* 4, no. 1 (1 January 2019): 88–104; Dorothy Makaza-Goede, 'Through the Contestation Looking-Glass: State Immunity and (Non)Compliance with the International Criminal Court', *Third World Approaches to International Law Review (TWAILR)* 2 (2021): 59.

addressing concerns of selectivity and political bias.[20] In addition to the UNSC, civil society and public opinion exert significant influence on government behaviour towards the ICC. Grassroots movements, human rights advocates, and media scrutiny can pressure governments to cooperate with the Court,[21] with social media platforms increasingly mobilising public support for international justice initiatives and holding governments accountable.[22] However, the crux remains that if a government proves unwilling to cooperate with the Court, the only way to execute ICC rulings remains threatening (or delivering) punishment for non-cooperation.

While economic sanctions and military interventions are commonly cited examples, subtler forms of coercion, such as diplomatic pressure and economic incentives, also warrant consideration. Understanding how these various tools interact with different state actors' motivations and perceptions is crucial for crafting effective strategies to promote ICC compliance while mitigating unintended consequences. In summary, the literature above highlights that the relationship between the efficacy of the ICC and the threat of coercive enforcement of international norms gives birth to a second conceptual paradox that is explored in detail in Chap. 4. This contends that while the ICC should be more effective in encouraging domestic authorities to abandon their criminal intents when coupled with the threat of international punitive measures, the presence of such a threat can make governments even less likely to engage cooperatively with the Court. This, in turn, can encourage authoritarian governments to use any instrument at their disposal to cling to power to avoid international condemnation, making them potentially more prone to the escalation of violence.

[20] Theresa Reinold, 'Constitutionalization? Whose Constitutionalization? Africa's Ambivalent Engagement with the International Criminal Court', *International Journal of Constitutional Law* 10, no. 4 (1 October 2012): 1076–1105; Leslie Vinjamuri, 'The International Criminal Court and the Paradox of Authority', *Law and Contemporary Problems* 79, no. 1 (2016): 275–87.

[21] Christine Bjork and Juanita Goebertus, 'Complementarity in Action: The Role of Civil Society and the ICC in Rule of Law Strengthening in Kenya', *Yale Human Rights & Development Law Journal* 14 (2011): 205; Marlies Glasius, 'What Is Global Justice and Who Decides? Civil Society and Victim Responses to the International Criminal Court's Investigations', *Human Rights Quarterly* 31 (2009): 496; Glasius, 'Does the Involvement of Global Civil Society Make International Decision-Making More Democratic?'

[22] Shannon Raj Singh, 'Move Fast and Break Societies: The Weaponisation of Social Media and Options for Accountability under International Criminal Law', *Cambridge International Law Journal* 8, no. 2 (1 December 2019): 331–42; Paul J. Zwier, 'Social Media and Conflict Mapping in Syria: Implications for Peacemaking, International Criminal Prosecutions and for TRC Processes', *Emory International Law Review* 30 (2016 2015): 169.

This paradox has an immediate implication on the relationship between the UNSC and the Court. While in the heyday of the ICC, the ability of the UNSC to refer situations that concern non-member states was perceived to be a fundamental feature to allow the Court the possibility of prosecuting crimes committed by non-member states, and to grant it the punitive threat it allegedly necessitates, the conceptual tension highlighted above suggests that the reliance on the UNSC can be a burden for the Court. This is because authorising any form of coercive power to force states to comply with ICC rulings is likely to exacerbate the tension between powers prone to intervention, often Western members of the UNSC, and the rest of the Council. However, it would be naïve to think that only UNSC-referred cases are influenced by the existence of this paradox. The reality seems to be remarkably different, as only self-referrals (and not all of them) are conceptually immune to this paradoxical dynamic, since these are the only cases in which governmental cooperation can be assumed and, in turn, the threat of punishment unnecessary.

The ICC and the Symbolism Paradox

Beyond its material capabilities, and the conceptual complexities that derive from the paradoxes of democracy and enforcement of justice, it is undeniable that the ICC operates within a complex web of symbolic meanings, both on a global scale and within regional and local contexts. Scholars have delved into this symbolic power, highlighting how the ICC's interventions, but the architecture of international law in general, can serve as poignant global condemnations of human rights abuses.[23] Such symbolic values and interpretations, once more, hold an even more pronounced value when it comes to SHoS prosecutions. In such instances it is even more evident that the link between expressions of international justice such as the ICC and the symbolism that underpins them and that they, in turn, propagate, is a matter of political leverage among sources of power in international politics. And this is true both in terms of how

[23] Mikkel Jarle Christensen, 'The Symbolic Economy of International Criminal Justice: Shaping the Discourse of a New Field of Law', in *Strengthening the Validity of International Criminal Tribunals* (Brill Nijhoff, 2018), 74–98; Catherine Gegout, 'The International Criminal Court: Limits, Potential and Conditions for the Promotion of Justice and Peace', *Third World Quarterly* 34, no. 5 (1 June 2013): 800–818; Elisa Hoven and Saskia Scheibel, '"Justice for Victims" in Trials of Mass Crimes: Symbolism or Substance?', *International Review of Victimology* 21, no. 2 (1 May 2015): 161–85.

symbolic dyads emerge and the repercussions they have on the ability of international tribunals to deliver on their mandates.[24]

One of the dominant aspects of narratives that highlight the symbolic potential of the ICC is the fact that efforts against impunity by the Court have been described as holding a deterrent value, warning potential perpetrators that their deeds will not escape scrutiny or consequence.[25] This is something that was already introduced when discussing the complexities related to enforcement issues—but rather than its material manifestation, some believe that the ability of the ICC to prevent the emergence and proliferation of violence rests precisely on the fact that the Court can be perceived as a permanent beacon of justice ready to prosecute criminals and set the spotlight of international condemnation on them.

Yet, within this framework, the ICC often encounters resistance both from governments under scrutiny and their international allies, and this in itself carries profound symbolic implications. Local opposition can arise from a myriad of factors, but as already noted, usually highlights concerns over sovereignty, perceptions of external interference, and criticisms of the Court's selectivity in investigations and prosecutions.[26] The first section of this Chapter also highlighted that undoubtedly this resistance might come from matters of political opportunism. However, some leaders frame their opposition to the Court in ways that allow them to position themselves as champions against neo-colonial powers. Critics argue that this is fuelled by

[24] Marina Aksenova, 'Symbolism as a Constraint on International Criminal Law', *Leiden Journal of International Law* 30, no. 2 (June 2017): 475–99; Andrew J. Walker, 'When a Good Idea Is Poorly Implemented: How the International Criminal Court Fails to Be Insulated from International Politics and to Protect Basic Due Process Guarantees', *West Virginia Law Review* 106 (2004 2003): 245.

[25] Courtney Hillebrecht, 'The Deterrent Effects of the International Criminal Court: Evidence from Libya', *International Interactions* 42, no. 4 (2016): 616–43; Hyeran Jo and Beth A. Simmons, 'Can the International Criminal Court Deter Atrocity?', *International Organization* 70, no. 3 (ed 2016): 443–75; Christopher W. Mullins and Dawn L. Rothe, 'The Ability of the International Criminal Court to Deter Violations of International Criminal Law: A Theoretical Assessment', *Int'l Crim. L. Rev.* 10 (2010): 771.

[26] Darryl Robinson, 'Inescapable Dyads: Why the International Criminal Court Cannot Win', *Leiden Journal of International Law* 28, no. 2 (June 2015): 323–47; Schneider, 'The International Criminal Court (ICC)—A Postcolonial Tool for Western States to Control Africa?'; Jean-Baptiste Jeangène Vilmer, 'The African Union and the International Criminal Court: Counteracting the Crisis', *International Affairs* 92, no. 6 (1 November 2016): 1319–42.

the ICC's reliance on Western support, which can be perceived as perpetuating and replicating neo-colonial dynamics.[27] This is true not only from a scholarly perspective, but also from a policy-making one. A multiplicity of non-Western political leaders have, in fact, often accused the ICC of bias and selective targeting, prompting calls for mass withdrawal from the Court. While it would be easy to dismiss this kind of resistance as another attempt of criminal governments to deflect international condemnation, and there is little doubt that this plays a very significant role, it is important to highlight that the construction of an anti-colonial imagination that portrays the ICC as the zenith of Western imperialism carries an important symbolic weight. This is also reflected, for instance, in the difficulties that the ICC has not only in ensuring governmental cooperation, but also in communicating and liaising with local communities.[28]

This symbolic resistance is not limited to intra-state dynamics but, perhaps more importantly, because of its symbolic value, is likely to galvanise non-Western dissent for allegedly neo-colonial practices disguised as forms of humanitarianism. The main difference between this paradox and the democratic paradox is that it is not only states under scrutiny that oppose the Court and exploit anti-ICC narratives for political opportunism, but also their regional and international allies, and the IOs that represent them in the international arena. In this sense, opposition to the ICC becomes a form of agency, that can symbolise the assertion of autonomy and self-determination against external impositions.

In conclusion, the third paradox that this book uses as a conceptual benchmark for analysis can be summarised as being underpinned by the following duality: while ICC actions are often thought of symbolising

[27] Robert Cryer, 'Sudan, Resolution 1593, and International Criminal Justice', *Leiden Journal of International Law* 19, no. 1 (March 2006): 195–222; June Wanjiru Gichuki, 'African State Sovereignty and the International Criminal Court : Case Studies in Analytical Context', *African Journal of Democracy and Governance* 1, no. 4 (January 2014): 103–20; Mutua, 'The International Criminal Court in Africa'.

[28] Luigi D.A. Corrias and Geoffrey M. Gordon, 'Judging in the Name of Humanity: International Criminal Tribunals and the Representation of a Global Public', *Journal of International Criminal Justice* 13, no. 1 (1 March 2015): 97–112; Luke Moffett, 'Meaningful and Effective? Considering Victims' Interests Through Participation at the International Criminal Court', *Criminal Law Forum* 26, no. 2 (1 June 2015): 255–89; Sarah M. H. Nouwen, *Complementarity in the Line of Fire: The Catalysing Effect of the International Criminal Court in Uganda and Sudan* (Cambridge University Press, 2013); Barrie Sander, 'The Expressive Turn of International Criminal Justice: A Field in Search of Meaning', *Leiden Journal of International Law* 32, no. 4 (December 2019): 851–72.

universal justice and accountability, non-Western resistance against them can be construed as symbolic defiance against neo-colonialism and Western interventionism. This is significant because it suggests that even states that have no evident reason to oppose the ICC might decide to join an anti-ICC crusade if they perceive that they can make a symbolic difference in a non-Western fight against new forms of colonialism.

Conclusions

This Chapter serves as a conceptual benchmark for the analysis of specific cases that the book conducts in Chaps. 3, 4, and 5. It set out the three paradoxes that underpin ICC investigations on SHoS for the crimes covered by the Rome Statute. The starting point for this analysis is the idea that the Court seems to be powerless in delivering on the mandate of prosecuting SHoS. The democratic paradox, the enforcement of justice paradox, and the symbolism paradox serve, in this sense, an analytical purpose to understand the reasons why this is the case and some of the implications that these attempts carry for local and international realities. As already highlighted, it is important to remember that the book considers these three as often manifesting simultaneously in each case and, as such, should not be perceived as mutually exclusive but rather as phenomena that concur to the political complications that the Court faces in this revolutionary endeavour.

In addition to this, the existence of the three paradoxes suggests that while literature has rightly focused on the specificities of each case, as it will be elucidated in each Chapter, the three paradoxes confer to the limits of ICC prosecutions of SHoS a systemic value. In fact, being the three unresolved conceptual tensions, it may be considered that the Court is likely to face similar difficulties every time it attempts at holding SHoS accountable for their actions. This doesn't mean that peculiar dynamics are to be disregarded, but rather that these can be read as emerging from these systemic and conceptual fallacies. It is also important to underscore that while the book claims that the ICC has been ineffective in this domain, this doesn't mean that it is ineffective in all its actions. Due to the singular characteristics that SHoS occupy in international politics, it is expected that certain complexities are more evident in situations that involve them. In a way, the following Chapters also highlight that criticism directed at the ICC should acknowledge more the fact that the difficulties that the Court is facing in this area should pay more attention to the conceptual architecture that underpins international politics, while also questioning the possibility of actually delivering on this mandate as long as the international arena continues to be regulated by current norms.

References

Abtahi, Hirad, and Steven Arrigg Koh. 'The Emerging Enforcement Practice of the International Criminal Court'. *Cornell International Law Journal* 45 (2013): 1.

Aksenova, Marina. 'Symbolism as a Constraint on International Criminal Law'. *Leiden Journal of International Law* 30, no. 2 (June 2017): 475–99.

Barnes, Gwen P. 'The International Criminal Court's Ineffective Enforcement Mechanisms: The Indictment of President Omar Al Bashir'. *Fordham International Law Journal* 34 (2011 [2010]): 1584.

Benzing, Markus. 'The Complementarity Regime of the International Criminal Court: International Criminal Justice between State Sovereignty and the Fight against Impunity'. *Max Planck Yearbook of United Nations Law Online* 7, no. 1 (1 January 2003): 591–632.

Beresford, Alexander, and Daniel Wand. 'Understanding Bricolage in Norm Development: South Africa, the International Criminal Court, and the Contested Politics of Transitional Justice'. *Review of International Studies* 46, no. 4 (October 2020): 534–54.

Bjork, Christine, and Juanita Goebertus. 'Complementarity in Action: The Role of Civil Society and the ICC in Rule of Law Strengthening in Kenya'. *Yale Human Rights & Development Law Journal* 14 (2011): 205.

Bogdandy, Armin von, and Ingo Venzke. 'In Whose Name? An Investigation of International Courts' Public Authority and Its Democratic Justification'. *European Journal of International Law* 23, no. 1 (1 February 2012): 7–41.

Bower, Adam. 'Contesting the International Criminal Court: Bashir, Kenyatta, and the Status of the Nonimpunity Norm in World Politics'. *Journal of Global Security Studies* 4, no. 1 (1 January 2019): 88–104.

Buitelaar, Tom, and Gisela Hirschmann. 'Criminal Accountability at What Cost? Norm Conflict, UN Peace Operations and the International Criminal Court'. *European Journal of International Relations* 27, no. 2 (1 June 2021): 548–71.

Chapman, Terrence L., and Stephen Chaudoin. 'Public Reactions to International Legal Institutions: The International Criminal Court in a Developing Democracy'. *The Journal of Politics* 82, no. 4 (October 2020): 1305–20.

Christensen, Mikkel Jarle. 'The Borderlands between Punitive and Non-Punitive Transitional Justice: Distinct Elites and Diverging Patterns of Import/Export'. *International Journal of Transitional Justice* 14, no. 3 (1 November 2020): 464–82.

———. 'The Symbolic Economy of International Criminal Justice: Shaping the Discourse of a New Field of Law'. In *Strengthening the Validity of International Criminal Tribunals*, 74–98. Brill Nijhoff, 2018.

Clarke, Kamari M., Abel S. Knottnerus, and Eefje de Volder. *Africa and the ICC*. Cambridge University Press, 2016.

Cogan, Jacob Katz. 'International Criminal Courts and Fair Trials: Difficulties and Prospects'. *Yale Journal of International Law* 27 (2002): 111.

Corrias, Luigi D.A., and Geoffrey M. Gordon. 'Judging in the Name of Humanity: International Criminal Tribunals and the Representation of a Global Public'. *Journal of International Criminal Justice* 13, no. 1 (1 March 2015): 97–112.

Cryer, Robert. 'Sudan, Resolution 1593, and International Criminal Justice'. *Leiden Journal of International Law* 19, no. 1 (March 2006): 195–222.

Dancy, Geoff. 'Searching for Deterrence at the International Criminal Court'. In *Strengthening the Validity of International Criminal Tribunals*, 43–73. Brill Nijhoff, 2018.

Deitelhoff, Nicole. 'What's in a Name? Contestation and Backlash against International Norms and Institutions'. *The British Journal of Politics and International Relations* 22, no. 4 (1 November 2020): 715–27.

Deitelhoff, Nicole, and Lisbeth Zimmermann. 'Norms under Challenge: Unpacking the Dynamics of Norm Robustness'. *Journal of Global Security Studies* 4, no. 1 (1 January 2019): 2–17.

Donnelly, Michael P. 'Democracy and Sovereignty vs International Human Rights: Reconciling the Irreconcilable?' *The International Journal of Human Rights* 24, no. 10 (25 November 2020): 1429–50.

Dutton, Yvonne M. 'Explaining State Commitment to the International Criminal Court: Strong Enforcement Mechanisms as a Credible Threat'. *Washington University Global Studies Law Review* 10 (2011): 477.

Fehl, Caroline. 'Explaining the International Criminal Court: A "Practice Test" for Rationalist and Constructivist Approaches'. *European Journal of International Relations* 10, no. 3 (1 September 2004): 357–94.

Franceschet, Antonio. 'The International Criminal Court's Provisional Authority to Coerce'. *Ethics & International Affairs* 26, no. 1 (April 2012): 93–101.

García Iommi, Lucrecia. 'Whose Justice? The ICC "Africa Problem"'. *International Relations* 34, no. 1 (1 March 2020): 105–29.

Garcia Iommi, Lucrecia. 'Al-Bashir Didn't Start the Fire. Diversity, Low Contestedness, and the Adoption of the Rome Statute of the International Criminal Court'. *Cambridge Review of International Affairs* 34, no. 1 (2 September 2020): 105–36.

Gegout, Catherine. 'The International Criminal Court: Limits, Potential and Conditions for the Promotion of Justice and Peace'. *Third World Quarterly* 34, no. 5 (1 June 2013): 800–818.

Gichuki, June Wanjiru. 'African State Sovereignty and the International Criminal Court: Case Studies in Analytical Context'. *African Journal of Democracy and Governance* 1, no. 4 (January 2014): 103–20.

Gilligan, Michael J. 'Is Enforcement Necessary for Effectiveness? A Model of the International Criminal Regime'. *International Organization* 60, no. 4 (October 2006): 935–67.

Glasius, Marlies. 'Do International Criminal Courts Require Democratic Legitimacy?' *European Journal of International Law* 23, no. 1 (1 February 2012): 43–66.

———. 'Does the Involvement of Global Civil Society Make International Decision-Making More Democratic? The Case of the International Criminal Court'. *Journal of Civil Society* 4, no. 1 (1 June 2008): 43–60.

———. 'What Is Global Justice and Who Decides? Civil Society and Victim Responses to the International Criminal Court's Investigations'. *Human Rights Quarterly* 31 (2009): 496.

Hillebrecht, Courtney. 'International Criminal Accountability and the Domestic Politics of Resistance: Case Studies from Kenya and Lebanon'. *Law & Society Review* 54, no. 2 (2020): 453–86.

———. 'The Deterrent Effects of the International Criminal Court: Evidence from Libya'. *International Interactions* 42, no. 4 (2016): 616–43.

Hoven, Elisa, and Saskia Scheibel. '"Justice for Victims" in Trials of Mass Crimes: Symbolism or Substance?' *International Review of Victimology* 21, no. 2 (1 May 2015): 161–85.

Jo, Hyeran, and Beth A. Simmons. 'Can the International Criminal Court Deter Atrocity?' *International Organization* 70, no. 3 (2016): 443–75.

Kerr, Christa-Gaye. 'Sovereign Immunity, the AU, and the ICC: Legitimacy Undermined'. *Michigan Journal of International Law* 41 (2020): 195.

Kirsch, Philippe. 'The Role of the International Criminal Court in Enforcing International Criminal Law'. *American University International Law Review* 22 (2007 [2006]): 539.

Lohne, Kjersti. 'Penal Humanitarianism beyond the Nation State: An Analysis of International Criminal Justice'. *Theoretical Criminology* 24, no. 2 (1 May 2020): 145–62.

Makaza-Goede, Dorothy. 'Through the Contestation Looking-Glass: State Immunity and (Non)Compliance with the International Criminal Court'. *Third World Approaches to International Law Review / (TWAILR)* 2 (2021): 59.

Mayerfeld, Jamie. 'The Democratic Legacy of the International Criminal Court'. *The Fletcher Forum of World Affairs* 28, no. 2 (2004): 147–56.

———. 'Who Shall Be Judge?: The United States, the International Criminal Court, and the Global Enforcement of Human Rights'. *Human Rights Quarterly* 25, no. 1 (2003): 93–129.

Moffett, Luke. 'Meaningful and Effective? Considering Victims' Interests Through Participation at the International Criminal Court'. *Criminal Law Forum* 26, no. 2 (1 June 2015): 255–89.

Mullins, Christopher W., and Dawn L. Rothe. 'The Ability of the International Criminal Court to Deter Violations of International Criminal Law: A Theoretical Assessment'. *Int'l Crim. L. Rev.* 10 (2010): 771.

Mutua, Makau W. 'The International Criminal Court in Africa: Challenges and Opportunities'. SSRN Scholarly Paper. Rochester, NY: Social Science Research Network, 1 September 2010.

Nill, David A. 'National Sovereignty: Must It Be Sacrificed to the International Criminal Court?' *BYU Journal of Public Law* 14 (2000 [1999]): 119.

Nouwen, Sarah M. H. *Complementarity in the Line of Fire: The Catalysing Effect of the International Criminal Court in Uganda and Sudan*. Cambridge University Press, 2013.

Ochs, Sara L. 'Propaganda Warfare on the International Criminal Court'. *Michigan Journal of International Law* 42 (2021 [2020]): 581.

Oloka-Onyango, Joe. 'Unpacking the African Backlash to the International Criminal Court (ICC): The Case of Uganda and Kenya'. *Strathmore Law Journal* 4 (2020): 41.

Oosterveld, Valerie. 'The Cooperation of States with the International Criminal Court'. *Fordham International Law Journal* 25 (2002 [2001]): 767.

Penrose, Mary Margaret. 'Lest We Fail: The Importance of Enforcement in International Criminal Law'. *American University of International Law Review* 15 (2000 [1999]): 321.

Rastan, Rod. 'Testing Co-Operation: The International Criminal Court and National Authorities'. *Leiden Journal of International Law* 21, no. 2 (June 2008): 431–56.

Reinold, Theresa. 'Constitutionalization? Whose Constitutionalization? Africa's Ambivalent Engagement with the International Criminal Court'. *International Journal of Constitutional Law* 10, no. 4 (1 October 2012): 1076–1105.

Robinson, Darryl. 'Inescapable Dyads: Why the International Criminal Court Cannot Win'. *Leiden Journal of International Law* 28, no. 2 (June 2015): 323–47.

———. 'Serving the Interests of Justice: Amnesties, Truth Commissions and the International Criminal Court'. *European Journal of International Law* 14, no. 3 (1 June 2003): 481–505.

Sander, Barrie. 'The Expressive Turn of International Criminal Justice: A Field in Search of Meaning'. *Leiden Journal of International Law* 32, no. 4 (December 2019): 851–72.

Schneider, Lea. 'The International Criminal Court (ICC)—A Postcolonial Tool for Western States to Control Africa?' *Journal of International Criminal Law (JICL)* 1, no. 1 (2020): 90–109.

Simmons, Beth A., and Allison Danner. 'Credible Commitments and the International Criminal Court'. *International Organization* 64, no. 2 (April 2010): 225–56.

Simmons, Beth A, and Hyeran Jo. 'Measuring Norms and Normative Contestation: The Case of International Criminal Law'. *Journal of Global Security Studies* 4, no. 1 (1 January 2019): 18–36.

Singh, Shannon Raj. 'Move Fast and Break Societies: The Weaponisation of Social Media and Options for Accountability under International Criminal Law'. *Cambridge International Law Journal* 8, no. 2 (1 December 2019): 331–42.

Tilden, S. J. 'Africa's Conflict with the International Criminal Court: The African Court of Justice and Human and Peoples' Right as an Alternative to the ICC'. *Tulane Journal of International and Comparative Law* 27 (2019 [2018]): 201.

Vilmer, Jean-Baptiste Jeangène. 'The African Union and the International Criminal Court: Counteracting the Crisis'. *International Affairs* 92, no. 6 (1 November 2016): 1319–42.

Vinjamuri, Leslie. 'Deterrence, Democracy, and the Pursuit of International Justice'. *Ethics & International Affairs* 24, no. 2 (2010): 191–211.

———. 'The International Criminal Court and the Paradox of Authority'. *Law and Contemporary Problems* 79, no. 1 (2016): 275–87.

Walker, Andrew J. 'When a Good Idea Is Poorly Implemented: How the International Criminal Court Fails to Be Insulated from International Politics and to Protect Basic Due Process Guarantees'. *West Virginia Law Review* 106 (2004 [2003]): 245.

Weerdesteijn, Maartje, and Barbora Holá. '"Tool in the R2P Toolbox"? Analysing the Role of the International Criminal Court in the Three Pillars of the Responsibility to Protect'. *Criminal Law Forum* 31, no. 3 (1 September 2020): 377–414.

Zwier, Paul J. 'Social Media and Conflict Mapping in Syria: Implications for Peacemaking, International Criminal Prosecutions and for TRC Processes'. *Emory International Law Review* 30 (2016 [2015]): 169.

CHAPTER 3

The ICC and the Democracy Paradox: The Museveni Affair and the Kenyatta Exception

Background to the Investigation in Uganda

This Chapter delves into the ICC endeavours in Uganda and Kenya, scrutinising them through the lens of the democracy paradox. This paradox suggests that while the ICC aims to promote democracy by upholding the rule of law, governments facing ICC scrutiny can manipulate ICC actions to strengthen their hold on power. From this perspective, the reason why this book doesn't start with a SHoS prosecution, and rather begins with a situation where Ugandan President Museveni and members of his government weren't scrutinised by the ICC (or not as much as the rebels) is to highlight the fact that, despite being outlined in the Rome Statute, the practice of prosecuting SHoS is not something that emerged naturally in the initial ICC cases. The political leverage that domestic authorities have on the Court generally means that the ICC usually necessitates from the cooperation of local authorities to carry out its investigations. This led some to argue that the Court might be biased in favour of governmental forces, especially in intra-state conflicts and civil wars. As noted in Chap. 1, the debate on the politicisation of the Court has been present since the first draft of the Rome Statute was circulated. After all, despite being formally a judicial organ, the ICC has to operate in a political world where power, resources, wars, and peace-processes are daily events. Further to this, as

M. Cacciatori, *The International Criminal Court and the Prosecution of Sitting Heads of State*,
https://doi.org/10.1007/978-3-031-54646-4_3

Nouwen and Werner claim, “the Court was created by political decisions, it adjudicates crimes which are frequently related to politics, and it depends on a mysterious and seemingly magical “political will” for the enforcement of its decisions. The political is not something external to the Court, not just a force which potentially compromises the independence of the Court and needs to be overcome”.[1] Not only that, but also the fact that the Court was set up to investigate the most heinous crimes conceivable by the humankind, sustained by the liberal project that aimed at eradicating them internationally at least since the end of the Cold War, added a layer of inherent politicisation that spurred a florid debate among academics and practitioners. In fact, as we will see in the following sections, many argued that the reason why the ICC decided to focus on non-governmental forces in the context of the Ugandan Civil War is precisely because declaring the intent of prosecuting a SHoS could have derailed the entire investigation—which led to accusations of bias, partiality, and unfairness. Some even argued that the Museveni government successfully exploited the ICC to prolong the existence of the conflict and consolidate its dominance on Ugandan politics—in line with the democracy paradox outlined above.

Literature investigating the ICC actions in Uganda has been florid. For instance Akhvan focused on the reasons why the government decided to refer itself to the Court. He suggests that, along with other political calculations, the Museveni self-referral was also shaped by a desire for Uganda to be recognised as an international actor in the international arena.[2] Branch, on the other hand, suggested that the self-referral was mainly motivated by a desire of the Museveni government to be legitimised in its fight against the LRA, and that this can be considered as fuelling future intra-ethnic tensions.[3] This is naturally very relevant to the Chapter, that considers the self-referral as the starting point to understand the formation of the democracy paradox.

[1] Sarah M. H. Nouwen and Wouter G. Werner, ‘Doing Justice to the Political: The International Criminal Court in Uganda and Sudan’, *European Journal of International Law* 21, no. 4 (1 November 2010): 943.

[2] Payam Akhavan, ‘The Lord’s Resistance Army Case: Uganda’s Submission of the First State Referral to the International Criminal Court’, *American Journal of International Law* 99, no. 2 (April 2005): 403–21.

[3] Adam Branch, ‘Uganda’s Civil War and the Politics of ICC Intervention’, *Ethics & International Affairs* 21, no. 2 (July 2007): 179–98.

Other strands of literature questioned specific proceedings and how the Ugandan case, being the first, was to set the bar over the handling of specific crimes. Denov and Drumbl, for instance, suggest that the Ugandan investigation illuminated on how gender-related crimes happening during the Ugandan Civil War were prosecuted by the ICC, and the extent of governmental cooperation to aid the Court in its efforts.[4] Bameka, on similar lines, highlights that the effectiveness of the Court in delivering on its justice mandate rests, also, on the ability to accommodate substantive victims' concerns over specific crimes committed, such as child soldiers.[5] While apparently departing from such analyses on the peculiarities of the case, the Chapter also considers how specific cultural and religious practices impacted the Court's work in Uganda—and the role that the government played in galvanising these discrepancies. Lastly, an ever present undertone of anti-colonial narrative also sparked important questions about perceptions of neo-colonialism and how to counter them. One of the reasons why such perceptions propagated in Uganda, Bens suggests, is the lack of transparency that prevents the creation of positive atmospheres in the courtroom.[6] Kirabira goes even further, by claiming that the proceedings of the Court in the country have indeed sparked doubts of imperialism and neo-colonialism, and that only NGOs that operate in the country can mitigate such critics.[7]

All this literature is very important for the scope of this Chapter, and this book in general. However, this section offers an alternative explanation to the difficulties that the ICC faced in Uganda and, perhaps more importantly, to some of the implications that the investigation contributed to produce in the country. As already noted, the underpinning conceptual

[4] Myriam S. Denov and Mark A. Drumbl, 'The Many Harms of Forced Marriage: Insights for Law from Ethnography in Northern Uganda', *Journal of International Criminal Justice* 18, no. 2 (1 May 2020): 349–72.

[5] Christelle Molima Bameka, 'The Post-Ongwen Case Period and the Reconciliation Process in Northern Uganda: Local Communities as a Site of Knowledge', *International Criminal Law Review* 1, no. aop (1 February 2024): 1–24.

[6] Jonas Bens, 'Transitional Justice Atmospheres: The Role of Space and Affect in the International Criminal Court's Outreach Efforts in Northern Uganda', in *Normative Spaces and Legal Dynamics in Africa* (Routledge, 2020).

[7] Tonny Raymond Kirabira, 'NGOs and the Legitimacy of International Criminal Justice: The Case of Uganda', in *International Criminal Law—A Counter-Hegemonic Project?*, ed. Florian Jeßberger, Leonie Steinl, and Kalika Mehta (The Hague: T.M.C. Asser Press, 2023), 153–74.

framework that this Chapter advances can be summarised by a paradoxical inference: ICC actions should help the consolidation of democracy; but these actions can be exploited by governments to consolidate their, often authoritarian, grip on the country. In a way, the argument departs from the ones outlined above because it focuses on the systemic consequences of this unresolved, and maybe unresolvable, conceptual tension. The main purpose of the first part of the Chapter, therefore, is to show how political considerations about the feasibility of an ICC investigation were paramount in Uganda, and how these led the Court to operate in a manner that ensured cooperation from local authorities. The only way in which this cooperation could be achieved, it was thought, was through an implicit exclusion of senior members of the government from prosecution. This questions the feasibility of SHoS prosecutions in general, since the conditions in which the ICC has to operate are almost always the same and have to acknowledge the fact that if a SHoS is scrutinised by the Court, then governmental resistance to the institution is to be assumed. However, by legitimising the Musveni government, there is little doubt that the ICC also helped in a consolidation of power that is not akin to bottom-up democratic processes. And this contradicts one of the alleged purposes of the Court.

In the following sections the Chapter aims at highlighting that certain societal challenges were present before the ICC stepped in, which greatly shaped the relationship between the Court and President Museveni: first, Ugandan society (and in particular the Acholi community) often approaches matters of criminal justice through restorative practices and not retributive ones. Second, in an attempt to de-escalate the violence that was plaguing the country and as part of a broader restorative process, the Museveni government promulgated a large-scale Amnesty in 2000—which is *de facto* antithetic to the work of the ICC. These considerations became important options in the governmental acceptance to the Court and, maybe more saliently, in its opposition once the prospect of an investigation into governmental responsibilities emerged. In addition to these societal circumstances that were present well before the ICC decided to step in, three additional ones were to dictate the terms of the cooperation of the Government of Uganda with the Court: first, the investigation was initiated because the government itself decided to refer the situation to the ICC. This is commonly referred to as a self-referral, a practice that would become very common, and that would characterise several situations concerning African countries. However, self-referrals by their very nature impose certain informal limits to the Court, in terms of who can be prosecuted. In other terms, governments refer themselves *also* to avoid international scrutiny on their criminal responsibilities. Second, after the ICC stepped in the government initiated the most important series of negotiations with LRA rebels: the Juba Peace Talks, and the ICC was eventually depicted as an obstacle to their development. This, at least on the rhetorical dimension, seems to sustain the dilemma posed by the peace and/or justice dichotomy as well as sustaining the existence of a democracy paradox when the ICC intervenes. Finally, since 2009, the ICC started actively prosecuting SHoS, with the arrest warrants released against Sudanese President Omar al-Bashir, and this indicated that sitting governments were not systematically exempt from ICC scrutiny. The combination of (at least) these factors contributed to an intermittent support of the Museveni government for the efforts of the ICC in the country. And surely highlighted that Prosecuting the SHoS would require considerations about the feasibility of the operation, the ability of a SHoS to exploit the efforts of international actors to maintain power and silence opposition, and the international reaction to potentially unbalanced prosecutions that would exclude state actors from prosecutions.

The LRA Insurgency

The LRA insurgency is a resistance guerrilla movement that has shaped the contours of the social texture of Uganda since the mid-1980s, when the Tito Okello government was overthrown by current President Museveni who, at the time, led the National Resistance Army (NRA). The LRA was then led, and remains to be, by political and spiritual leader Joseph Kony who, as early as the 1980s, adopted guerrilla tactics to attack villages and civilians. The alignment of the movement with certain Acholi personalities, coupled with the fact that Museveni overthrew a government of Acholi inclinations, ensured that at least part of the population supported and granted logistical aid to the LRA.

The Government of Uganda started retaliating against the LRA militarily, by launching large-scale operations like the 1991 Operation North, and by empowering local militias to cut the popular support for the LRA while counter-acting the organisation's guerrilla tactics. Emblematic of this was the creation of the Arrow Groups, factions of local villagers armed with traditional weapons to fight against LRA attacks. Betty Bigombe, an eminent political figure in the Ugandan society, initiated in the mid-1990s a process of negotiation for the termination of hostilities with Kony himself. However, the process did not bear fruit due to mutual distrust between the warring factions. The breaking down of the peace talks coincided with an internationalisation of the conflict, since Kony was seeking (and would eventually be granted) support from neighbouring countries, especially Sudan.

Between 1994 and the starting of the ICC investigation, the LRA enjoyed the cooperation of the Al Bashir government, maybe in response to the Government of Uganda supporting the Sudan People Liberation Army (SPLA). The Museveni government responded by creating the so-called Displaced People's Camps, where the government forced all Acholis to leave in inhuman conditions. The conflict formally ended in 2006, although sparks of violence reappear constantly. It is in this context that events that will be described in subsequent sections, like the 2000 Amnesty Law, the Juba Talks, and the ICC investigation, took place.

Box 3.1 Biographical Sketch Museveni

Who Is Yoweri Museveni?

Museveni was probably born on 15 September 1944, and began his political career, deeply intertwined with his military allegiances, in the early 1970s when he formed the Front for National Salvation (FRONASA). From the 1970s Uganda has been in constant turmoil, with frequent changes in power and even more frequent internecine struggles for the control of the country. In this context, the FRONASA supported the counter-invasion rebel groups that opposed the Idi Amin regime, which ousted Milton Obote, Uganda's second President, in 1971. Amin's ruling had been characterised by unmatched brutality and ruthlessness, which fuelled the creation of a multiplicity of groups that aimed at overthrowing him. Among these, Museveni eventually became a leading figure of the Ugandan National Liberation Front (UNLF), which played a crucial role in the overthrowal of the President in 1979. After the coup, a contested national election gave the presidency to former President Obote, who was ousted eight years prior.

(*continued*)

Box 3.1 (continued)
The year 1980 is considered the start of the so-called Ugandan Bush War, an intra-state conflict between official governmental forces and rebel groups. Among these, Museveni was constantly a central presence.[8]

Dissatisfied with the outcome of the murky electoral process, Museveni became a leading opposition figure that contested the second term of Obote. He was part of a variety of groups such as the Popular Resistance Army (PRA) and the paramilitary NRA.[9] The Obote regime was eventually overthrown by a military coup led by Tito Okello, a military general of Acholi origins. Okello and Museveni both aimed at the presidency and held unsuccessful talks to find a peaceful resolve of their dispute for power. The PRA/NRA led, since 1985, a series of attacks that weakened the Okello government. His regime officially ended when the troops led by Museveni captured the capital Kampala on 26 January 1986. Museveni was sworn in as President on 29 January of the same year and has been the President of the country since then, having been re-elected for mandate six times, amidst constitutional reforms and a myriad of allegations of electoral fraud.

Ugandan Restorativism: *Mato Oput*, the 2000 Amnesty Law, and the ICC as an Impediment for Local Justice

This book already introduced the tension between restorative and punitive forms of justice, formalised in the peace and/or justice debate, in Chap. 1. The tension between these two seemingly alternative dimensions of justice, particularly prominent in the mid-1990s, re-emerged forcefully in Uganda and greatly shaped the relationship between the government and

[8] Thomas P. Ofcansky, 'Musevenis War and the Ugandan Conflict', Journal of Conflict Studies, 1 July 1999, https://journals.lib.unb.ca/index.php/JCS/article/view/4386.

[9] Gérard Prunier, 'Rebel Movements and Proxy Warfare: Uganda, Sudan and the Congo (1986–99)', African Affairs 103, no. 412 (1 July 2004): 359–83.

the ICC. At this stage, it must be remembered, that the ICC's aim is to work in conjunction with local governments where possible, and not supersede them. The Court essentially provides with a safety net when domestic prosecutions are impossible because of collapsed national legal systems or because governments are unwilling to prosecute alleged perpetrators, whatever the reason.[10] Commentators argued that this creates a conceptual and practical environment in which either the ICC lets domestic criminal systems take precedence, or tensions would always arise from an implicit accusation that these domestic actors are either incompetent or complicit to the crimes.[11] These issues are particularly acute when local practices seem to be incompatible with the scope and remit of the Court, or when the ICC is perceived as alien to local realities. Also, this perceived incompatibility can become a powerful tool for governments to garner political support should they decide to oppose the ICC.

Among the various local practices typical of Uganda, *Mato Oput* stands out as one of the main restorative ceremonies that have been continuously employed, especially by the Acholi community, to come to terms with crimes that affect the fabric of society. The ceremony is conceptually similar to the work of a truth commission. During the *Mato Oput*, elders conduct truth-seeking processes and compensation rituals to restore communal relationship between the clan of the offender and the clan of the victim. Bangura describes the rite as a ritual that "[...]involves a murderer facing relatives of the victim and admitting his crime before the murderer and the relatives drink a bitter brew made from a tree root mixed with sheep's blood".[12] The tension between such forms of justice and the work of the ICC is evident, and opposed the Court to local communities. On one side international actors through the ICC pushed for a criminal trial,[13] in line with the progressive hostility towards truth-seeking mechanisms and amnesties as *alternatives* to retributive justice.[14] On the other, influent

[10] M. Cherif Bassiouni, 'The ICC—Quo Vadis?', *Journal of International Criminal Justice* 4, no. 3 (1 July 2006): 422.

[11] Claus Kress, 'Self-Referrals and Waivers of Complementarity—Some Considerations in Law and Policy', *Journal of International Criminal Justice* 2 (2004): 944.

[12] Abdul Karim Bangura, 'The Politics of the Struggle to Resolve the Conflict in Uganda: Westerners Pushing Their Legal Approach versus Ugandans Insisting on Their Mato Oput', 2008, 143.

[13] Steven C. Roach, 'Multilayered Justice in Northern Uganda: ICC Intervention and Local Procedures of Accountability', *International Criminal Law Review* 13, no. 1 (1 January 2013): 249.

[14] Ruti G. Teitel, 'Transitional Justice Genealogy', *Harv. Hum. Rts. J.* 16 (2003): 69.

intra-societal groups like the Acholi pushed for restorative approaches evidently incompatible with such international efforts. The Acholi community, in fact, consistently challenged any form of prosecution on the basis that this was an impediment for local restorative processes.[15] Considering how this approach has been a cornerstone of the Ugandan system for a long time, it is not difficult to understand why the government decided, in 2000, to promulgate an amnesty law for the crimes committed since 1986. It has been historically noted how restorative practices and amnesties tend(ed) to go hand in hand, with examples emerging for instance in the South American and the Balkan contexts of the mid-1990s. Amnesties are not conceptually as incompatible with restorative processes as criminal trials, and, it has been argued, *de facto* to encourage perpetrators to give up arms and participate in restorative ceremonies if they are not threatened with retributive punishment for their actions.

The amnesty initiative was launched at the request of the victims, in the hope that the process would encourage all combatant factions to abandon the protests and avoid an escalation of violence. It was formalised by the promulgation of the Amnesty Act that provided that all those involved in the conflict who renounced violence were to be shielded from prosecution and could return to their communities as free men. The Amnesty specifically postulated that "[a]n amnesty is declared in respect of any Ugandan who has at any time since the 26th day of January, 1986, engaged in or is engaging in war or armed rebellion against the government of the Republic of Uganda [...]"[16] if the offender "renounces and abandons involvement in the war or armed rebellion".[17] The difficulty in reconciling the Act and the purpose of the ICC is clear and the Chairman of the Amnesty Commission, Justice Peter Onega, claimed that"[s]ince the ICC takes precedence over our national laws, even people already granted amnesty could be taken for trial before the ICC—if this happens, the amnesty process and the law will be rendered useless".[18] Onega even

[15] Katherine Southwick, 'Investigating War in Northern Uganda: Dilemmas for the International Criminal Court', *Yale Journal of International Affairs* 1, no. 1 (2005): 116.

[16] Law Reform Commission of Uganda, 'Amnesty Act' (2000), pt. 2 (1), https://ulii.org/akn/ug/act/2000/2/eng@2000-12-31.

[17] Law Reform Commission of Uganda, pt. 3 (1)(b).

[18] Manisuli Ssenyonjo, 'Accountability of Non-State Actors in Uganda for War Crimes and Human Rights Violations: Between Amnesty and the International Criminal Court', *Journal of Conflict and Security Law* 10, no. 3 (1 December 2005): 427.

suggested that any Court investigation would have hampered the possibility of a peaceful resolution of the conflict and would have encouraged more atrocities, by claiming that LRA leaders could have acted as "desperately as a wounded buffalo".[19] This stance was reinforced by Acholi leaders who tried to lobby Moreno-Ocampo to drop the investigation.[20] For instance the Information Minister of the time, Nsaba Buturo, claimed that those who took part in the amnesty process would be shielded from any future prosecution by the ICC—seeding the initial germ for a *de facto* withdrawal of governmental support for the ICC.[21] The leader of the Acholi Religious Leaders' Peace Initiative (ARLPI), Archbishop John Baptist Odama, later asked "how can we tell the LRA soldiers to come out of the bush and receive amnesty when at the same the threat of arrest by the ICC hangs over their heads?".[22]

However, there was widespread scepticism already present among LRA ranks related to the sincerity of the governmental backing of the Amnesty Act. Many LRA combatants claimed that Kony himself declared that the Amnesty was just another governmental strategy to invite them in the open so that the resistance could be crushed.[23] These doubts, fuelled by a dubious governmental military strategy, have shaped the discourse around the Amnesty Law since it was introduced. For instance, Hovil and Lomo argued that the fact that the government launched the controversial Operation Iron Fist in March 2002, is an indication that the Museveni government was not really committed to a peaceful resolution of the conflict against the LRA. The operation not only contradicted the aims of the

[19] Sara Darehshori and Elizabeth Evenson, 'Peace, Justice, and the International Criminal Court', *Oxford Transitional Justice Research Papers*, 19 March 2010, https://www.law.ox.ac.uk/sites/default/files/migrated/darehshoriandevenson20101.pdf.

[20] Kasaija Phillip Apuuli, 'The ICC Arrest Warrants for the Lord's Resistance Army Leaders and Peace Prospects for Northern Uganda', *Journal of International Criminal Justice* 4, no. 1 (1 March 2006): 184.

[21] Bassiouni, 'The ICC—Quo Vadis?', 424.

[22] 'Waiting for Elusive Peace in the War-Ravaged North', *The New Humanitarian* 9 June 2005, https://www.thenewhumanitarian.org/report/54852/uganda-waiting-elusive-peace-war-ravaged-north.

[23] Relief Web, 'Uganda: Forgiveness as an Instrument of Peace—Uganda', 9 June 2005, https://reliefweb.int/report/uganda/uganda-forgiveness-instrument-peace.

Amnesty Act, but also "unleashed renewed attacks against the civilian population and gave Kony increased justification for using violence".[24] To add fuel to the fire, the Ugandan government also urged neighbouring countries, Sudan especially, to cut ties with the LRA rebels and sustain the governmental retaliation against them. The Sudanese government eventually signed a protocol that allowed the Ugandan armed forces to attack LRA camps in Sudan.[25] Consequently, Operation Iron Fist deprived the rebels from the ability to cultivate crops in Sudan, which sparked the worst cycle of violence in the history of the conflict.[26] Following Operation Iron Fist, and as a consequence of the renewed activity of LRA groups within Uganda, the number of displaced people quadrupled from ca. 400000 to 1.6 million. This led Jan Eagland, Under-Secretary General for Humanitarian Affairs and Emergency Relief in 2004, to describe the situation as the "biggest neglected humanitarian emergency in the world". The British Ambassador to the UN, Sir Emyr Jones Parry, reinforced this view by claiming that Uganda was "one of the great crises out there which is not recognised enough".[27] In addition to the dubious aims and outcomes of the Operation, the LRA was also included as a Terrorist organisation in the Anti-Terrorism Act promulgated by the government and was included in the US list of terrorist organisations after the Twin Towers attacks. The combination of these elements raised questions about the environment that surrounded the promulgation of the Amnesty, which effectively contributed to the creation of a climate of distrust that was not conducive to an effective enforcement of the Act to mitigate the effects of the conflict.

So, the context in which the ICC had to operate in was extremely problematic, well *before* the Court initiated any investigation in the case. Historic societal practices which prioritised restoration against retribution, and a governmental approach to the pacification of the conflict that

[24] Lucy Hovil and Zachary Lomo, 'Whose Justice? Perceptions of Uganda's Amnesty Act 2000', *Refugee Law Project Working Paper No. 15*, no. 15 (2005): 19–20.

[25] Darehshori and Evenson, 'Peace, Justice, and the International Criminal Court', 8.

[26] Ssenyonjo, 'Accountability of Non-State Actors in Uganda for War Crimes and Human Rights Violations', 417.

[27] The Guardian, 'Northern Uganda "World's Biggest Neglected Crisis"', 22 October 2004, sec. World news, https://www.theguardian.com/world/2004/oct/22/2.

swinged from amnesty offerings to brutal retaliatory military missions, created a situation in which the ICC had to cooperate with the Museveni government, allow for domestic redressing of the crimes, and not contradict its own Statute. Considerable parts of the societal fabric of Uganda seemed to be inherently hostile to any prosecution, not only SHoS ones. But prosecuting Museveni and his government would have been, on one side, alien to local practices like *Mato Oput*, and on the other in clear opposition to the 2000 Amnesty Law. Without even considering the reaction of the government to such a scenario, the ground was not particularly fertile for the ICC, and this was to be further complicated by three additional factors: the fact that the Court initiated the investigation upon the request of Museveni himself in 2004, the Juba Peace Talks that occurred between 2006 and 2008, and the release of the warrants of arrest against Sudanese President Al Bashir. The combination of these factors can be read as indicating a societal incompatibility with ICC prosecutions or, alternatively, as forming an optimal ground for the government to justify its opposition to the Court while harnessing popular support. In fact, the Museveni government was able to initially accommodate the differences outlined above by suggesting that the ICC would have helped the Ugandan society against a terrorist group. However, as the following sections will outline, the narrative quickly turned to exacerbate these tensions once the government perceived it could be prosecuted. This seems to sustain the idea that the ability of a government to swing the narrative to consolidate its power significantly influences perceptions of the ICC in a country, regardless of the societal preconditions in which the investigation occurs.

The Self-Referral and the Legitimisation of the Museveni Government

This section explores issues related to the practice of self-referrals in Uganda and how this shaped the Ugandan investigation by implicitly shielding Museveni and his officials from prosecution. ICC operations in Uganda formally began in July 2004. Even though many commentators were asking questions about the admissibility of the case according to the Rome Statute, given the nature of self-referrals and the fact that the LRA is a non-state actor, Chief Prosecutor Moreno-Ocampo initiated an investigation into the crimes committed by the LRA in the northern part of the country. It is of extreme importance for the scope of this Chapter, and this book in general, to note that a florid discussion about the legitimacy of self-referrals has been shaping the role of the Court in international politics since the very beginning, and the Ugandan case is often cited as one of the primary instances of this practice.[28] In fact, "[...] but few at the Rome Conference had anticipated that a state would refer to the Court a situation on its own territory and concerning its own nationals. The debate had focused on how states could prevent ICC intervention. It had been assumed that states would consider such intervention as costly to their sovereignty and reputation".[29] So, in the initial iterations, most thought that no state would refer itself to the ICC, given the fact that in unbiased circumstances this would have meant drawing international attention to the potential responsibility of state actors for the crimes covered by the Court. It seemed to be assumed that, on the other hand, a member-state could witness suspicious activity in a neighbouring country and refer that case to the ICC. However, in the case of self-referrals, a government asks the Court to investigate something that is happening within its borders and, assuming that states do not engage in conscious self-destructive practices, this gave birth to two systemic problematics: "first, in states in which civil war is taking place, it may be that a state's request for an investigation is chiefly motivated by the will to expose internationally the crimes allegedly being perpetrated by the other side" and "second is that it is likely to be difficult to achieve full cooperation of the referring state in cases where the state is torn apart by internecine war".[30] So only when a government perceives ICC interventions as potentially aligning with its own interests self-referrals become a viable option.[31] The decision to refer a case to the ICC is ultimately subject to the vetting of the sitting government, but if

[28] Payam Akhavan, 'Self-Referrals before the International Criminal Court: Are States the Villains or the Victims of Atrocities?', *Criminal Law Forum* 21 (2010): 103; Giorgio Gaja, 'Issues of Admissibility in Case of Self-Referrals', in *The International Criminal Court and National Jurisdictions* (Routledge, 2008); Kress, 'Self-Referrals and Waivers of Complementarity - Some Considerations in Law and Policy'.

[29] Nouwen and Werner, 'Doing Justice to the Political', 948.

[30] P. Gaeta, 'Is the Practice of "Self-Referrals" a Sound Start for the ICC?', *Journal of International Criminal Justice* 2, no. 4 (1 December 2004): 951–52.

[31] Sarah M. H. Nouwen, *Complementarity in the Line of Fire: The Catalysing Effect of the International Criminal Court in Uganda and Sudan* (Cambridge University Press, 2013), 116–40.

members of the government are likely to be impacted directly by the investigation, the likelihood of a self-referral happening becomes quite slim. This, if the Court doesn't strike a tacit and implicit deal with the government, where basically the investigation would mainly focus on anti-governmental forces. This seems to have underpinned the relationship between the Ugandan government and the Court. In 2004, after Museveni referred the case to the ICC, Moreno-Ocampo praised the Ugandan government for "[...] exhaust[ing] very other means of bringing an end to this terrible suffering",[32] and was photographed shaking hands with the Ugandan President. Initially, Museveni pledged its "full cooperation to the Prosecutor in the investigation and prosecution of the LRA crimes",[33] already underlining that governmental cooperation with the Court was limited to the prosecution of Kony and his soldiers. Naturally, such considerations make the ICC subject to the volatility of local political opportunism that are likely to either support or contest the Court depending on what course of action ensures maximal legitimisation. If this is true, then the hope that the ICC would encourage and sustain democratic processes seems to be ill placed at least when SHoS are concerned.

It is true that since 1986, as already noted, the LRA and the Government of Uganda attempted several times to engage in peace negotiations, unsuccessfully. In November 2004, the government even announced a unilateral ceasefire in the northern parts of the nation, but the talks broke down in December of the same year.[34] In this context, the Prosecutor decided to step in and issue five mandates for the arrest of LRA leaders: Joseph Kony, Vincent Otti, Okot Odhiambo, Dominic Ongwen, and Raska Luwyia. The debate on the politicisation and potential bias of the Court was exacerbated considering the release of the warrants, given that in Uganda the Court was involved in a civil conflict that, by definition, involves both governmental and non-governmental forces.[35] Only indicting LRA

[32] Renée Jeffery, *Amnesties, Accountability, and Human Rights* (University of Pennsylvania Press, 2014), 87.

[33] United Nations, 'President of Uganda Refers Situation Concerning Lord's Resistance Army (LRA) To International Criminal Court', 2004, accessed 13 June 2023, https://press.un.org/en/2004/afr821.doc.htm.

[34] Apuuli, 'The ICC Arrest Warrants for the Lord's Resistance Army Leaders and Peace Prospects for Northern Uganda', 183.

[35] Adam Branch, 'Uganda's Civil War and the Politics of ICC Intervention', *Ethics & International Affairs* 21, no. 2 (July 2007): 179–80.

leaders, "put the ICC in an awkward position in acting on behalf of the Ugandan state, which is involved in the war. Certainly the perception of some observers [was] that the ICC has allowed itself to be subject to the political needs of the Ugandan state".[36] Despite this, Museveni became increasingly sceptical about the possibility of being able to comply with the warrants for the arrest against the members of the LRA that the ICC named.[37] As such, the underpinning discrepancies between the overall goals of the Museveni government (to crush LRA opposition and legitimise its rule) and the ICC's (to combat impunity and be perceived as an impartial and unbiased court) were bound to culminate in a struggle to determine which actor held the leverage in the relationship.

The fact that the Prosecutor only named LRA commanders as primary suspects, *de facto* excluded Museveni and senior members of his government from investigation. Naturally, the ICC couldn't openly admit that, since it would defeat the purpose of being perceived as an impartial institution. In a statement released in 2005, Moreno-Ocampo clarified that after reviewing the evidence, and after 20 missions in Uganda to listen to victims and members of the civil society (including members of the Acholi group), the crimes "committed by the LRA were much more numerous and of much higher gravity than alleged crimes committed by the UPDF".[38] This statement, however, was not taken at face value and was heavily contested by several civil society groups including Human Rights' Watch (HRW) and the Refugee Law Project (RLP). The RLP claimed that the Court actively ignored crimes of similar magnitude of those committed by the LRA, showing prosecutorial bias.[39] HRW, after publishing an extensive report that detailed many atrocities committed by UPDF forces, urged the ICC to investigate both state and non-state actors.[40] While the Prosecutor clarified

[36] Paul Jackson, '"Negotiating with Ghosts": Religion, Conflict and Peace in Northern Uganda', *The Round Table* 98, no. 402 (1 June 2009): 327.

[37] Jeffery, *Amnesties, Accountability, and Human Rights*, 87.

[38] International Criminal Court, 'Statement by Chief Prosecutor Luis Moreno Ocampo', 14 October 2005, https://www.icc-cpi.int/sites/default/files/NR/rdonlyres/2919856F-03E0-403F-A1A8-D61D4F350A20/277305/Uganda_LMO_Speech_141020091.pdf.

[39] Apuuli, 'The ICC Arrest Warrants for the Lord's Resistance Army Leaders and Peace Prospects for Northern Uganda', 185.

[40] Human Rights Watch, 'Uprooted and Forgotten', 20 September 2005, https://www.hrw.org/report/2005/09/20/uprooted-and-forgotten/impunity-and-human-rights-abuses-northern-uganda.

that he would continue examining allegations against all groups to determine if the Court needed to take action against members of the Uganda's People Defence Force (UPDF) as well,[41] doubts remained. Richard Dicker, director of the International Justice programme at HRW, stated that the necessity of collaborating with local authorities could have hampered the possibility of an impartial investigation by the ICC, "[b]ut the ICC prosecutor cannot ignore the crimes that Ugandan government troops allegedly have committed" and added "President Museveni's referral does not limit the prosecutor's investigation only to crimes allegedly committed by the LRA [...] The prosecutor should operate independently and has the authority to look at all ICC crimes committed in Uganda".[42] This was reiterated by Goldston, who argued that "Moreno Ocampo should make clear that while he welcomes governments' cooperation, his office operates independently. A President cannot immunize himself from prosecution simply by referring a case against his opponents".[43] These statements were highlighted locally by one of the suspects as well, Otti, who told Voice of America that "[t]he Museveni government indicted the LRA leadership and some of its top commanders. We were indicted without being questioned. We were not even investigated. That is why we decided to at least first of all send some of our delegates to go and find it properly from the Hague and from the court prosecutor to explain to them or we would like the prosecutor to send his staff to come here and hear from us whether we have really committed crimes".[44] Otti associated the government with the ICC directly, hinting at the fact that the Court was subjugated to Museveni's will. While the Museveni government rejected the allegations, it is undeniable that the focus on LRA commanders created a sense of acrimony towards the ICC which, at least internationally, was seen as consolidating a

[41] International Criminal Court, 'Statement by Chief Prosecutor Luis Moreno Ocampo'.

[42] Human Rights Watch, 'ICC: Investigate All Sides in Uganda', 4 February 2004, https://www.hrw.org/news/2004/02/04/icc-investigate-all-sides-uganda.

[43] James A. Goldston et al., 'Opinion | Justice for Uganda : A Crucial Case for the International Criminal Court', *The New York Times*, 27 February 2004, sec. Opinion, https://www.nytimes.com/2004/02/27/opinion/justice-for-uganda-a-crucial-case-for-the-international-criminal.html.

[44] Voice of America, 'LRA Rebels to Send Delegates to the ICC', 1 November 2009, https://www.voanews.com/a/a-13-2007-01-24-voa3/351110.html.

government allegedly complicit in the escalation of violence in northern Uganda. And given the ambivalent governmental attitude towards past peace talks and the intermittent support for the 2000 Amnesty Act, the exclusion of governmental officials from investigation did indeed question the impartiality of the Court, to the point that Kony himself declared that he would not engage in any talks about peace until the ICC lifted the warrants of arrest.[45]

Admittedly, the Ugandan case has been shaped by a unique relationship between the Court and the Government of Uganda since the very beginning. Müller and Stegmiller claimed that, while still voluntary, the government was strongly encouraged by the Prosecutor to refer the situation in the country "warning that he would otherwise consider opening an investigation *proprio motu*".[46] However, it would be naïve to claim that the Museveni government only acted out of the pressure made by the ICC Prosecutor. In fact, as outlined earlier, the deterioration of the humanitarian situation in the country brought it to the spotlight of UN attention and questions about the legitimacy of Museveni and the involvement of the government and the UPDF in the escalation of the civil war started to surface at the international level. So, it seems plausible, that on the one hand the government attempted at shaping the Court' action by willingly submitting a referral. On the other it also attempted to use the ICC as part of a rehabilitation strategy that aimed at restoring the credibility of the government internationally while, as a government official put it in 2008, "intimidate[ing] these thugs [the LRA], to show that they were sought by many more".[47] This view was reinforced by the President himself, who was reported saying during an radio interview: "[t]he removal of the indictments will be a reward for [the LRA] signing the [June] Agreement. Otherwise you [the rebels] will die in our hands or in the hands of the ICC".[48]

[45] Janine Natalya Clark, 'The ICC, Uganda and the LRA: Re-Framing the Debate', *African Studies* 69, no. 1 (1 April 2010): 147.

[46] Andreas Th. Müller and Ignaz Stegmiller, 'Self-Referrals on Trial: From Panacea to Patient', *Journal of International Criminal Justice* 8, no. 5 (1 November 2010): 1271.

[47] Nouwen and Werner, 'Doing Justice to the Political', 949.

[48] The New Humanitarian, 'ICC Indictments against Rebels Should Stay, Says President', 21 September 2006, https://www.thenewhumanitarian.org/report/61142/uganda-icc-indictments-against-rebels-should-stay-says-president.

Bassiouni highlighted that the Ugandan case underscored in many ways the dependence of the ICC on the goodwill of national authorities, adding that this was especially true when the UNSC "[did not] land its weight to the ICC's efforts".[49] Even years after the initiation of the investigation in Uganda, commentators still argue that the prosecution showed certain fallacies. Mark Kersten claimed that "[p]rosecuting Government and military officials would be a welcome move. But it would also represent an admission that the ICC should have—but didn't—do so initially".[50] The most publicised reaction to the non-indictment of the President started when Ugandan musician-turned-politician Bobi Wine founded the National Unity Platform party in 2020. Wine stood as the opposition leader in the same year and called for an investigation on the crimes of Museveni on several occasions.[51] So, it seems that the fact that the ICC started its operations in Uganda because of a self-referral of the Museveni government had two corollaries. On the positive side, the ICC was able to initiate an investigation in one of the gravest situations in the world, which gives credit to the Court. On the negative, because the Court was invited in from the Museveni government, and the support of the government was conditional to its objectives, the ICC wasn't free to investigate fully both parties—at least initially.

The Museveni Reversal and the ICC as a Threat for Peace

This section explores the nexus between the peace negotiations that started in 2006 and the efforts of the Court, highlighting that the support for the ICC by the Museveni government was continuously

[49] Bassiouni, 'The ICC—Quo Vadis?', 425.

[50] Mark Kersten, 'Why the ICC Won't Prosecute Museveni', *Justice in Conflict* (blog), 19 March 2015, https://justiceinconflict.org/2015/03/19/why-the-icc-wont-prosecute-museveni/.

[51] The East African, 'Bobi Wine Asks ICC to Investigate Museveni over Human Rights Abuses', 8 January 2021, https://www.theeastafrican.co.ke/tea/news/east-africa/bobi-wine-asks-icc-to-investigate-museveni-over-human-rights-abuses-3250734; Peter Clottey, 'Uganda Opposition Demands ICC Action Against President', *Voice Of America*, 11 June 2013, https://www.voanews.com/a/uganda-opposition-demands-icc-action-against-president/1679859.html; Abdi Latif Dahir, 'Uganda Opposition Candidate, Citing Abuses, Petitions International Court', *The New York Times*, 8 January 2021, sec. World, https://www.nytimes.com/2021/01/08/world/africa/uganda-election-bobi-wine-icc.html.

subdued to other political considerations and namely the attempt of the government to disband the rebel group while conducting peace talks in Juba. Further to this, the section also highlights how Museveni completely changed his stance towards the Court after the release of the warrants of arrest for Al Bashir in Sudan, signalling that the idea that the ICC would prosecute African SHoS was met with total hostility by a President that, at least initially, thought that the Court was a valuable ally in his hunt for Kony.

After the release of the arrest warrants, the ICC requested the governments of Uganda, the Democratic Republic of Congo (DRC), and Sudan to comply with these. Two of these states, Uganda, and DRC, are bound by the Rome Statute being member parties to it. However, the request has been met with some scepticism. While it is true that the DRC refused to offer asylum to Otti after he asked for a safe base to continue LRA operations, the request made by the Court sounded, at the time, optimistic at best. The Ugandan government attempted to capture Kony and crush the LRA resistance for more than 19 years at that point, never succeeding. And Sudan had a history of supporting the LRA. Some commentators even argued that the Court's request was motivated by the idea of drawing attention to the situation in the country, while also incentivising Sudan to cut ties with the group especially considering what was unfolding in Karthoum,[52] which will be explored in Chap. 5 of this book. Regardless, the Government of Sudan signed a memorandum of understanding with the ICC agreeing to enforce the arrest warrants for the suspected.[53] To many, the willingness of the Sudanese government to cooperate with the Court isolated the LRA, "forcing [the rebels] to talk about peace".[54] And this is indeed, what happened.

[52] Apuuli, 'The ICC Arrest Warrants for the Lord's Resistance Army Leaders and Peace Prospects for Northern Uganda', 187.

[53] Darehshori and Evenson, 'Peace, Justice, and the International Criminal Court', 9.

[54] Tim Allen, 'War and Justice in Northern Uganda', *Crisis States Research Center*, February, 2005, 58.

The Juba Peace Talks were a series of negotiations between the LRA and the Government of Uganda that initiated in 2006 and lasted for two whole years, and had five agenda items: the cessation of hostilities; comprehensive solutions to the conflict; accountability and reconciliation; formal cease-fire; and disarmament, demobilisation, and reintegration.[55] The talks were however underpinned by a general distrust among the parties, both of which were apparently unwilling to give up arms.[56] The aims of the talks, while not formally incompatible with the mandate of the ICC, emphasised the importance of a de-escalation of the conflict between the government and the LRA before any discussion on potentially investigating those who were allegedly most responsible for the atrocities. In addition to this, LRA officials demanded the withdrawal of the arrest warrants for the five suspected to even engage in any discussion. Otti was recorded saying that the ICC was the greatest obstacle to the negotiations.[57] He went further claiming that the LRA was ready to kill anyone who attempted at enforcing the arrest warrants and, he added, that the rebels would not sign anything in Juba that would send them to prison.[58] To complicate the talks even further, the LRA approached the talks as a disjointed organisation with different factions claiming to be the representatives of the rebel group, with some willing to accept the Amnesty offer for instance, and others totally opposed to it.[59]

As a result of LRA lobbying, and the government's progressive delegitimisation of the self-referral, the rebels and the government eventually signed the Agreement on Accountability and Reconciliation, on 29 June 2007. The agreement prioritised domestic forms of accountability,

[55] Kasaija Phillip Apuuli, 'The ICC's Possible Deferral of the LRA Case to Uganda', *Journal of International Criminal Justice* 6, no. 4 (1 September 2008): 804.

[56] Anna Macdonald, '"In the Interests of Justice?" The International Criminal Court, Peace Talks and the Failed Quest for War Crimes Accountability in Northern Uganda', *Journal of Eastern African Studies* 11, no. 4 (2 October 2017): 634.

[57] Apuuli, 'The ICC's Possible Deferral of the LRA Case to Uganda', 804.

[58] Paul Harera and Emmanuel Gyezaho, 'Uganda: LRA's Otti Vows to Kill ICC Captors', *The Monitor*, 13 October 2006, sec. News, https://allafrica.com/stories/200610130276.html.

[59] Jackson, '"Negotiating with Ghosts"', 329.

including *Mato Oput*, and concluded that if a person had been subject to the forms of accountability included in the Agreement for any conduct in the course of the conflict, "that person shall not be subjected to any other proceedings".[60] The Court's scepticism towards the accountability mechanisms provided in the June Agreement and its Annexes manifested when the Court demanded the government to clarify the meaning of the deal for the arrest warrants .[61] It is beyond the scope of this Chapter and this book to investigate the details of this Agreement. What is important, instead, is to highlight the fact that after the self-referral, the Museveni government has consistently displayed an opportunistic attitude towards the ICC and the warrants of arrest. While on the one hand the President initially sustained the efforts of the Court, on the other he repeatedly acted against it either through the support for the 2000 Amnesty Law, or through the apparent establishment of alternative mechanisms of justice after the Juba talks.

This opportunistic attitude signalled that governmental support for the Court was subdued to its short-term political goals. This was clarified by Museveni himself, who argued that the ICC would not enforce the arrest warrants if the Government of Uganda found an internal solution—arguing that even Kony would benefit from an amnesty. To corroborate this Museveni claimed that: "[...] because [Kony] was not under our jurisdiction, we sought the assistance of the ICC. If he signs the peace agreement and returns to our jurisdiction, it becomes our responsibility not any other party's, including the ICC".[62] He further confirmed that this solution could include the *Mato Oput* ceremony, hinting at the fact that the government could easily withdraw its referral if this sustained the peace talks.[63] Already in 2006 Stephen Kagoda, Permanent Secretary to the Ministry of Internal Affairs, sustained the idea that the ICC was only instrumental to the government by claiming that "we thought only a military operation would get rid of Kony but our military did not have jurisdiction in Sudan. That is why we listened to the ICC: how else do we handle this? The ICC

[60] Government of Uganda, 'Agreement on Accountability and Reconciliation between the Government of the Republic of Uganda and the Lord's Resistance Army', 29 June 2007, art. 3(10), https://peacemaker.un.org/uganda-accountability-reconciliation2007.

[61] Apuuli, 'The ICC's Possible Deferral of the LRA Case to Uganda', 806.

[62] Apuuli, 801.

[63] New Vision, 'Museveni Gives Kony Amnesty', 2006, accessed 20 June 2023, https://www.newvision.co.ug/articledetails/1145443.

can help us".[64] This followed mainly considerations based on the necessity of creating a fertile ground for the peace negotiations which, in the eyes of governmental officials, could have been hampered if the ICC was investigating one of the warring factions. [65] The Juba talks were finalised in 2008, although Kony was not present to the signing of the final agreement.

The conditional support for the Court by the Museveni government ended in 2009—year of the release of the warrants of arrest against Sudanese President Al Bashir. This was followed by Museveni's statements on the alleged bias of the institution that decided to target only African leaders, promoting a culture of impunity for non-African criminals.[66] In 2014 he reiterated this view when he said "I supported the court at first because I like discipline. I don't want people to err without accountability", and added "[...] [b]ut they have turned it into a vessel for oppressing Africa again so I'm done with that court. I won't work with them again".[67] In 2016, while sharing the stage with the Sudanese President, Museveni was reported stating: "[w]hen they started, we used to take the ICC serious but not anymore. They are a bunch of useless people who should not be taken serious[ly]. We have no business with the ICC".[68]

Throughout the Juba Talks Museveni was undoubtedly able to exploit the ICC for his own political gains. Just as much as the ICC attempted at exploiting the relationship with the Ugandan President to assert its legitimacy in international politics.[69] However, anytime in which the Court moved against the government's political objectives, Museveni would clarify that the ICC was a guest in Uganda. And that the welcome that the government extended to it was limited, and subjugated to the goals of the President. As soon as the Court was to step outside the limits delineated

[64] Macdonald, '"In the Interests of Justice?"', 635.

[65] Müller and Stegmiller, 'Self-Referrals on Trial', 1290.

[66] Alexander Kay, 'President Museveni Wants Uganda to Leave the ICC', *Bradford Law International,* 25 February 2016, http://9bri.com/president-museveni-wants-uganda-to-leave-the-icc/.

[67] Reuters, 'Uganda's Museveni Calls on African Nations to Quit the ICC', 12 December 2014, sec. Emerging Markets, https://www.reuters.com/article/us-africa-icc-idUSKBN0JQ1DO20141212.

[68] Omar Kafia, 'Presidents Museveni, Bashir and the International Criminal Court', *International Rights and Refugee Initiative*, 13 May 2016, http://refugee-rights.org/presidents-museveni-bashir-and-the-international-criminal-court/.

[69] Joe Oloka-Onyango, 'Unpacking the African Backlash to the International Criminal Court (ICC): The Case of Uganda and Kenya', *Strathmore Law Journal* 4 (2020): 41.

by the government any form of support would cease. The final Chapter in the cooperation between the two actors was the Court's attempt to hold Al Bashir responsible for his crimes, which was perceived as an utmost affront to the sovereign statehood of African states, that could not be forgiven by Museveni.

All in all this section has shown that even when the ICC doesn't directly target a SHoS, cooperation with local authorities is always volatile and subject to calculations by governments in pursuit of legitimacy. When the Museveni government perceived the ICC to be useful to that end, it fully sustained the Court's efforts. As soon as the ICC was seen as an impediment for the consolidation of governmental power, Museveni started opposing the Court by invoking its incompatibility with local practices, and by declaring that justice efforts should be postponed to prioritise peace. In the context of the democratic paradox this sheds a grim light on the possibility that ICC actions actually promote democratic values in the countries that host them. If anything, when SHoS are involved, these can be construed and re-construed by local authorities to consolidate their power on the country and, in this manner, derail ICC actions.

Background to the Investigation in Kenya

The investigation in Kenya followed the tumultuous biennium of 2007 and 2008, which characterised one of the most violent eruptions of post-electoral dissatisfaction in history. The situation in Kenya is different to the one in Uganda in terms of who the Court attempted to put on trial, since it would eventually prosecute the President of the country, Uhuru Kenyatta. Procedurally, the ICC didn't act following a self-referral and the investigation initiated *proprio motu*. Some would argue that because Kenya ratified the Rome Statute, the country should have been more prone to ensure cooperation with the Court, similarly to what Uganda did at least in the initial stages. However, in occasion of the Al Bashir prosecution in Sudan in 2009, the Kenyan political elite already started expressing hostility to SHoS prosecutions by the ICC. This dissatisfaction would eventually turn to total opposition after the ICC indicted Kenyatta, which was exemplified by the lack of cooperation that the SHoS, once summoned, displayed towards the trial. The charges against the President were eventually withdrawn for lack of cooperation of Kenyan authorities,[70] amidst claims of evidence tampering and witness intimidation. The repercussions of a second failed attempt to hold SHoS accountable for their actions were not limited to the ability of the ICC to conclude the proceedings but impacted the internal dynamics of the country as well as rippling through Africa and international politics in general.

Literature has dissected this hostility, with authors like Chaudoin sustaining that local contestation is one of the factors that limited the ability for the ICC to be more effective in Kenya. And that local contestation is mainly shaped by a dissonance between the values projected by the ICC and the values that shape the life of Kenyan people.[71] On this, Cherono highlights that the indictment of SHoS is one of the crucial factors that encourages states not to cooperate with the Court.[72] Other scholars, on the other hand, find that this bias towards the ICC is fuelled by group attachments, but also that Kenyans mostly exposed to violence are more likely to sustain the efforts of the Court.[73] Aloyo, Dancy, and Dutton sustain this view, arguing that while certain individuals might prefer reparative over punitive measures, the majority of Kenyans who were directly affected by the post-electoral violence would prefer the alleged criminals to be prosecuted.[74] Other strands of research focused more on the domestic implications of the investigation. Dutton and Alleblas, for instance, suggest that the ICC has, through its actions, attempted at preventing the

[70] International Criminal Court, 'Notice of Withdrawal of the Charges against Uhuru Muigai Kenyatta', 2014, accessed 11 July 2023, https://www.icc-cpi.int/court-record/icc-01/09-02/11-983.

[71] Stephen Chaudoin, 'How Contestation Moderates the Effects of International Institutions: The International Criminal Court and Kenya', *The Journal of Politics* 78, no. 2 (April 2016): 557–71.

[72] 'The Principle of Complementarity: Comprehending the Motives behind States' Neglect to Cooperate with the ICC (Case Study of the Situations in Kenya and Sudan)', accessed 14 March 2024, https://su-plus.strathmore.edu/items/69cc3b17-07cf-4ac2-9e6c-95635cfc29d1.

[73] Geoff Dancy et al., 'What Determines Perceptions of Bias toward the International Criminal Court? Evidence from Kenya', *Journal of Conflict Resolution* 64, no. 7–8 (1 August 2020): 1443–69.

[74] Eamon Aloyo, Geoff Dancy, and Yvonne Dutton, 'Retributive or Reparative Justice? Explaining Post-Conflict Preferences in Kenya', *Journal of Peace Research* 60, no. 2 (1 March 2023): 258–73.

re-escalation of conflict in the country.[75] However, authors like Oduor and Ikachoi indicated that the ability of the government to influence the media played a crucial role in fuelling anti-ICC sentiment in the country, de facto hampering the investigation.[76] Jjuko rightly highlights that this was also possible because an ineffective victim-protection programme allowed the government to encourage potential witnesses not to cooperate with the ICC.[77] Once more, this literature is incredibly helpful in unpacking the peculiarities of the events that characterised the Kenyan investigation. However, read through the lens of the democracy paradox, the situation in Kenya also sustains the view that SHoS are able to exploit ICC actions to consolidate or, in this case, facilitate their access to power. And that once in power through governments can easily derail ICC endeavours, often through authoritarian measures. Once more, the book argues, this is a systemic condition that manifests when the ICC moves against SHoS.

This section of the Chapter starts by outlining the events that led to the opening of the ICC investigation, and namely the wave of post-electoral turmoil that characterised 2007 and 2008. It analyses the situation in Kenya before and after the election of Kenyatta, to identify patterns of replicability that would corroborate the idea that SHoS reactions to prosecutions share certain systemic traits that can be read through the democracy paradox. It further links ICC operations with the creation of the Jubilee Alliance that eventually won the elections in Kenya in 2013. The birth of the Jubilee Alliance constitutes a pivotal moment in recent Kenyan history since it forged an electoral party that brought together individuals who stood on opposite political and ethnic sides, that is still dominating the political environment of the country. In this sense, Kenyan dynamics appear to complement the analysis of the Ugandan investigation. In addition to this, another element that is explored in this section is the discriminate targeting of NGOs after the opening of the ICC investigation,

[75] Yvonne M. Dutton and Tessa Alleblas, 'Unpacking the Deterrent Effect of the International Criminal Court: Lessons from Kenya', *St. John's Law Review* 91 (2017): 105.

[76] Juliet Atieno Oduor and Denis Ikachoi, 'Social Representations of the 2011 Kenyan-Related ICC Court Proceedings by Mainstream Kenyan Print Media', 2023, https://saspublishers.com/media/articles/SJAHSS_117_154-163.pdf.

[77] Dennis Jjuuko, 'Double Victimization? Using a Human Security Framework to Assess the Effectiveness of the Witness Protection Regime in Kenya', *African Security* 15, no. 3 (3 July 2022): 189–212.

something that would also happen in Sudan. The Chapter then highlights the growth of anti-ICC sentiments in Africa that coincided with the Kenyan situation, which led several countries to announce their withdrawal from the Rome Statute.

The 2007 Post-Electoral Violence

Since the introduction of multi-party politics in 1991, Kenyan political climate around elections has historically been characterised by waves of violence of different magnitudes—with prominent examples emerging in 1992 and 1999. However, the 2007/2008 post-electoral violence exceeded by far the scale of anything that happened before.[78] The reintroduction of competitive electoral processes destabilised the monolithically, one-party system, that shaped the country for almost three decades. This was welcomed as a turning point for the improvement of the democratic prospects of Kenya. However, some argued that the reintroduction of competitive politics wasn't followed by constitutional, legal, and administrative reforms, which created an aleatory competitive system that led to extremely unstable and violent elections.[79] To complicate things even further, Kenyan electoral preferences are still largely determined by ethnicity, kinship, and neighbourhood.[80] With the three major ethnic groups constituting the vast majority of the electorate (the Kalenjin, the Kikuyu, and the Luo), usually political formations that encompass two of the three win the elections. The composition of the political arena in Kenya makes it compulsory, in order to understand the peculiarities of the 2013 elections and the influence that the ICC had on them, to focus on the domestic fluctuations of power also in relation to their ethnic dimension. Furthermore, to understand the issue in its complexity, it is necessary to start from the tensions that arose in 2007, for which the ICC decided to open an investigation.

[78] Department for International Development, 'Elections in Kenya in 2007—GOV.UK', 2010, 1, https://www.gov.uk/government/publications/elections-in-kenya-in-2007.

[79] Department for International Development, 'Elections in Kenya in 2007', 1–2.

[80] Mba Chidi Nmaju, 'Violence in Kenya: Any Role for the ICC in the Quest for Accountability?', *African Journal of Legal Studies* 3, no. 1 (2009): 80.

In 2002 the long-standing authority of President Daniel Arap Moi was eventually overthrown by a coalition led by former Vice-President Mwai Kibaki. Kibaki was elected after promising important constitutional reforms to mitigate the volatility of the Kenyan electoral system, as well as highlighting the necessity of curtailing presidential powers in the country. However, such promises were not maintained, and it is in a context of widespread popular malcontent that Kenya held its 2007 elections. The Election Commission of Kenya (ECK) monitored the elections, despite Kibaki's "last minute appointment of 18 out of 21 new Commissioners without consulting the opposition (as they formerly agreed) and the refusal of the ECK to carry out several technical improvements recommended by the donor-provided experts assisting it".[81] Three individuals competed for presidency: Mwai Kibaki represented the Kikuyus of Central Kenya. Raila Odinga stood for the Luos, mainly supported in the West of the country, in the Rift Valley, and along the Coast Province, and Kalonzo Musyoka. At the time of the electoral campaign, the Orange Democratic Movement (ODM)-Kenya coalition was widely considered the fiercest opponent of Kibaki. However, some months before the elections, in August 2007, the coalition broke down and was replaced by the Party of National Unity (PNU) with Kenyatta at the head. Kenyatta turned from opposing Kibaki to supporting him. The new PNU encompassed members of Kibaki political party and former members of the opposition drew support from different ethnic groups. The opposition was composed mainly of members of the original ODM, including William Ruto. The reason why it is important to mention this is that in the 2007 elections, Kenyatta and Ruto (who were to become President and Vice-President of Kenya in 2013) stood on opposite sides. Kenyatta and Ruto were political opponents supported by different ethnic groups, Kenyatta by the Kikuyus, while Ruto represented the Kalenjin.[82] The election followed poll-predictions and confirmed that

[81] Department for International Development, 'Elections in Kenya in 2007—GOV.UK', 4.

[82] Susanne D. Mueller, 'Kenya and the International Criminal Court (ICC): Politics, the Election and the Law', *Journal of Eastern African Studies* 8, no. 1 (2014): 27.

Kenya's most influential ethnic groups supported the ODM.[83] However, in a surprising turn of events, the ECK declared Kibaki winner, and he was sworn in at the State House in Nairobi on 30 December 2007. The Kriegler Commission set up to investigate the fairness of the contested electoral process, concluded that "[…] the errors made in the various stages of the tallying process were so great and widespread that it is impossible to reconstruct from the formal record who in fact won the presidential contest".[84] Kibaki's victory, which was followed by allegations of electoral fraud that questioned the fairness of the ECK, was the spark to fuel the 2007/2008 post-electoral violence.[85]

Over a period of two months after the presidential elections, more than 1000 people were killed and at least 700,000 were displaced.[86] Three distinct groups were involved in the escalation of violence. First, Kikuyu families and members of the PNU were targeted in Nairobi and Kisumu by those who contested the fairness of the elections. Second, violence organised before the elections by ODM and tribal leaders in the case of Kibaki's re-election spurred after the counting of votes. Third, and perhaps more worrying, the government supported Kikuyus' militias to repress any form of contestation, mainly in the Rift Valley, the Central Province, and Nairobi. The police was also allegedly responsible for choosing not to prevent the violence or using excessive force in dealing with protesters.[87] As Siriam and Brown noted, "[…] this was the type of crime that the ICC was supposed to prevent or at least prosecute".[88]

[83] Gerard Prunier, 'Kenya: Roots of Crisis', *Open Democracy*, 2008, http://www.opendemocracy.net/article/democracy_power/kenya_roots_crisis.

[84] Johann Kriegler, *Report of the Independent Review Commission on the General Elections Held in Kenya on 27th December 2007* (Govt. Printer, 2008).

[85] Nmaju, 'Violence in Kenya', 81.

[86] Gabrielle Lynch and Misa Zgonec-Rožej, 'The ICC Intervention in Kenya', *Chatham House Programme Paper AFP/ILP* 1 (2013): 2.

[87] Department for International Development, 'Elections in Kenya in 2007—GOV.UK', 4.

[88] Chandra Lekha Sriram and Stephen Brown, 'Kenya in the Shadow of the ICC: Complementarity, Gravity and Impact', *International Criminal Law Review* 12, no. 2 (2012): 220.

Box 3.2 Biographical Sketch Kenyatta

Who Is Uhuru Kenyatta?

Uhuru Muigai Kenyatta, born on 26 October 1961, is the second-born of Kenya's first President Jomo Kenyatta. His family has historically been considered one of the most prominent ones among the Kikuyus, which gave him access to the Kenyan high society from a very young age.Such privileges entailed the possibility of studying in the US, where he attended the Amherst College majoring in political science. He was firstly elected to government in 2001, with former President Moi suggesting that Kenyatta would be his natural successor. With Moi's support, Kenyatta ran as candidate for the 2002 presidential elections, which he lost against Kibaki. Following this considerable defeat, Kenyatta started leading the opposition group in Parliament until 2007, when he decided to switch sides to back his former opponent for the 2007 electoral campaign. When Kibaki won the elections, Kenyatta became one of the most important figures in the new government—as Deputy Prime Minister, Minister of Trade, and Minister of Finances between 2008 and 2012. The electoral campaign that led to the election of Kibaki, and Kenyatta's appointment as Minister, was characterised by the wave of post-electoral violence that the ICC was set out to investigate. In the 2013 Elections, Kenyatta, in concomitance with the ICC investigation, would become the fifth President of Kenya, a position that he retained until 2022 when he was succeeded by his former Vice-President, William Ruto. Kenyatta became, after Al Bashir, the second SHoS ever investigated by the ICC even though, it must be noted, he became President after the investigation started.

Kenyatta Faces Trial: Becoming a SHoS and the ICC

Because of international pressures, the ICC opened an investigation *proprio motu* to shed some light on the violent events that characterised the aftermath of the 2007 election on 31 March 2010, after two years since the wave of violence ended. This was the first time in the short history of the ICC that the Court's investigation was not triggered by a self-referral (like the case of Uganda) or a referral from the UNSC (like the case of Sudan). In early April 2011, the deputy prime minister, two cabinet ministers, and the former head of the police force appeared voluntarily at The Hague.[89] On four of them, charges were confirmed by the Pre-Trial Chamber on 23 January 2012.[90] This group of individuals formed the so-called Ocampo Six, who were accused of being mostly responsible for the violence of 2007/2008. Among the six, the ICC first accused Ruto, Henry Kiprono Kosgey, and Joshua Arap Sang, who belonged to the Kalenjin community, of targeting Kikuyu supporters of Kibaki in the north of the Rift Valley.[91] These crimes were allegedly committed against PNU members as part of a plan to take control of the northern parts of the Rift Valley Province, and to punish and drive out PNU supporters.[92] The second case was directed against Muthaura, Kenyatta, and Ali for allegedly hiring a Kikuyu militia to retaliate against ODM's anti-Kikuyu electoral violence.[93] While the investigation was ongoing, another wave of electoral turmoil hit Kenya, with the 2013 general elections approaching. So, Kenyatta was at the same time one of the Ocampo Six and considered among the most prominent candidates for the Kenyan presidency.

Commentators noted how "[...] winning the election was [for Kenyatta] part of a key defence strategy to undercut the ICC by seizing political power, flexing it to deflect the ICC, and opening up the

[89] The confirmation of charges hearings in *Prosecutor v. William Samoei Ruto, Henry Kiprono Kosgey, and Joshua Arap Sang* ICC-01/09-01/11 took place on 1–8 September 2011; the confirmation of charges hearings in *Prosecutor v. Francis Kirimi Muthaura, Uhuru Muigai Kenyatta and Muhammed Hussein Ali* ICC-01/09-02/11 took place on 21 September–5 October 2011. However, one of the three PTC judges issued a dissenting opinion, arguing that it was not clear that the alleged crimes against humanity were committed as part of a calculated 'organizational policy' to attack civilians, as stipulated in the Rome Statute, see Dissenting Opinion by Judge Hans-Peter Kaul; Article 7(2)(a) of the Rome Statute of the International Criminal Court, http://untreaty.un.org/cod/icc/statute/99_corr/2.htm; L. Muthoni Wanyeki, *The International Criminal Court's Cases in Kenya: Origin and Impact*, Institute for Security Studies, 2013.

[90] *Prosecutor v. William Samoei Ruto, Henry Kiprono Kosgey, and Joshua Arap Sang* Decision on the Confirmation of Charges Pursuant to Article 61(7)(a) and (b) of the Rome Statute (ICC-01/09-01/11 23-01-2012 1/173 FB PT) 23 January 2012 and International Criminal Court transcript (ICC-01/09-02/11-T-17-ENG ET WT 23-01-2012 1/9 SZ PT) 23 January 2012. Judge Kaul issued a dissenting opinion in both cases on the grounds that the crimes committed during post-election violence were not crimes against humanity but were common crimes in Kenya.

[91] Mueller, 'Kenya and the International Criminal Court (ICC)', 28.

[92] Gabrielle Lynch and Misa Zgonec-Rožej, 'The ICC Intervention in Kenya'.

[93] Mueller, 'Kenya and the International Criminal Court (ICC)', 28.

possibility of not showing up for trial if all else failed".[94] In other terms, the ICC investigation raised the stakes for Kenyatta to win the elections. However, he had to ensure he would be elected President. In the second case of the Ocampo Six, Kenyatta identified in Ruto—a long-standing antagonist – a strategic ally to ensure his presidential victory. That is how the Jubilee Alliance came onto the Kenyan political scene as part of a strategy for both Kenyatta and Ruto to escape prosecution. As Kenyatta himself pointed out, politics is "[...] a game of numbers, and every politician should understand that there is no other route to winning an election but getting more votes",[95] and the ability of derailing an international investigation comes with the presidential seat.[96] In light of these considerations, Kenyatta and Ruto have demonstrated to be more than willing to bury the hatchet of political and ethnic contestation. However, if the ICC succeeded in passing the message that a fair international investigation was ongoing in relation to Kenyatta and Ruto's implications in crimes against humanity, the expected outcome would have been a clear loss in the polling station for the Jubilee Alliance. To understand how it is possible that instead Kenyatta and Ruto were elected as President and Vice-President of Kenya even with allegations of this magnitude, it is crucial to understand the Kenyan voters' perspective on the ICC's investigation.

Initially, it seems that the ICC was welcomed in Kenya to shed light on the disastrous events of 2007–2008, and to deal with the thorny ECK case. However, once the ICC named, summoned, and charged the first suspects, popular support dropped significantly especially in Central Province and in the Rift Valley, the strongholds of the accused. In October 2010, before the names of the defendants came out, 68% of the country wanted the ICC to prosecute the suspects, including 73% in Central Province and 61% in the Rift Valley. By February 2012 total support fell to 60% overall and to only 42% in Central Province and 50% in the Rift Valley.[97] This compared unfavourably with support for the ICC in Odinga

[94] Mueller, 26.

[95] *Nation Africa*, 'Uhuru Kenyatta: JAP Now Ready for Take-Off', 2014, accessed 3 December 2015, http://www.nation.co.ke/news/politics/Uhuru-Kenyatta-Jubilee-Alliance-Party/-/1064/2856232/-/122iciaz/-/index.html.

[96] Christine Bjork and Juanita Goebertus, 'Complementarity in Action: The Role of Civil Society and the ICC in Rule of Law Strengthening in Kenya', *Yale Human Rights & Development Law Journal* 14 (2011): 205.

[97] 'Ipsos-Synovate Poll, "Confirmation Hearings Boost Support for ICC Process"', 4 November 2011.

strongholds of 75% and 74% in Coast and Nyanza provinces.[98] This decrease in the support for the ICC is explained by understanding that the names of the indicted didn't reflect, in the eyes of the Kenyan electorate, an impartial proceeding. Questions about Odinga being left out from the Ocampo Six, or about a radio station leader being indicted (Sang) while others remained free to voice their concerns, strengthened the view that the trial was as politicised as Kenyatta and Ruto frequently stated.[99] This shift in popular support also pressured Odinga to start opposing the Court, promising that if he was elected the investigation would have been carried out on Kenyan soil. Kenyatta, on his side, was even clearer. Counting on an anti-ICC sentiment that was quickly spreading from the heart of the country, he promised a referendum to withdraw from the Rome Statute. By mid-July 2013, only 39% of those polled wanted trials to take place in The Hague, falling to only 7% in Central Province and 24% in Rift Valley Province.[100] In concomitance with this decreased support, Kenyatta and Ruto both gained popularity since the ICC's charges against them were announced.[101] This, again, is due to a commonly expressed opinion (echoed by Kenyatta and Ruto themselves) that the ICC's intervention was a political ploy by Odinga and his purported Western allies to ensure his electoral victory. In this narrative, Kibaki and Odinga are seen to bear greater responsibility for the 2007–08 post-election violence.[102] The idea that the ICC was a political puppet set up by international actors against Kenyatta and Ruto led to all kinds of conspiracy theories, to the point of associating the Luo background that US President Barack Obama shares with Odinga as proof of international interferences in the Kenyan political sphere.[103]

In this context, the 2013 elections were dominated by two voters' rationales: for those who believed Kenyatta and Ruto's accusations to the Court, that they described as racist and neo-imperialist on several occasions, the election was a referendum on the ICC's intervention. So, by

[98] 'Ipsos-Synovate Poll, "Confirmation Hearings Boost Support for ICC Process"'.

[99] International Crisis Group, 'Kenya's 2013 Elections', 2013, http://www.crisisgroup.org/en/regions/africa/horn-of-africa/kenya/197-kenyas-2013-elections.aspx.

[100] 'Ipsos-Synovate Poll, "Confirmation Hearings Boost Support for ICC Process'.

[101] Lynch and Zgonec-Rožej, 'The ICC Intervention in Kenya', 2.

[102] International Crisis Group, 'Kenya's 2013 Elections'.

[103] Lynch and Zgonec-Rožej, 'The ICC Intervention in Kenya', 10.

electing Kenyatta, they would also oppose the Court and any foreign meddling in Kenyan affairs. Those who supported Odinga on the other hand, saw the elections as a possibility to reject the candidacy of Kenyatta and Ruto, given the allegations leveraged against them by the Court. From this perspective there is no denying that the ICC's intervention in Kenya has been one of the major factors that contributed to the formation of these political perspectives. The ICC fuelled the creation of the Jubilee Alliance between two oppositional political and ethnic forces. The alleged partiality of the ICC investigation in Kenya, that made clear *a priori* that Odinga was not to be investigated (much like what happened with Museveni in Uganda), allowed members of the Jubilee Alliance to rally against the former President and blame him of cooperation with neo-imperialist Western powers. The marginalisation of Odinga, and the normalisation of the relationship between Kenyatta and Ruto, led to the victory of the Jubilee Alliance in 2013. Since the Jubilee Alliance won by a very narrow margin, it seems legitimate to think that this wouldn't have happened without the formation of this coalition. With Odinga's loss of influence, and Ruto and his supporters on his side, Kenyatta was able to set the ground for ruling the country for almost ten years, until 2022. He defeated Odinga again in 2017 (in another very heated election) and was eventually succeeded by his former Vice-President, cofounder of the Jubilee Alliance and member of the Ocampo Six, William Ruto. It must be noted that Kenyatta deployed "[d]elaying tactics for about a year before the prosecutor requested approval to open an investigation" even before he faced trial.[104] However, when the trial started, such tactics progressively escalated, to include victim intimidation[105] and bribery.[106] As a result of the impossibility of obtaining evidence in Kenya, the charges were formally withdrawn in 2015, once more highlighting that when prosecuting a SHoS, hostility from local authorities is to be expected, and can produce poignant consequences for those who might cooperate with the Court.

[104] Sriram and Brown, 'Kenya in the Shadow of the ICC', 219.

[105] Nicholas Kulish and Marlise Simons, 'Setbacks Rise in Prosecuting the President of Kenya', *The New York Times*, 19 July 2013, sec. World, https://www.nytimes.com/2013/07/20/world/africa/dwindling-witness-list-threatens-case-against-kenyan-president.html.

[106] Catrina Stewart, 'ICC on Trial along with Kenya's Elite amid Claims of Bribery and Intimidation', *The Guardian*, 1 October 2013, sec. World news, https://www.theguardian.com/world/2013/oct/01/icc-trial-kenya-kenyatta-ruto.

Victims associations released a statement in response to the withdrawal and claimed that: "[t]he surviving victims received no justice from the Kenyan criminal justice system. If the Prosecution now also walks away from them, it will betray thousands who have already had their lives torn asunder".[107] President Judge Fatou Bensouda's statement on the decision to withdraw the charges against Kenyatta sums up perfectly the thorny relationship between a SHoS and the Court:

> several people who may have provided important evidence regarding Mr. Kenyatta's actions, have died, while others were too terrified to testify for the Prosecution; key witnesses who provided evidence in this case later withdrew or changed their accounts, in particular, witnesses who subsequently alleged that they had lied to my Office about having been personally present at crucial meetings; and the Kenyan Government's non-compliance compromised the Prosecution's ability to thoroughly investigate the charges, as recently confirmed by the Trial Chamber.[108]

It is important, once more, to reiterate that when the ICC unsealed the warrants for the arrest of Kenyatta and Ruto they were not President and Vice-President of Kenya, and the Court might have been unaware that they would be elected three years after the investigation started. However, instead of undermining some of the propositions of the book, this situation corroborates them in two manners. First, it shows that the warrants increased the stakes for the accused who, as we have seen, started considering winning the political elections not only as a matter of internal power accumulation, but also to escape international prosecution. Second, once in power Kenyatta and Ruto retaliated against those who might have aided the Prosecutor's efforts to establish a trial. This section highlighted that ICC actions do have a concrete impact on the societies in which they take place, that can be understood as emerging from the conceptual tension outlined in the democracy paradox. Sometimes this impact is incredibly

[107] International Criminal Court, 'Victims' Response to the "Prosecution's Notice of Withdrawal of the Charges against Uhuru Muigai Kenyatta"', accessed 11 July 2023, https://www.icc-cpi.int/court-record/icc-01/09-02/11-984.

[108] Fatou Bensouda, 'Statement of the Prosecutor of the International Criminal Court, Fatou Bensouda, on the Withdrawal of Charges against Mr. Uhuru Muigai Kenyatta', International Criminal Court, 5 December 2014, https://www.icc-cpi.int/news/statement-prosecutor-international-criminal-court-fatou-bensouda-withdrawal-charges-against-mr.

easy to observe, like in Uganda where the Museveni government benefitted from the ICC investigation against the LRA at least in terms of legitimacy. Sometimes, like Kenya, this impact is more subtle and requires understanding the internal political dynamics that shape a country.[109] Regardless, it seems evident that treating the Court as a pure legal instrument would be myopic—especially in cases like this one, where the ICC is not only unable to effectively put an alleged criminal on trial, but also somehow shapes the alliances and coalition strategies in domestic electoral processes.

Governmental Retaliation Against NGOs

In Kenya, the climate for civil society groups after the ICC initiated its proceedings against Kenyatta and Ruto (and after the two became President and Vice-President of the country) became quite dire. Prior to that, Kenya had been the host of a florid civil society environment with a plethora of NGOs being highly effective, for instance, in voter education and electoral observation. However, as indicated in the section above and along the establishment of the ECK, these groups did not perform as well in 2007, perhaps because they now found themselves divided in their political allegiances.[110] Following the events that succeeded the election, and with the Court openly targeting Kenyatta and Ruto, the debate around the role of NGOs became much more heated. This eventually fuelled the perception that some of those NGOs and civil society groups represented the interests of international actors attempting at meddling with the internal affairs of Kenyan politics, with national elections, and with the management of resources in the country.[111]

It would be short-sighted to claim that the hostility towards NGOs was something that emerged abruptly after the ICC intervention. Lynch, in fact, identified at least three rounds that characterised the tension between various Kenyan governments and NGOs. The first signs of hostility

[109] Mattia Cacciatori, 'When Kings Are Criminals: Lessons from ICC Prosecutions of African Presidents', *International Journal of Transitional Justice* 12, no. 3 (1 November 2018): 390–391.

[110] Department for International Development, 'Elections in Kenya in 2007—GOV. UK', 3–4.

[111] Sriram and Brown, 'Kenya in the Shadow of the ICC', 224.

emerged in the 1990s, in concomitance with the global proliferation of international and national NGOs. International NGOs represented new and fresh funding opportunities for Kenya, while being looked at suspiciously for how much they could influence Kenya's internal political agenda.[112] On the matter, then President Moi introduced a state-based NGO Coordination Board to monitor NGOs, and ensure that their activities wouldn't constitute infringements on the sovereignty of the country.[113] This ever-present tension between governments' protection of national sovereignty and the financial and logistic opportunities that NGOs provide is often exacerbated, as happened in Sudan, when NGOs are perceived as aiding the efforts of the ICC. On one side, the role of NGOs has become quintessential for developing states. On the other side, NGOs have their own agendas that often encourage democratic transitions and a generally more transparent stance of governments, clearly clashing with the intents of authoritarian ones. In this light, as already stated, the relationship between governments and NGOs can be used as a barometer for assessing authoritarian pushes in specific countries.

In the mid-2000s the second round between the Kenyan government and NGOs manifested. African Press reported that during that time, NGOs and their networks alone provided roughly 70% of health-care assistance and promotion of secondary education in Kenya.[114] At this stage however, several NGOs named officials in the Kenyan government as heavily involved in the wave of violence that characterised the 2007 elections. This was the manifestation of all the fears expressed by Al Bashir before, and Kenyatta and Ruto (but the Ocampo Six in general) after. It is never clear how deliberate is the decision of NGOs to sustain prosecutions, but the mere fact that these bodies produce reports and statements to highlight the existence of humanitarian crises, and their calls for international help, is often perceived as a way in which international institutions like the ICC can obtain the necessary proof to sustain their accusations

[112] Cecelia Lynch, 'Kenya vs. NGOs: Round 3?', *CIHA Blog*, 2015, accessed December 3, 2015, http://www.cihablog.com/kenya-vs-ngos-round-3/.

[113] Institute for Strategic Studies, 'Democracy and Development under Siege in Kenya', *ISS Africa*, 2014, https://www.issafrica.org/iss-today/democracy-and-development-under-siege-in-kenya.

[114] Rose Calnin Kagawa, Andrew Anglemyer, and Dominic Montagu, 'The Scale of Faith Based Organization Participation in Health Service Delivery in Developing Countries: Systemic Review and Meta-Analysis', *PLoS ONE* 7, no. 11 (12 November 2012): e48457.

against specific individuals. It is, in other words, the very existence and mandate of international humanitarian NGOs that heighten the tension between them and governments allegedly involved in crimes included in the Rome Statute. The situation deteriorated after the election of Kenyatta and Ruto. At this stage the duo obtained the power necessary not only to hamper the work of NGOs, but also to retaliate against the ones that allegedly helped the ICC in the setting up of the cases against them.

Formally, the 2013 Public Benefits Organisations Act (PBOA) was drafted by the Kenyan government for security reasons, that is to prevent foreign infiltration and control of NGOs work. In this sense it was not too dissimilar to what former President Moi did in the 1990s. However, commentators like Aling'o and Gatimu, claim that the PBOA was an act of governmental retaliation against those agencies that helped the efforts for accountability for the 2007 electoral violence. In their words "[...] the current siege on NGOs can be traced back to the 2007/8 post-election violence and the subsequent indictment by the ICC of President Kenyatta and his Deputy, William Ruto. NGOs are perceived by the ruling Jubilee coalition and its supporters to have provided critical help to the ICC in collecting evidence and preparing witnesses in the ongoing Kenyan ICC cases, and consistently advocating for accountability and justice through the continuation of the cases".[115] The act resulted in the expulsion of 525 NGOs in the country, and the freezing of their accounts.[116] The Kenyan NGOs Co-Ordination Board Executive Director Fazul Mahamed Yusuf declared that 15 of these 525 were linked to "criminal activities including terrorism. The investigations are being finalised and the people behind them will be prosecuted soon".[117] Aling'o and Gatimu further commented on this by saying that "[t]his kind of clampdown on civil society is the hallmark of authoritarian governments with a low tolerance for independent critical voices. The NGO Bill does not offer alternative funding for the sector; and neither is the government committing to cater for the 85% deficit that a mass expulsion of NGOs entails. The move would thus be an effective means of silencing civil society activism, leaving Kenya with a dearth of independent voices".[118] Chebusiri confirmed this by harnessing

[115] Institute for Strategic Studies, 'Democracy and Development under Siege in Kenya'.

[116] Ally Jamah, 'Jobs to Go as Uhuru Administration Revokes Registrations of 525 NGOs in Kenya, Freezes Their Accounts', *Standard Digital News*, 2014, http://standardmedia.co.ke/article/2000144966/govt-revokes-registrations-of-510-ngos-freezes-their-accounts.

[117] Ally Jamah.

[118] Institute for Strategic Studies, 'Democracy and Development under Siege in Kenya'.

a general malcontent with the PBOA, claiming that the major concern was how the government was using security to curb democratic values and freedoms.[119]

The Kenyan case supports the idea that ICC's investigations against SHoS are likely to trigger authoritarian retaliation on civil society groups. In fact, even though the Kenyan scepticism towards NGOs can be traced back to the mid-1990s and is not dissimilar to many international reactions to the proliferation of these entities, the 2013 NGO clampdown was unprecedented both in magnitude and in terms of the justification provided. The fact that this came just after Kenyatta and Ruto managed were elected, is also not to be underestimated. The 2013 PBOA constituted a governmental retaliation on many of those groups that helped in setting up the investigation for the 2007/2008 wave of electoral violence. In essence, as soon as Kenyatta and Ruto had the power to do so, they immediately sent a message to those who sustained their indictments. This supports the idea that a pattern exists between the indictment of SHoS and authoritarian shifts in governments. In fact, very few other comparable case exist across the spectrum of the entire international arena. One of these will be analysed in Chap. 5 of this book, and happened in Sudan in occasion of another SHoS prosecution. Further to this, the case also sustains the idea that a democracy paradox exists for the ICC, one in which the ICC should promote democracy at the intra-state level, but ICC actions can be exploited by local political elites to either maintain or access power. And then, once in power, consolidate authoritarian practices to derail the Court's attempts to deliver on its mandate.

Conclusions

This Chapter sets the basis to understand how SHoS prosecutions, despite being formally admitted and encouraged by the Rome Statute, have been a controversial issue for the ICC since the inception of the Court. Further to this, the Chapter also aimed at corroborating the existence of the democracy paradox and show how local authorities can exploit ICC efforts to either legitimise their authority or to consolidate their domestic power. After 17 years since the beginning of the investigation the Court, on 6

[119] BBC News, 'Kenya "deregisters" NGOs in Anti-Terror Clampdown', 2014, http://www.bbc.co.uk/news/world-africa-30494259.

May 2021, was able to sentence Dominic Ongwen to 25 years in prison for a total of 61 crimes comprising crimes against humanity and war crimes, committed in northern Uganda between July 2002 and December 2005. Operations against two of the five initial accused, Odhiambo and Lukwiya, were terminated because of the confirmed passing of the accused. Kony and Otti remain at large, even though there are speculations on the latter's passing as well. Despite numerous calls for an investigation on the responsibilities of the Government of Uganda in the escalation of the conflict by international agencies and human rights' activists, the President remains solidly in power.

Even in the context of a de-escalated conflict, questions about the right timing of a prosecution remains debated, and leaves commentators wondering about what the ICC has compromised in its quest for efficiency.[120] This resonates with the peace and/or justice dilemma which has been exploited by the Ugandan government in various stages to justify its momentary hostility towards the Court—at least rhetorically. This was particularly evident between 2006 and 2008, during the Juba Peace talks, and underpinned both governmental and LRA rationales for not cooperating with the Court. This Chapter also dealt with (some of) the effects and influences of domestic politics on ICC investigations and *vice versa*. In the Ugandan case, the struggle between the Government of Uganda and the LRA and, more importantly, the position of power that Museveni enjoyed *vis a vis* the rebels, greatly shaped not only the outcome of the investigation, but the process that led to the naming of the five LRA commanders that followed the initiation of the Court's proceedings in the country. For the purpose of this Chapter, it is important to highlight two elements that emerged since the beginning of the ICC investigation in Uganda. First, Museveni remains the President of the country. This makes him one of the longest-serving presidents in the world, having been in power for 37 years. Despite many reports, comments, and calls, the ICC never opened a formal investigation against him. Considering that the ICC is formally designed to sustain the domestic enforcement of the Rule of Law, and for that it requires governmental complacency, the likelihood of a government cooperating with the Court in its own prosecution is

[120] Kimberly Hanlon, 'Peace or Justice: Now That Peace Is Being Negotiated in Uganda, Will the ICC Still Pursue Justice', *Tulsa Journal of Comparative & International Law* 14 (2007): 295–96.

extremely slim. And this is perhaps the main reason why self-referrals became so popular in the first years of the Court. Second, in Uganda, a prosecution against the President, but more in general prosecutions understood as the ICC understands them, seem to be incompatible with local forms of justice that prioritised the restorative dimension of the concept—another extension of the peace and/or justice debate. This is not something to be easily dismissed. Just because a certain view of justice has permeated recent (or even less recent) evolutions in international law, it is not granted that societies will perceive them to be legitimate or serving a country's interests. And the ability of governments to emphasise these differences is also likely to play a crucial role in the legitimisation of SHoS. This creates an important practical issue, because there are several countries that signed and ratified the Rome Statute abiding formally to its view of justice, but domestically might have certain sets of practices that are in manifest opposition to what the ICC stands for. The reasons why they signed the Rome Statute are varied but the fact that the ICC almost inevitably needs domestic cooperation is likely to cause more than one headache in the future.

The situation in Kenya is in many ways similar, although it remains unclear the extent to which the Court knew that the investigation in Kenya would end up focusing on the President and Vice-President of the country. In fact, when it started, Kenyatta was simply a minister (albeit a very important one) of Kibaki's government. Kibaki himself was not part of the Ocampo Six—the six individuals that were initially named by the Court as the ones carrying the most responsibility for the 2007–2008 wave of electoral violence. Despite this, Kenyatta has since 2001 been one of the central figures in Kenyan politics—already running for President as KANU representative in 2002. Further to this, he is also the son of Kenya's former President Jomo Kenyatta. So, the idea that he would potentially become President didn't seem far-fetched even in 2010. The development of the Kenyan investigation suggests that the Museveni case was not an isolated one. States remain the most important actor in international politics, and without the cooperation of local authorities, it is extremely hard for the ICC to effectively bring alleged perpetrators to trial. When the accused is (or becomes) a SHoS, the tension between international law and domestic politics is exacerbated. Something that is also worth noticing is that the investigation raised the stakes for Kenyatta (and Ruto) in the 2013 presidential elections. As many noticed, winning the elections became part of a strategy to fend off the attempts of the Court to set up and conduct a trial. Unfortunately, when Kenyatta became the President of Kenya, he became virtually untouchable—and this risks to spread the message that if the ICC opens an investigation against an individual, their best option to avoid going to jail is either to retain or obtain political power with any means necessary. Meanwhile, when Kenyatta rose to presidential status, he ensured to minimise the potential of the prosecution by marginalising political opponents like Odinga, deregistering more than 500 NGOs, and allegedly threatening potential witnesses.

The Chapter has ultimately shown that the ICC is facing a conundrum in relation to the idea of the promotion of democracy. While having an international institution that promotes the rule of law should encourage states to democratise, governments under scrutiny have the ability of exploiting ICC investigation to consolidate their (often authoritarian) power. This, on one side suggests that ICC investigations can have the opposite effect and encourage authoritarian practices, on the other that the Court might be limited to the prosecution of non-governmental actors, or low- and mid-level perpetrators. Such an aprioristic choice, naturally, would be a perversion of a mechanism of true justice that should be evaluated on the basis that it can prosecute the most powerful. After all, the motto of contemporary justice is "equal justice under law".

References

Akhavan, Payam. 'Self-Referrals before the International Criminal Court: Are States the Villains or the Victims of Atrocities?' *Criminal Law Forum* 21 (2010): 103.

———. 'The Lord's Resistance Army Case: Uganda's Submission of the First State Referral to the International Criminal Court'. *American Journal of International Law* 99, no. 2 (April 2005): 403–21.

Alexander Kay. 'President Museveni Wants Uganda to Leave the ICC', *Bedford Raw International*, 25 February 2016. http://9bri.com/president-museveni-wants-uganda-to-leave-the-icc/.

Ally Jamah. 'Jobs to Go as Uhuru Administration Revokes Registrations of 525 NGOs in Kenya, Freezes Their Accounts'. *Standard Digital News*, 2014. http://standardmedia.co.ke/article/2000144966/govt-revokes-registrations-of-510-ngos-freezes-their-accounts.

Aloyo, Eamon, Geoff Dancy, and Yvonne Dutton. 'Retributive or Reparative Justice? Explaining Post-Conflict Preferences in Kenya'. *Journal of Peace Research* 60, no. 2 (1 March 2023): 258–73.

Apuuli, Kasaija Phillip. 'The ICC Arrest Warrants for the Lord's Resistance Army Leaders and Peace Prospects for Northern Uganda'. *Journal of International Criminal Justice* 4, no. 1 (1 March 2006): 179–87.

———. 'The ICC's Possible Deferral of the LRA Case to Uganda'. *Journal of International Criminal Justice* 6, no. 4 (1 September 2008): 801–13.

Associated Press. 'Northern Uganda "World's Biggest Neglected Crisis"'. *The Guardian*, 22 October 2004, sec. World news. https://www.theguardian.com/world/2004/oct/22/2.

Bameka, Christelle Molima. 'The Post-Ongwen Case Period and the Reconciliation Process in Northern Uganda: Local Communities as a Site of Knowledge'. *International Criminal Law Review* 1, (1 February 2024): 1–24.

Bangura, Abdul Karim. 'The Politics of the Struggle to Resolve the Conflict in Uganda: Westerners Pushing Their Legal Approach versus Ugandans Insisting on Their Mato Oput', 2008.

Bassiouni, M. Cherif. 'The ICC—Quo Vadis?' *Journal of International Criminal Justice* 4, no. 3 (1 July 2006): 421–27.

BBC News. 'Kenya "deregisters" NGOs in Anti-Terror Clampdown', 2014. http://www.bbc.co.uk/news/world-africa-30494259.

Bens, Jonas. 'Transitional Justice Atmospheres: The Role of Space and Affect in the International Criminal Court's Outreach Efforts in Northern Uganda'. In *Normative Spaces and Legal Dynamics in Africa*. Routledge, 2020.

Bjork, Christine, and Juanita Goebertus. 'Complementarity in Action: The Role of Civil Society and the ICC in Rule of Law Strengthening in Kenya'. *Yale Human Rights & Development Law Journal* 14 (2011): 205.

Branch, Adam. 'Uganda's Civil War and the Politics of ICC Intervention'. *Ethics & International Affairs* 21, no. 2 (July 2007): 179–98.

Cacciatori, Mattia. 'When Kings Are Criminals: Lessons from ICC Prosecutions of African Presidents'. *International Journal of Transitional Justice* 12, no. 3 (1 November 2018): 386–406.

Cecelia Lynch. 'Kenya vs. NGOs: Round 3?' *Critical Investigations into Humanitarianism in Africa* (blog), 2015. http://www.cihablog.com/kenya-vs-ngos-round-3/.

Chaudoin, Stephen. 'How Contestation Moderates the Effects of International Institutions: The International Criminal Court and Kenya'. *The Journal of Politics* 78, no. 2 (April 2016): 557–71.

Clark, Janine Natalya. 'The ICC, Uganda and the LRA: Re-Framing the Debate'. *African Studies* 69, no. 1 (1 April 2010): 141–60.

Clark, Janine Natalya. 'Peace, Justice and the International Criminal Court: Limitations and Possibilities'. *Journal of International Criminal Justice* 9, no. 3 (2011): 521–45.

Clottey, Peter. 'Uganda Opposition Demands ICC Action Against President'. *Voice of America*, 11 June 2013. https://www.voanews.com/a/uganda-opposition-demands-icc-action-against-president/1679859.html.

Dahir, Abdi Latif. 'Uganda Opposition Candidate, Citing Abuses, Petitions International Court'. *The New York Times*, 8 January 2021, sec. World. https://www.nytimes.com/2021/01/08/world/africa/uganda-election-bobi-wine-icc.html.

Dancy, Geoff, Yvonne Marie Dutton, Tessa Alleblas, and Eamon Aloyo. 'What Determines Perceptions of Bias toward the International Criminal Court? Evidence from Kenya'. *Journal of Conflict Resolution* 64, no. 7–8 (1 August 2020): 1443–69.

Darehshori, Sara, and Elizabeth Evenson. 'Peace, Justice, and the International Criminal Court'. *Oxford Transitional Justice Research Papers*, 19 March 2010. https://www.law.ox.ac.uk/sites/default/files/migrated/darehshoriandevenson20101.pdf.

Denov, Myriam S, and Mark A Drumbl. 'The Many Harms of Forced Marriage: Insights for Law from Ethnography in Northern Uganda'. *Journal of International Criminal Justice* 18, no. 2 (1 May 2020): 349–72.

Department for International Development. 'Elections in Kenya in 2007—GOV.UK', 2010. https://www.gov.uk/government/publications/elections-in-kenya-in-2007.

Dutton, Yvonne M., and Tessa Alleblas. 'Unpacking the Deterrent Effect of the International Criminal Court: Lessons from Kenya'. *St. John's Law Review* 91 (2017): 105.

Fatou Bensouda. 'Statement of the Prosecutor of the International Criminal Court, Fatou Bensouda, on the Withdrawal of Charges against Mr. Uhuru Muigai Kenyatta'. International Criminal Court, 5 December 2014. https://www.icc-cpi.int/news/statement-prosecutor-international-criminal-court-fatou-bensouda-withdrawal-charges-against-mr.

Gaeta, P. 'Is the Practice of "Self-Referrals" a Sound Start for the ICC?' *Journal of International Criminal Justice* 2, no. 4 (1 December 2004): 949–52.

Gaja, Giorgio. 'Issues of Admissibility in Case of Self-Referrals'. In *The International Criminal Court and National Jurisdictions.* Routledge, 2008.

Goldston, James A., Chidi Anselm Odinkalu, Jeremiah Smith Jr. 'Opinion | Justice for Uganda : A Crucial Case for the International Criminal Court'. *The New York Times*, 27 February 2004, sec. Opinion. https://www.nytimes.com/2004/02/27/opinion/justice-for-uganda-a-crucial-case-for-the-international-criminal.html.

Government of Uganda. 'Agreement on Accountability and Reconciliation between the Government of the Republic of Uganda and the Lord's Resistance Army', 29 June 2007. https://peacemaker.un.org/uganda-accountability-reconciliation2007.

Hanlon, Kimberly. 'Peace or Justice: Now That Peace Is Being Negotiated in Uganda, Will the ICC Still Pursue Justice'. *Tulsa Journal of Comparative & International Law* 14 (2007 [2006]): 295.

Harera, Paul, and Emmanuel Gyezaho. 'Uganda: LRA's Otti Vows to Kill ICC Captors'. *The Monitor*, 13 October 2006, sec. News. https://allafrica.com/stories/200610130276.html.

Human Rights Watch. 'ICC: Investigate All Sides in Uganda', 4 February 2004. https://www.hrw.org/news/2004/02/04/icc-investigate-all-sides-uganda.

Human Rights Watch: 'Uprooted and Forgotten', 20 September 2005. https://www.hrw.org/report/2005/09/20/uprooted-and-forgotten/impunity-and-human-rights-abuses-northern-uganda.

Institute for Strategic Studies. 'Democracy and Development under Siege in Kenya'. *ISS Africa*, 2014. https://www.issafrica.org/iss-today/democracy-and-development-under-siege-in-kenya.

International Criminal Court, 'Statement by Chief Prosecutor Luis Moreno Ocampo', 14 October 2005. https://www.icc-cpi.int/sites/default/files/NR/rdonlyres/2919856F-03E0-403F-A1A8-D61D4F350A20/277305/Uganda_LMO_Speech_141020091.pdf.

International Criminal Court. 'Notice of Withdrawal of the Charges against Uhuru Muigai Kenyatta', 2014. Accessed 11 July 2023a. https://www.icc-cpi.int/court-record/icc-01/09-02/11-983.

International Criminal Court. 'Victims' Response to the "Prosecution's Notice of Withdrawal of the Charges against Uhuru Muigai Kenyatta"', 2014. Accessed 11 July 2023b. https://www.icc-cpi.int/court-record/icc-01/09-02/11-984.

International Crisis Group. 'Kenya's 2013 Elections', 2013. http://www.crisisgroup.org/en/regions/africa/horn-of-africa/kenya/197-kenyas-2013-elections.aspx.

Ipsos-Synovate Poll, "Confirmation Hearings Boost Support for ICC Process'. Ipsos-Synovate, 4 November 2011.

Jackson, Paul. '"Negotiating with Ghosts": Religion, Conflict and Peace in Northern Uganda'. *The Round Table* 98, no. 402 (1 June 2009): 319–31.

Jeffery, Renée. *Amnesties, Accountability, and Human Rights*. University of Pennsylvania Press, 2014.

Jjuuko, Dennis. 'Double Victimization? Using a Human Security Framework to Assess the Effectiveness of the Witness Protection Regime in Kenya'. *African Security* 15, no. 3 (3 July 2022): 189–212.

Kagawa, Rose Calnin, Andrew Anglemyer, and Dominic Montagu. 'The Scale of Faith Based Organization Participation in Health Service Delivery in Developing Countries: Systemic Review and Meta-Analysis'. *PLoS ONE* 7, no. 11 (12 November 2012): e48457.

Kersten, Mark. 'Why the ICC Won't Prosecute Museveni'. *Justice in Conflict* (blog), 19 March 2015. https://justiceinconflict.org/2015/03/19/why-the-icc-wont-prosecute-museveni/.

Kirabira, Tonny Raymond. 'NGOs and the Legitimacy of International Criminal Justice: The Case of Uganda'. In *International Criminal Law—A Counter-Hegemonic Project?*, edited by Florian Jeßberger, Leonie Steinl, and Kalika Mehta, 153–74. The Hague: T.M.C. Asser Press, 2023.

Kress, Claus. 'Self-Referrals and Waivers of Complementarity - Some Considerations in Law and Policy'. *Journal of International Criminal Justice* 2 (2004): 944.

Kriegler, Johann. *Report of the Independent Review Commission on the General Elections Held in Kenya on 27th December 2007*. Govt. Printer, 2008.

Kulish, Nicholas, and Marlise Simons. 'Setbacks Rise in Prosecuting the President of Kenya'. *The New York Times*, 19 July 2013, sec. World. https://www.nytimes.com/2013/07/20/world/africa/dwindling-witness-list-threatens-case-against-kenyan-president.html.

Law Reform Commission of Uganda. Amnesty Act (2000). https://ulii.org/akn/ug/act/2000/2/eng@2000-12-31.

Lucy Hovil and Zachary Lomo. 'Whose Justice? Perceptions of Uganda's Amnesty Act 2000'. *Refugee Law Project Working Paper No. 15*, no. 15 (2005).

Lynch, Gabrielle, and Misa Zgonec-Rožej. 'The ICC Intervention in Kenya'. *Chatham House Programme Paper AFP/ILP* 1 (2013): 2013.

Macdonald, Anna. '"In the Interests of Justice?" The International Criminal Court, Peace Talks and the Failed Quest for War Crimes Accountability in Northern Uganda'. *Journal of Eastern African Studies* 11, no. 4 (2 October 2017): 628–48.

Mueller, Susanne D. 'Kenya and the International Criminal Court (ICC): Politics, the Election and the Law'. *Journal of Eastern African Studies* 8, no. 1 (2014): 25–42.

Müller, Andreas Th., and Ignaz Stegmiller. 'Self-Referrals on Trial: From Panacea to Patient'. *Journal of International Criminal Justice* 8, no. 5 (1 November 2010): 1267–94.

Nation Africa: 'Uhuru Kenyatta: JAP Now Ready for Take-Off'. 2015 Accessed 3 December 2024. http://www.nation.co.ke/news/politics/Uhuru-Kenyatta-Jubilee-Alliance-Party/-/1064/2856232/-/122iciaz/-/index.html.

New Vision. 'Museveni Gives Kony Amnesty', 2006. Accessed 20 June 2023. https://www.newvision.co.ug/articledetails/1145443.

Nmaju, Mba Chidi. 'Violence in Kenya: Any Role for the ICC in the Quest for Accountability?' *African Journal of Legal Studies* 3, no. 1 (2009): 78–95.

Nouwen, Sarah M. H. *Complementarity in the Line of Fire: The Catalysing Effect of the International Criminal Court in Uganda and Sudan*. Cambridge University Press, 2013.

Nouwen, Sarah M. H., and Wouter G. Werner. 'Doing Justice to the Political: The International Criminal Court in Uganda and Sudan'. *European Journal of International Law* 21, no. 4 (1 November 2010): 941–65.

Oduor, Juliet Atieno, and Denis Ikachoi. 'Social Representations of the 2011 Kenyan-Related ICC Court Proceedings by Mainstream Kenyan Print Media', 2023. https://saspublishers.com/media/articles/SJAHSS_117_154-163.pdf.

Ofcansky, Thomas P. 'Musevenis War and the Ugandan Conflict'. *Journal of Conflict Studies*, 1 July 1999. https://journals.lib.unb.ca/index.php/JCS/article/view/4386.

Oloka-Onyango, Joe. 'Unpacking the African Backlash to the International Criminal Court (ICC): The Case of Uganda and Kenya'. *Strathmore Law Journal* 4 (2020): 41.

Omar Kafia. 'Presidents Museveni, Bashir and the International Criminal Court'. *International Rights and Refugee Initiative*, 13 May 2016. http://refugee-rights.org/presidents-museveni-bashir-and-the-international-criminal-court/.

Opongo, Elias O. 'The International Criminal Court and Electoral Justice in Kenya and Côte d'Ivoire'. In *Elections, Violence and Transitional Justice in Africa*. Routledge, 2021.

Prunier, Gérard. 'Rebel Movements and Proxy Warfare: Uganda, Sudan and the Congo (1986–99)'. *African Affairs* 103, no. 412 (1 July 2004): 359–83.

———. 'Kenya: Roots of Crisis'. *Open Democracy*, 2008. http://www.opendemocracy.net/article/democracy_power/kenya_roots_crisis.

Relief Web: 'Uganda: Forgiveness as an Instrument of Peace', 9 June 2005. https://reliefweb.int/report/uganda/uganda-forgiveness-instrument-peace.

Reuters. 'Uganda's Museveni Calls on African Nations to Quit the ICC'. 12 December 2014, sec. Emerging Markets. https://www.reuters.com/article/us-africa-icc-idUSKBN0JQ1DO20141212.

Roach, Steven C. 'Multilayered Justice in Northern Uganda: ICC Intervention and Local Procedures of Accountability'. *International Criminal Law Review* 13, no. 1 (1 January 2013): 249–68.

Southwick, Katherine. 'Investigating War in Northern Uganda: Dilemmas for the International Criminal Court'. *Yale Journal of International Affairs* 1, no. 1 (2005): 105–19.

Sriram, Chandra Lekha, and Stephen Brown. 'Kenya in the Shadow of the ICC: Complementarity, Gravity and Impact'. *International Criminal Law Review* 12, no. 2 (2012): 219–44.

Ssenyonjo, Manisuli. 'Accountability of Non-State Actors in Uganda for War Crimes and Human Rights Violations: Between Amnesty and the International Criminal Court'. *Journal of Conflict and Security Law* 10, no. 3 (1 December 2005): 405–34.

Stewart, Catrina. 'ICC on Trial along with Kenya's Elite amid Claims of Bribery and Intimidation'. *The Guardian*, 1 October 2013, sec. World news. https://www.theguardian.com/world/2013/oct/01/icc-trial-kenya-kenyatta-ruto.

Teitel, Ruti G. 'Transitional Justice Genealogy'. *Harv. Hum. Rts. J.* 16 (2003): 69.

The East African. 'Bobi Wine Asks ICC to Investigate Museveni over Human Rights Abuses', 8 January 2021. https://www.theeastafrican.co.ke/tea/news/east-africa/bobi-wine-asks-icc-to-investigate-museveni-over-human-rights-abuses-3250734.

The New Humanitarian. 'ICC Indictments against Rebels Should Stay, Says President', 21 September 2006. https://www.thenewhumanitarian.org/report/61142/uganda-icc-indictments-against-rebels-should-stay-says-president.

The New Humanitarian. 'Waiting for Elusive Peace in the War-Ravaged North', 9 June 2005. https://www.thenewhumanitarian.org/report/54852/uganda-waiting-elusive-peace-war-ravaged-north.

'The Principle of Complementarity: Comprehending the Motives behind States' Neglect to Cooperate with the ICC (Case Study of the Situations in Kenya and Sudan)'. Accessed 14 March 2024. https://su-plus.strathmore.edu/items/69cc3b17-07cf-4ac2-9e6c-95635cfc29d1.

Tim Allen. 'War and Justice in Northern Uganda'. *Crisis States Research Center*, February 2005.

United Nations. 'President of Uganda Refers Situation Concerning Lord's Resistance Army (LRA) to International Criminal Court', 2004. Accessed 13 June 2023. https://press.un.org/en/2004/afr821.doc.htm.

Voice of America. 'LRA Rebels to Send Delegates to the ICC', 1 November 2009. https://www.voanews.com/a/a-13-2007-01-24-voa3/351110.html.

CHAPTER 4

The ICC and the Enforcement of Justice Paradox: The Downfall of Gaddafi and the Assad Impasse

Background to the Investigation in Libya

The differences and peculiarities of the Ugandan and Kenyan cases revived the idea that the major issue that the Court faces is the lack of an enforcement mechanism that can impose international rules on states.[1] After all, what good is a Court that cannot enforce the laws it was designed to uphold? Naturally, the ICC doesn't have its own police force, and considering that resistance by local authorities is to be assumed for SHoS prosecutions, the Court is reliant on international cooperation to sustain its rulings. And if this cooperation is subdued to political considerations in regional contexts, like Africa, then it is up to the broader international community and especially powerful members of the UN to aid the ICC in its quest for accountability. This Chapter is dedicated to illustrating the paradox of the enforcement of justice and how this has manifested in Libya and Syria. This paradox contends that while the ICC should be more effective in encouraging domestic authorities to abandon their criminal intents when coupled with the threat of international punitive measures, the presence of such a threat can make governments even less likely to

[1] Aidan Hehir and Anthony Lang, 'The Impact of the Security Council on the Efficacy of the International Criminal Court and the Responsibility to Protect', *Criminal Law Forum* 26, no. 1 (1 March 2015): 179.

M. Cacciatori, *The International Criminal Court and the Prosecution of Sitting Heads of State*,
https://doi.org/10.1007/978-3-031-54646-4_4

engage cooperatively with the Court. This, in turn, can encourage authoritarian governments to use any instrument at their disposal to cling to power and avoid international condemnation. The existence of this paradox, it will be shown, is related to the justice and/or order dilemma and has the potential of galvanising opposition to Western interventionary practices by non-Western actors.

Following this and assessing the ICC intervention in Libya, literature has mostly focused on how ICC actions can be linked to punitive measures and, eventually, regime change. Jurdi, for instance, claims that the lack of a true strategy for complementarity and cooperation with local authorities has contributed to the creation of the Libyan quagmire.[2] This kind of reasoning effectively sparked a lively debate on the priorities that the Court should pursue when launching an investigation. Authors like Walker claim that whether or not the ICC should care about promoting peace instead of justice is still up for debating due to the architecture of the Rome Statute.[3] This is echoed by Stahn, who focuses on unresolved tensions in the Rome Statute that affected the application of the principle of complementarity in the situation.[4] On similar notes, Lubaale and Carkeek suggest that it is the punitive nature of the mandate that encountered widespread resistance in Libya.[5] Another strand of literature, on the other hand, advanced the idea that ICC interventions do have a dampening effect on violence in a country,[6] and this is one of the most salient features of the Court. Naturally, because of the specificity of the situation, many focused on the relationship between the UNSC and

[2] Nidal Nabil Jurdi, 'The Complementarity Regime of the International Criminal Court in Practice: Is It Truly Serving the Purpose? Some Lessons from Libya', *Leiden Journal of International Law* 30, no. 1 (March 2017): 199–220.

[3] Angela Walker, 'The Icc Versus Libya: How to End the Cycle of Impunity for Atrocity Crimes by Protecting Due Process', *UCLA Journal of International Law and Foreign Affairs* 18, no. 2 (2014): 303–54.

[4] Carsten Stahn, 'Libya, the International Criminal Court and Complementarity: A Test for "Shared Responsibility"', *Journal of International Criminal Justice* 10, no. 2 (1 May 2012): 325–49.

[5] Emma Charlene Lubaale and James Carkeek, 'African Restorative Justice Approaches as Complementarity: The Case of Libya', in *National Accountability for International Crimes in Africa*, ed. Emma Charlene Lubaale and Ntombizozuko Dyani-Mhango (Cham: Springer International Publishing, 2022), 207–45.

[6] Courtney Hillebrecht, 'The Deterrent Effects of the International Criminal Court: Evidence from Libya', *International Interactions* 42, no. 4 (2016): 616–43.

the ICC when dissecting the Libyan case. Scharf and Graham, for instance, claim that the difficulties in carrying out the Libyan intervention lie precisely in the fractious relationship between the UNSC and the ICC, which have characterised the nexus between these two organs since the drafting of the Rome Statute.[7] Peskin and Boduszynski echo such worries, highlighting that the major deficiency of the Libyan case lies in the fact that initial state supporters of the ICC withdrew their support for the Court's actions, leaving the ICC powerless.[8] Finally, Saba and Akbarzadeh claim that the ICC has become too entangled with the UNSC in Libya,[9] becoming a legitimising tool for Western powers to promote regime change. The first section of the Chapter departs from such analyses while acknowledging their importance, and it does so by highlighting the fact that the enforcement of justice paradox suggests that punitive measures are both essential and counter-productive for the Court. Essential because non-cooperative governments are not going to willingly comply with ICC rulings when a SHoS is indicted. Counter-productive because the threat of punishment makes them even less likely to cooperate with the ICC and, in turn, can encourage them to become even more violent to hold on to power. This, it is argued, also bolsters non-Western resistance against Western interventionary policies and, as such, it is vital to acknowledge the importance of the UNSC in the mosaic, while also suggesting that the emergence of the paradox is not limited to UNSC-referred cases, but shapes all situations in which a SHoS is investigated. Such unresolved paradoxical inferences make the fallacies emerging from the cases presented in this book systemic, and not particular to the cases so far initiated by the ICC.

The first section of the Chapter focuses on the complications that arose during the ICC prosecution of Libyan President Muammar Gaddafi, to show that while the international community was able to muster the will to act decisively in Libya, with the ICC, the UN, and NATO seemingly aligned to protect Libyan civilians from authoritarian violence, the

[7] Michael Scharf and Laura Graham, 'Bridging the Divide between the ICC and UN Security Council', *Georgetown Journal of International Law* 52 (2021 2020): 977.

[8] Victor Peskin and Mieczyslaw P. Boduszynski, 'The Rise and Fall of the ICC in Libya and the Politics of International Surrogate Enforcership', *International Journal of Transitional Justice* 10, no. 2 (1 July 2016): 272–91.

[9] Arif Saba and Shahram Akbarzadeh, 'The ICC and R2P: Complementary or Contradictory?', *International Peacekeeping* 28, no. 1 (1 January 2021): 84–109.

situation deteriorated due to a combination of local unwillingness to cooperate with the ICC and selective international support. In particular, it discusses the relationship between the UN and the ICC, the nexus between coercive enforcement of the warrants of arrest, the Court, and R2P, and how the institution has been accused of focusing on regime change, a taboo idea in international politics. In the following sections the Chapter reviews such issues by exploring the Libyan Civil War and Muammar Gaddafi, to contextualise the international reactions to the events that unfolded in the country since 2011. Further to this, the section explores the notion of regime change as intimately linked with the issuing of the warrant for the arrest of Gaddafi, and the debate about Western support for the ICC, especially in relation to the behaviour of Western members of the P-5 before transitioning to the situation in Syria.

The 2011 Civil War in Libya

On 15 February 2011 the streets of Benghazi and Bediya were stormed by thousands of protesters demanding the release of an imprisoned human right campaigner. The protest quickly turned violent, with the insurgents attacking security forces and government supporters. In the first 48 hours, 38 people were injured—with 10 among them belonging to the police or security forces.[10] Following this, the National Front for the Salvation of Libya (NFSL) called for accountability of the Gaddafi Regime on what they labelled as "National Day of Rage". The NSFL, a long-standing secular opposition group, urged citizens to aid the effort of removing the Libyan President, which manifested in the attack of the police headquarters in the capital, and an attempt of crowd control through violent means by governmental forces, resulting in numerous civilian deaths across the country. It must be noted that the Libyan situation emerged after the deposition of Tunisian President Ben Ali, on 14 February 2011, in the context of the Arab revolution. While many celebrated the collapse of the 23-year-long Tunisian regime, Gaddafi expressed grief and regret about the fall of the Tunisian leader, anticipating what was to come in his own country.[11] What distinguishes the Libyan events from other protests hap-

[10] James Siebens and Benjamin Case, 'The Libyan Civil War: Context and Consequences', *THINK International and Human Security* 4 (2012): 14.

[11] Tim Dunne and Jess Gifkins, 'Libya and the State of Intervention', *Australian Journal of International Affairs* 65, no. 5 (1 November 2011): 519.

pening at the same time in North Africa and the Middle East, constituting the so-called Arab Spring, is not the violent governmental response to the protests. In fact, in numerous instances, the governments of Tunisia, Egypt, Bahrain, Yemen, and Syria, all responded violently to the protests that were spreading through their countries. However, while in these governments responded violently to mainly peaceful protests, in Libya the insurgents made it clear from the beginning that they wanted to overthrow the Gaddafi regime. Through violent means if necessary. This is sustained by the fact that the Libyan uprising was initiated, underpinned, and conducted by organisations and individuals who opposed their governments for years through subversive strategies. So, in Libya, one could observe a unique combination of protestors calling for more respect for human rights and insurgents directing and orchestrating a *coup d'état.*[12]

The government very quickly lost control of Benghazi, after the rebel's occupation of the Katiba Military base on 20 February 2011. From that moment on, the entirety of the country saw multiple battles between governmental forces and insurgents to retain or gain control of nodal cities, with the rebels managing to progressively control the Eastern front of the country. The Gaddafi regime then initiated wide-scale, indiscriminate attacks on both peaceful and violent protestors—escalating the conflict to a full-blown civil war. By the end of February, the rebels counted more than 1000 deaths among their ranks. The governmental response resulted in governmental re-capturing of the city of Misarata, the biggest city controlled by rebels, and marched towards Benghazi. At this stage, Libya was a war-torn country with the Gaddafi government struggling to assert its territorial dominance, while outgunned rebel groups were seemingly unprepared to face the human and economic costs of waging a prolonged civil war.[13] This wave of violence was characterised by multiple allegations of war crimes and human rights violations committed by the government, and was the main reason why, eventually, the UNSC referred the situation to the ICC.

[12] Hugh Roberts, 'Who Said Gaddafi Had to Go?', *London Review of Books*, 17 November 2011, https://www.lrb.co.uk/the-paper/v33/n22/hugh-roberts/who-said-gaddafi-had-to-go.

[13] Maria Golovnina and Patrick Worsnip, 'Gaddafi Orders Storm of Benghazi; U.N. Meets', *Reuters*, 17 March 2011, sec. World News, https://www.reuters.com/article/idINIndia-55642620110317.

Box 4.1 Biographical Sketch Gaddafi

Who Was Muammar Gaddafi?

Muammar Muhamma Abu Minyaar al-Gaddafi was born in 1942 near Sirte, while the city was still under Italian colonial control. From very modest origins, he found the perfect avenue to fulfil his nationalistic aspirations within the Royal Military Academy in Benghazi. Gaddafi played a major role in the 1969 Libyan coup, that deposed monarch Idris Senussi. From the revolution until his death in 2011, Gaddafi had been the uncontested ruler of Libya which, under his command, formally became a republic. Among his many policies, worth of notice are the deportation off the entire Italian population from the country as well as his resistance to the establishment and maintenance of Western military bases on Libyan soil.

In 1977 Libya became a so-called Islamic Socialist State, the Jamahiriya (state of the masses). Through a series of policies directed at tightening governmental control over the means of production, such as the nationalisation on the oil industry, Gaddafi was able to bolster the country's reputation on the world stage also by continuously augmenting military suspending. However, a series of regional conflicts, such as the ones against Egypt and Chad, as well as international incidents, such as the bombing of Pan Am flight 103, heavily damaged his reputation in the eyes of Western political elites. Topical of this is the 1986 US-led bombing of the country, as well as the imposition of economic sanctions by the UN. In the early 2000 Gaddafi remodelled his pan-Arab ideas to ease mounting international tensions over his ruling with mixed results. In 2011, during the revolts, Gaddafi was captured by a rebel militia from the city of Misrata and was eventually found dead. The details of his death are still debated, with official accounts claiming that he was caught in crossfire, while others claim that rebels shot him in the stomach.

The UNSC Responds Swiftly: Warrant of Arrest, R2P, and NATO Bombings as International Threats

Following the tragic escalation of the Libyan conflict, the international community reacted with horror and disdain to the violence being perpetrated against civilians. It became clear quite soon that an international response was required on one side to condemn the violence, on the other to halt the propagation of the conflict. To fulfil this mandate the ICC and R2P seemed to be the adequate international mechanisms to achieve simultaneously both goals. As Ramesh Thakur pointed out, the emergence and development of the humanitarian crisis in Libya became the first test to see how well these two institutions worked with each other.[14] Even officials at the ICC shared this view, with Fatou Bensouda arguing that the ICC is the legal arm of the R2P norm.[15] Also, since the ICC was criticised not because of what it stands for, but because of its lack of efficiency (resulting from a lack of enforcement mechanisms), Libya constituted the perfect instance to see what the Court could do with the full support of the UNSC, and most vitally in this case, NATO. After all, one of the major lines of criticism moved to the ICC, but to international law in general, has constantly revolved around the idea that the international community lacks an enforcement mechanism like a domestic police force to ensure compliance with international norms and praxes. For these reasons, the multi-agent intervention in Libya was hailed by many as the "successful implementation of the R2P framework adopted at the 2005 UN world summit".[16] In a certain sense, the way through which the international community reacted to the situation in Libya can be read as the materialisation of those punitive threats set out by the ICC and the R2P norm, and as a manifestation of the first inference of the enforcement of justice paradox.

In a subtle invoking of the R2P principles, the UNSC demanded that the Libyan government fulfil its responsibility to protect its population,

[14] Ramesh Thakur, 'R2P after Libya and Syria: Engaging Emerging Powers', *The Washington Quarterly* 36, no. 2 (2013): 61.

[15] Arif Saba and Shahram Akbarzadeh, 'The ICC and R2P: Complementary or Contradictory?', *International Peacekeeping* 28, no. 1 (1 January 2021): 88.

[16] Christopher Zambakari, 'The Misguided and Mismanaged Intervention in Libya: Consequences for Peace', *African Security Review* 25, no. 1 (2 January 2016): 45.

following a suspension of Libya from the League of Arab States in late February 2011. Many praised the actions taken by the UNSC following these incidents as being a signal of swiftness and effectiveness that saw very few precedents in the history of the UN. American Ambassador Susan Rice, for one, stated "I can't remember a time in recent memory when the Council has acted so swiftly, so decisively, and in unanimity on an urgent matter of international human rights".[17] The intervention, despite raising some controversies both at the discussion stage and, most notably, at the implementation stage, was seemingly justified by the emerging humanitarian discourse that followed Gaddafi's infamous speeches that "for many people, resonated with the genocide in Rwanda in 1994".[18] The international response took physical form in two official steps: resolutions 1970, which comprised the UN referral of the Libyan situation to the ICC to trigger an investigation and prosecute those most responsible for the crimes committed during the war, and resolution 1973.

Resolution 1970, approved unanimously during the February escalation of the civil war, focused on the immediate cessation of hostilities through the imposition of sanctions on the regime, and the issuing of travel bans on prominent members of the Libyan government. In the same resolution, the UN also referred the attacks on civilians to the ICC.[19] This was the second time in which the UNSC referred a case to the ICC, and, unlike Sudan, this followed a 15–0 vote by members of the Council to trigger an investigation, even though five members of the UNSC were not party members of the Rome Statute.[20] The fact that even non-members of the ICC voted in favour of this has been often heralded as an indication of the fact that the situation in Libya was so unique that even those states that were unconvinced about the role of the Court in international society felt that the international community should have used all its means to produce an immediate ceasefire.[21] This, however, also had repercussions

[17] U. N. Insider, 'UN Maintains Focus on Libya in NY, Geneva & D.C., Amos Briefs on Humanitarian Situation, Pascoe Wraps-up Egypt Visit and More from UN Direct', *UN Dispatch*, 28 February 2011, https://www.undispatch.com/un-maintains-focus-on-libya-in-ny-geneva-d-c-amos-briefs-on-humanitarian-situation-pascoe-wraps-up-egypt-visit-and-more-from-un-direct/.

[18] Zambakari, 'The Misguided and Mismanaged Intervention in Libya', 46.

[19] S/RES/1970 (2011)

[20] Dunne and Gifkins, 'Libya and the State of Intervention', 524–25.

[21] Ruti G. Teitel, 'Transitional Justice Genealogy', *Harvard Human Rights Journal* 16 (2003): 90.

on the Court's ability to act independently. In fact, the wording and language of the resolution greatly shaped how the Court could operate. It excluded, for instance, the possibility of prosecution for crimes committed by non-Libyan nationals and emphasised that the Court could not prosecute non-member states' individuals for crimes committed in Libya, *de facto* attempting to prevent an "investigation into crimes committed by mercenaries or other states, and notably of crimes potentially committed by NATO forces".[22] Tiemessen argued convincingly that the politicisation of the Libyan situation resulted from a tacit support of international actors for the Libyan rebels, and that the ICC would have risked both local and international cooperation if it defied the language of the resolution.[23] This view seems to be further legitimised by the issuing of the warrants of arrest for Gaddafi, his son, and the Libyan head of military intelligence. This is not because there wasn't enough evidence to trigger the warrants against these individuals but, much like what happened in Uganda, because the focus of the Court seemed to be one-sided. This time it excluded non-state and most importantly international actors, to concentrate solely on governmental forces. The support of the international community for the rebels will be of dramatic importance for the evolution of the ICC prosecution as well.

Further to this, on 27 February 2011, one day after the passing of resolution 1970, the rebels formed an opposition government based in Benghazi—under the name of National Transitional Council (NTC).[24] While the NTC seemed to welcome NATO's support, it vehemently opposed the ICC. For instance, both the ICC and the NTC attempted to put Gaddafi's son to trial in relation to the crimes committed during the war—but the NTC openly disputed the ICC's jurisdiction over such crimes. When ICC personnel were sent to monitor the situation regarding another detainee, Seif al-Islam, mainly to ensure that his legal rights were protected, they were arrested and detained for a month.[25] Furthermore, in an exacerbation of these tensions, in April 2012, the NTC passed amnesty laws to grant immunities to those who might have committed war crimes and human rights violations, justifying this by saying that they were made

[22] Alana Tiemessen, 'The International Criminal Court and the Politics of Prosecutions', *The International Journal of Human Rights* 18, no. 4–5 (4 July 2014): 456.

[23] Tiemessen, 456–57.

[24] Siebens and Case, 'The Libyan Civil War', 16.

[25] Siebens and Case, 36.

necessary by the February revolution.[26] The Rome Statute was signed, and the ICC established, precisely against the notion that immunities and amnesties could be granted for the crimes of this kind. Once more, this is an exemplification of the tensions that arise naturally when the Court attempts at superseding local authorities, especially evident in cases that concern SHoS. The detaining of ICC personnel and the issuing of widespread, rebel-oriented amnesties constituted crucial nodes in the development of the case. On one side, the international community supported and sustained the idea of a prosecution in Libya which included top officials of the Gaddafi government, on the other it also showed its support for the NTC for the post-Gaddafi era. But now the NTC showed manifest hostility towards the ICC, and this led to a quick and progressive abandonment of the Court and its efforts by international actors.

The international community couldn't support both actors at the same time, since they were in clear opposition one with the other. As Peskin and Boduszynskii write,

> [w]hile the ICC had been a useful tool in the early days of the war to oust [Gaddafi], the vagaries of Libya's fragile postconflict political transition rendered the Court, in the eyes of many western and non-western diplomats, at best a distraction and at worst a threat to the central goal of bolstering a fragile new Libyan state.[27]

This, naturally, questions the nature of international support for the ICC and its praxes. If at the beginning of operations it looked like the international community was ready to accept the fact that the ICC, in conjunction with R2P, was the most legitimate form of international response to the Libyan atrocities, this U-turn seemed to signal that the Court had only been instrumental to legalise and legitimise an international military action against the Gaddafi regime. This kind of selective support left the Court not only virtually powerless, and subject to the ever-present accusations of lacking coercive mechanisms to enforce its rulings, but also contributed to a heightening of the debate on its role in promoting regime change and neo-imperialism.

[26] Victor Peskin and Mieczyslaw P. Boduszynski, 'The Rise and Fall of the ICC in Libya and the Politics of International Surrogate Enforcership', *International Journal of Transitional Justice* 10, no. 2 (1 July 2016): 288.

[27] Peskin and Boduszynski, 288.

To complicate matters even further, on 31 March 2011, the UN passed Resolution 1973 authorising the establishment of a no-fly zone and the taking all means necessary to protect Libyan civilians.[28] The Resolution was supported by evident violations that failed to heed the UNSC that urged for a "[...] utmost restraint and respect for human rights and international law".[29] Interestingly, the staunchest supporters of the sovereignty and non-intervention norms among the P-5, Russia and China, abstained from vetoing UNSCR 1973, which eventually "[c]leared the road for NATO military intervention in Libya".[30] This, in open contrast with a long-standing opposition to violations of national sovereignty, could be read as a sign that international community was, for a brief moment, moving towards a more interventionist configuration, where even the most vocal opposers of international interventions recognised that certain crimes exist where such actions are legitimate, if supported by regional organisations and international actors.[31] In particular, to justify this monumental change in their traditional stance, China and Russia claimed that the position of the AU and the Arab League was a crucial reason why they decided to abstain, and this was necessary given Obama's commitment to have the entire UNSC on board for an intervention.[32] Despite the reasons why this happened, it is hard to minimise such an event that broke an uninterrupted pattern that shaped the UNSC since the Cold War. So, to recall the justice versus order debate introduced in Chap. 1, it seemed that the Libyan situation cleared the way to the possibility of prioritising the former in the early 2010s. In fact, for the first time, the UN authorised military intervention on the grounds of a state that expressly manifested

[28] A/63/677 (2011).

[29] S/RES/1973 (2011).

[30] Yun Sun, 'Syria : What China Has Learned from Its Libya Experience', Report (Washington, D.C. : *East-West Center in Washington*, 27 February 2012), 1, http://scholarspace.manoa.hawaii.edu/handle/10125/22208.

[31] Courtney J. Fung, 'Global South Solidarity? China, Regional Organisations and Intervention in the Libyan and Syrian Civil Wars', *Third World Quarterly* 37, no. 1 (2 January 2016): 33–50; Andrew Garwood-Gowers, 'China and the "Responsibility to Protect": The Implications of the Libyan Intervention', *Asian Journal of International Law* 2, no. 2 (July 2012): 375–93.

[32] Hehir and Lang, 'The Impact of the Security Council on the Efficacy of the International Criminal Court and the Responsibility to Protect', 166–67.

an opposed will.[33] It must be noted, however, that Western powers were heavily criticised especially by Russia, China, and several African states on the way in which UNSC resolution 1973 was implemented. In particular, the intervening powers were accused of having exceeded the mandate granted by the UNSC by authorising the NATO bombings of the country.[34] Thus, while the resolution formally passed a UNSC vote, it is hard to argue that Russia, China, and the AU actually supported an international military intervention. To corroborate this, as the book will show in the next section of the Chapter, the unfolding of the Libyan situation was going to become the ground for the two non-Western members of the P-5 to veto a potential resolution in Syria.

The passing of resolution 1973 carries some important implications for the ICC. As the book has shown, the Court has constantly been criticised for lacking the coercive power to act against inimical governments, which led to questionable prosecutorial decisions like Uganda. In this case, the mandate of the ICC not only aligned formally with the UN, but its efforts were also militarily supported by NATO. However, if cooperating with local governments attracted criticism on the partiality of the ICC, aligning with international actors who militarily intervened against local governments reinforced views on the politicisation of the Court and, most notably, was seen as a way for international actors, especially Western ones, to legitimise regime change. So, what started as a promising situation that could finally demonstrate that with adequate international support the ICC could be an effective international instrument to ensure that the most heinous crimes in international politics don't go unpunished, turned out to be another instance in which the Court was accused of being ineffective *and* a neo-imperialist tool for Western powers to decide the fate of African countries. In addition to this, given the fact that the situation in Libya in all its articulations was framed under the R2P banner, it is necessary to question if the international community did manage to de-escalate the tensions in the country and create a more secure environment for civilians. If that was the case, then the situation could resonate with those solidarist views that advocated for ex-post evaluations of humanitarian missions.

[33] Justin Morris, 'Libya and Syria: R2P and the Spectre of the Swinging Pendulum', *International Affairs* 89, no. 5 (2013): 1271.

[34] Geir Ulfstein and Hege Føsund Christiansen, 'The Legality of the Nato Bombing in Libya', *The International and Comparative Law Quarterly* 62, no. 1 (2013): 159–71; Julian Borger, 'Libya No-Fly Resolution Reveals Global Split in UN', *The Guardian*, 18 March 2011. https://www.theguardian.com/world/2011/mar/18/libya-no-fly-resolution-split.

Unfortunately, this wasn't the case, and the 2011 intervention remains one of the most controversial ones in the post-Cold War era also because the death-toll and the internal stability of the country worsened exponentially since the intervention. As Kuperman puts it

> [the] grim math leads to a depressing but unavoidable conclusion. Before NATO's intervention, Libya's civil war was on the verge of ending, at the cost of barely 1,000 lives. Since then, however, Libya has suffered at least 10,000 additional deaths from conflict. In other words, NATO's intervention appears to have increased the violent death toll more than tenfold.[35]

So, the situation in Libya created a paradoxical precedent for the ICC. On one side, it highlighted that the Court can formally investigate a SHoS if the international community backs the investigation, and that SHoS can effectively be removed from a position in which they can exert violence on their own citizens. On the other, the instance in which the ICC received the greatest international support, at least initially, is the one in which actions of the Court are associated with a worsening of one of the greatest humanitarian tragedies of our times—questioning the old assumption that the ICC is inefficient because it lacks coercive measures to back up its judiciary dimension. This is an echo of the peace and/or justice debate introduced in Chap. 1 as well as sustaining the existence of an enforcement of justice paradox, and highlights that ICC interventions can in fact have a detrimental effect on peace prospects in a state when they are supported by dubious international military interventions.

The ICC, Regime Change, and Selective International Support

Along with *ex-post* evaluations on the efficacy of the ICC in terms of bringing perpetrators to trial, and the fact that after the 2011 intervention the conflict in Libya escalated, another thorny issue emerged during and after ICC operations in Libya. As already noted, the nexus between the ICC, SHoS prosecutions, and regime change, has been a controversial point of debate since the drafting of the Rome Statute. However, to use the ICC

[35] Alan J. Kuperman, 'A Model Humanitarian Intervention? Reassessing NATO's Libya Campaign', *International Security* 38, no. 1 (1 July 2013): 106.

as a threat to encourage a SHoS to alter his behaviour "[l]ies at the heart if the argument that tribunals can advance global governance and other political interests".[36] The involvement of the UN and NATO in the fight against Gaddafi, heightened the controversies derived by such an intersection—as well as confirming the existence of the enforcement of justice paradox. After all, if an international institution is tasked with the prosecution and potential jailing of SHoS, then talking about regime change does not constitute a logical stretch. If a parallel with domestic situations can be drawn, limiting the freedom of a criminal is a quintessential aspect of modern legislative systems to halt the crime being perpetrated or curtail its repetition. But regime change is always a taboo word in international politics. When this coercive support manifests only at times in which the removal of a specific leader is perceived as a priority for Western states, the role of the Court in legalising and legitimising regime change becomes quite problematic.[37]

The issue lies at the heart of the IR discipline and questions the authority that the international community has in carrying out operations clearly designed to influence the internal dynamics of a country. The fact that the ICC issued an arrest warrant that demanded enforcement can be read as the ICC implicitly calling for the removal of the former Libyan President and, despite early warnings about how the ICC involvement in Libya could hinder the prospects of a peaceful resolution of the conflict,[38] Western political elites seemed determined to prioritise the criminalisation of Gaddafi over such concerns. First, British and French authorities clarified, through a statement released by French foreign minister Alain Juppe, that France and the UK were in "perfect co-operation in Libya"—so any operation in the country was to be considered as agreed upon.[39] Such a statement also received formal endorsing from US President Barack Obama, who saw the opportunity of having European powers taking the

[36] Peskin and Boduszynski, 'The Rise and Fall of the ICC in Libya and the Politics of International Surrogate Enforcership', 279.

[37] Saba and Akbarzadeh, 'The ICC and R2P', 85.

[38] Simon Tisdall, 'This Arrest Warrant Could Make Gaddafi More Dangerous', *The Guardian*, 27 June 2011, sec. Opinion, http://www.theguardian.com/commentisfree/2011/jun/27/gaddafi-international-criminal-court-arrest-warrant.

[39] The Independent, 'Gaddafi Must Relinquish Power Says William Hague', 26 July 2011, http://www.independent.co.uk/news/world/africa/gaddafi-must-relinquish-power-says-william-hague-2326152.html.

lead in the operations in Libya.[40] The nature of these operations and their most evident mandate was the removal of Gaddafi, which took precedence over any other consideration, whether humanitarian, concerning the orderly conduct of international politics, or legal. This is encapsulated by the statement released by William Hague, then British foreign secretary, who claimed that "[...] the warrants demonstrate why Gaddafi has lost all his legitimacy and why he should go immediately".[41] The statement is of incredible importance because it explicitly links the efforts of the ICC with the operations led by Western forces to remove Gaddafi, ascribing to the arrest warrants a legitimising role for international actors to adopt coercive policies to oust Gaddafi. With the proceeding of the situation against the Libyan President, which eventually led to his death, the debate on the release of the warrants of arrest focused on the relationship between the ICC, the practice of prosecuting SHoS, and regime change. Interestingly, at least in most Western responses, Gaddafi's death was met with a sense of justice achieved, evident in the American, French, and British reactions, which gave credit to the idea that these prioritised the removal of the leader over a trial.[42] This is conceptually problematic for an international tribunal whose aim should be to conduct a trial to assess the charges made against an accused.

Practically, the situation in Libya might have underlined that the lack of enforcement power is not the major concern for the Court that, in this instance, found international support but still failed to hold a perpetrator accountable if we don't consider the death of Gaddafi as a legitimate form of punishment for his crimes. As elucidated by the enforcement of justice paradox, SHoS are expected to be even more hostile to the Court when faced with the threat of coercive punishment for their actions. And this might mean that the only international response left to the table is their removal. However, to be perceived as legitimate, international support for the ICC cannot be *a la carte*, and only manifest when the desires of powerful states align with prosecutions. As Bosco highlighted: "the [...] court

[40] BBC News, 'Libya: Obama, Cameron and Sarkozy Vow Gaddafi Must Go', 15 April 2011, sec. Africa, http://www.bbc.co.uk/news/world-africa-13089758.

[41] Tisdall, 'This Arrest Warrant Could Make Gaddafi More Dangerous'.

[42] Columbia Broadcasting System/Associated Prest October 20, 2011, 'Qaddafi's Death Met with Little Sadness', accessed 27 March 2017, http://www.cbsnews.com/news/qaddafis-death-met-with-little-sadness/; Luke Harding, 'Gaddafi's Will Tells Libyans: We Chose Confrontation as a Badge of Honour', *The Guardian*, 23 October 2011, sec. World news, https://www.theguardian.com/world/2011/oct/23/gaddafi-will-libya.

operates in a turbulent world where power matters. [...] In the abstract, the powerful states leading the intervention [in Libya] all endorsed international justice. In practice, as the prosecutor discovered, there were distinct limits to their support".[43] However, many argued that Libya "[...] proved to be almost a textbook illustration justifying R2P principles".[44] Yet, the fragmentation between those who believed that interventions on humanitarian grounds constitute acts of solidarity and those who claim that they conceal regime-change aspirations by the international community did not dissolve because of international support but was rather heightened by it. Çubukçu outlined this dilemma in 2013, by writing

> humanitarian operations' themselves, are they to be considered acts of solidarity or acts of intervention? In the case of Libya, this problem was particularly relevant as opponents and proponents of the international military operation defined it as an act of 'foreign intervention' and 'transnational solidarity' respectively.[45]

The Chapter already highlighted how support for the investigation faded as soon as Gaddafi was removed, but the discrepancy is more deeply institutionalised than this, and goes back to when the ICC in 2010 introduced a fourth crime to the three that were originally covered in the 1998 Rome Statute. And it is important to note that this amendment was discussed just one year prior to the intervention in Libya. In Kampala, member-states voted on the inclusion of the crime of aggression among the ones over which the Court has jurisdiction. About 35 states ratified the crime of aggression, "making their leaders liable to prosecution if they start a war".[46] However, several states including the UK and France, failed to ratify it. This failure attracted widespread criticism,[47] and fuelled the

[43] David Bosco, *Rough Justice: The International Criminal Court in a World of Power Politics* (Oxford University Press, 2013), 1–2.

[44] Thakur, 'R2P after Libya and Syria', 61.

[45] Ayça Çubukçu, 'The Responsibility to Protect: Libya and the Problem of Transnational Solidarity', *Journal of Human Rights* 12, no. 1 (1 January 2013): 54.

[46] Owen Shaun Walker Bowcott, 'ICC Crime of Aggression Comes into Effect without Key Signatories', *The Guardian*, July 17, 2018, sec. Law, http://www.theguardian.com/law/2018/jul/17/icc-crimeof-aggression-comes-into-effect-without-key-signatories-uk-law-war.

[47] Ian Davis, 'If NATO Cares about International Crimes of Aggression, Why Have Only 14 Member States Ratified the New ICC Statute?', *Nato Watch*, 2018, accessed 8 August 2018, http://www.natowatch.org/default/2018/if-nato-cares-about-international-crimes-aggression-why-have-only-14-member-states; correspondent, 'ICC Crime of Aggression Comes into Effect without Key Signatories'.

idea that the Court can only be effective if it projects the interests of Western states. There is a tendency to isolate these hostile actions towards the ICC as being actor- or time-specific.[48] Robertson condemned this decision by stating "[a]ny criminal court that takes itself seriously must outlaw war-making", and added "aggression is the supreme crime. Many other deaths and maimings follow from an act of war".[49] While both the UK and France often reiterated support for "[...] the universalization of the Rome Statute"[50] and renewed their calls for cooperation "with the ICC and abide by their obligations under the Rome Statute",[51] they refused to sign the inclusion of the crime of aggression among the core crimes that the Court could investigate. Despite their decision not to sign, both states achieved formally what they had been advocating for more than a year, that: "[...] any agreement to amend the crimes set out in the [ICC's] statute may not bind state already party to the statute which does not become party to the agreement".[52] The final version of the amended Statute in relation to the crime of aggression reads as follows

> [I]n accordance with the Rome Statute, the amendments to the Statute regarding the crime of aggression adopted at the Kampala Review Conference enter into force for those States Parties which have accepted the

[48] See for instance Kirsten Ainley, 'The Responsibility to Protect and the International Criminal Court: Counteracting the Crisis', *International Affairs* 91, no. 1 (2015): 37–54; Jason Ralph, 'International Society, the International Criminal Court and American Foreign Policy', *Review of International Studies* 31, no. 1 (2005): 27–44; Jean-Baptiste Jeangène Vilmer, 'The African Union and the International Criminal Court: Counteracting the Crisis', *International Affairs* 92, no. 6 (November 1, 2016): 1319–42; Kurt Mills and Alan Bloomfield, 'African Resistance to the International Criminal Court: Halting the Advance of the Anti-Impunity Norm', *Review of International Studies* 44, no. 1 (January 2018): 101–27.

[49] Cain Burdeau, 'International Court Makes War of Aggression a Crime', *Courthouse News*, 17 July 2018, https://www.courthousenews.com/international-court-makes-war-of-aggression-a-crime/.

[50] Ministère des Affaires étrangères et du Développement international, 'France and the International Criminal Court (ICC)', France Diplomatie: Ministry for Europe and Foreign Affairs, accessed 6 August 2018, https://www.diplomatie.gouv.fr/en/french-foreign-policy/international-justice/france-and-the-international-criminal-court-icc/.

[51] Susan Dickinson, 'The International Criminal Court's Role to Achieve Justice for Darfur Victims', GOV.UK, 2018, accessed 6 August 2018, https://www.gov.uk/government/speeches/iccs-role-to-achieve-justice-for-victims-in-darfur.

[52] Owen Shaun Walker Bowcott, 'UK Calls for "greater Clarity" on ICC's New Crime of Aggression', *The Guardian*, 15 November 2017, sec. Law, http://www.theguardian.com/law/2017/nov/15/uk-calls-for-greater-clarity-on-iccs-new-of-aggression.

> amendments one year after the deposit of their instruments of ratification or acceptance and that in the case of a state referral or *proprio motu* investigation the Court shall not exercise its jurisdiction regarding a crime of aggression when committed by a national or on the territory of a state party that has not ratified or accepted these amendments.[53]

So, among the P-5, the US, China, and Russia currently challenge the jurisdiction of the Court on their citizens by failing to be parties to the Rome Statute. Furthermore, in 2010, the UK and France also clarified that they won't accept the ICC jurisdiction on the crimes that they are most likely to be prosecuted for. All this while supporting the Court's efforts up until the removal of Gaddafi, but then siding with the NTC when the former Libyan President was removed from power. The combination of all these stances doesn't help the ICC's quest for legitimacy and gives credit to those states that claim that the Court is nothing more than a tool for powerful states to finally legitimise and legalise regime-change aspirations that are traditionally seen as criminal in international politics, exacerbating the enforcement of justice paradox.

A situation that was initially heralded as a turning point for both the ICC, and the future of international humanitarianism, has evolved to be another addition to the idea that international justice is limited by the same power constraints that always shaped the course of international politics. Further to this, the escalation of violence in the country suggests that while the threat of punishment has been described as a fundamental weapon in the international justice arsenal to enforce compliance by non-cooperative states, the materialisation of such threats can fuel the spread of violence instead of curtailing it, because SHoS know that if they lose power, the chances of being jailed increase dramatically. As such, and as outlined by the enforcement of justice paradox, the threat of punishment might disincentivise governments to halt their criminal activities instead of incentivising them.

Background to the Attempted Investigation in Syria

This second section of the Chapter is different in nature from the previous ones because it can't focus on the mechanisms that aid or hamper a specific ICC intervention, but rather an exploration of the reasons why the

[53] International Criminal Court, 'Review Conference', accessed 6 August 2018, https://asp.icc-cpi.int/en_menus/asp/reviewconference/pages/review%20conference.aspx.

international community, in the form of the UNSC, couldn't muster a consensus to involve the Court in the context of the Syrian crisis. This is particularly important considering the sentiment that pervaded the international community in occasion of the prosecution against Gaddafi, and the claims for a renewed international humanitarianism that emerged in that context. In this sense the previous section and this one focus more on the international dimension of prosecuting SHoS, indicating that the practice is not only being contested by local authorities that host ICC investigations, or by regional actors that prioritise their interests instead of complying with their legal obligations, but also at the international level.

Literature has debated such matters extensively. For instance, Gutman claims that the international deadlock in Syria is indicative of a retrenchment of international humanitarian law,[54] with Aloklah claiming that the reason behind such a deadlock is still due to the friction among great powers in the UNSC.[55] Sweeney underscores that the difficulties of investigating states that are non-signatories to the Rome Statute suggesting that the UNSC unwillingness to refer the situation is only one of the many roadblocks towards accountability in the country.[56] Unpacking this, Macmillan and Mickler claim that one of the major issues in addressing the violence that emerged in Syria is linked to the notion of regime change, especially when the ICC and the UNSC—through the R2P umbrella—operate in conjunction.[57] Following this, Whiting argues that the 2016 UNGA creation of the Mechanism to investigate and preserve evidence of international crimes in Syria, while to be praised for keeping the idea of justice alive, reflects the inability to pursue accountability through a UNSC referral.[58]

[54] Roy Gutman, 'The View from Syria: In War on Terror, Humanitarian Law Takes the Back Seat', *Case Western Reserve Journal of International Law* 52 (2020): 9.

[55] Wissam Aldien Aloklah, 'International Efforts Against Impunity for the Use of Chemical Weapons in Syria: Is There Hope for International Justice?', *Journal of International Criminal Justice* 20, no. 3 (1 July 2022): 541–69.

[56] Caroline Sweeney, 'Accountability for Syria: Is the International Criminal Court Now a Realistic Option?', *Journal of International Criminal Justice* 17, no. 5 (1 December 2019): 1083–1115.

[57] Nesam Macmillan and David Mickler, 'From Sudan to Syria: Locating "Regime Change" in R2P and the ICC*', *Global Responsibility to Protect* 5, no. 3 (1 January 2013): 283–316.

[58] Alex Whiting, 'An Investigation Mechanism for Syria: The General Assembly Steps into the Breach', *Journal of International Criminal Justice* 15, no. 2 (1 May 2017): 231–37.

Other strands of literature analysed the meaning of such a deadlock, and potential ways to overcome it. On this Russo suggested that Syria, while broadly considered as a case where the UNSC deadlock prevented more decisive action, can be useful to remind states in international politics about their commitment to R2P.[59] Beigi argues that the only way to address the Syrian situation remains an investigation by the ICC.[60] Doumit advances that local justice initiatives coupled with notions of universal jurisdiction are helping to keep the prospects of justice in the country alive.[61] Omar adds that along with the difficulties of making the UNSC refer the situation to the ICC, proving intent from governmental forces is also a difficult legal question.[62] From this perspective there is, finally, a corpus of scholarship that has focused on the specificities of the Syrian situation, especially dealing with the heinous use of chemical weapons by the government on civilians. Edwards and Cacciatori, for instance, claimed that the specificity of the use of chemical weapons made the conflict more publicised even though the UNSC remained deadlocked also because of what happened in Libya.[63] Blake and Mahmud dissect the difficulties in understanding international legislation on the use of chemical weapons focusing on the distinctions between international and non-international conflicts.[64]

While this body of literature certainly provides with a useful background for this section of the Chapter, the main argument advanced here is that many of the shortcomings identified above are underpinned by the systemic nature of the enforcement of justice paradox. Questions about a deadlocked UNSC, and the legal implications of overriding it, become

[59] Jenna B. Russo, 'R2P in Syria and Myanmar: Norm Violation and Advancement', *Global Responsibility to Protect* 12, no. 2 (8 May 2020): 211–33.

[60] Jamal Beigi, 'Crimes Committed in Syria and the Referral Mechanism to the International Criminal Court', *International Criminal Law* 1, no. 1 (21 March 2023): 31–43.

[61] Jessica Doumit, 'Accountability in a Time of War: Universal Jurisdiction and the Strive for Justice in Syria', *Georgetown Journal of International Law* 52 (2021 2020): 263.

[62] Abdulaziz Omar, 'Understanding and Preventing Attacks on Health Facilities During Armed Conflict in Syria', *Risk Management and Healthcare Policy* 13 (18 March 2020): 191–203.

[63] Brett Edwards and Mattia Cacciatori, 'The Politics of International Chemical Weapon Justice: The Case of Syria, 2011–2017', *Contemporary Security Policy* 39, no. 2 (3 April 2018): 280–97.

[64] Jillian Blake and Aqsa Mahmud, 'A Legal Red Line: Syria and the Use of Chemical Weapons in Civil Conflict', *UCLA Law Review Discourse* 61 (2013): 244.

paramount when acknowledging the fact that punitive measures are perceived to be at the same time inevitable and counter-productive. To this, it is important to add that the manifestation of the paradox in Libya created a fertile rhetorical ground for those states that aimed deliberately at deadlocking the UNSC.

Before venturing into the analysis, it is necessary to introduce a little caveat. When discussing the opposition to an intervention in Syria and to a potential referral of the case to the ICC, it might be tempting to consider it as a criminal act *per se*. Just as much as the failures to comply with ICC requests to arrest al Bashir constituted, for some, violations comparable to the crimes for which the warrants of arrest were released. Many commentators stigmatised the opposition to the prosecution of Assad severely on these grounds, by claiming that those who are allegedly opposing the prosecution of a criminal should be treated as criminals themselves, and there is some grounding for this. Bull, for instance, argued that "[...] it is wrong not merely to engage in an unlawful war, such as one that involves deliberate killing of the innocent, but also to engage in conditional preparation for it".[65] By extension, for some, it is not only unlawful to commit genocide, war crimes, gross human rights violations, or the crime of aggression, but it is also unlawful to allow the perpetrators of these crimes to escape prosecution, or impede those proceedings that aim at shedding light on potential abuses of such magnitude.

Russian and Chinese behaviour in the Syrian context is undoubtedly hostile to a practice of international law established in the wake of WWII (SHoS prosecutions) and its institutional poster-child, the ICC. Also, the vetoes can be read as not deterring the recurrence of the crimes committed in Syria. However, vetoing the referral of the Syrian situation does not constitute a violation of international law *per se*, nor notions of ethics and morality should be attached to it lightly.[66] This is particularly relevant because it lays the foundations to understand Russian and Chinese actions not as mere strategies to defend a strategic ally, undoubtedly important, but also as indicating a profound dissatisfaction on certain aspects of international law that have, according to them, proven to be fallacious. And because certain injunctions of international law are fundamentally

[65] Hedley Bull, 'Natural Law and International Relations', *Review of International Studies* 5, no. 2 (1979): 172.

[66] Philippa Webb, 'Deadlock or Restraint? The Security Council Veto and the Use of Force in Syria', *Journal of Conflict and Security Law* 19, no. 3 (December 1, 2014): 486.

associated with the expansion of Western views on morality and ethics, such actions also reassert the centrality of state sovereignty and non-intervention as fundamental pillars of inter-state behaviour to preserve the ontological diversity of the international arena. The next section deals with these tensions in the context of the paradox of the enforcement of justice and, as such, doesn't focus solely on those violations of international law allegedly committed by the Assad regime, but draws more attention to those initiatives that aim at challenging a legal order associated with specific hegemonic traits.

The 2013 Syrian Civil War

The Syrian Civil War exploded in the context of the wider 2011 Arab Spring and was characterised by the contraposition of the Syrian Arab Republic of President Assad and a heterogeneous group of forces that opposed it. On 15 March 2011, the protesters took the unrest to the streets of Deraa, Damascus, and Aleppo, demanding the removal of the President amidst calls for wider democratic reforms and the release of political prisoners. In July 2011 dissatisfied members of the Syrian Arab Republic formed the Free Syrian Army, galvanising the protests. The protests escalated in 2012 and in 2013 with the multiplication of rebel actors in contraposition to the government and, sometimes, themselves. Such movements were met with brutal governmental crackdowns[67] in which the Assad government was accused of directly targeting civilians and peaceful protesters.[68] This was coupled with the progressive involvement of foreign powers, which included pro-governmental actors like Russia, and anti-governmental ones like the US. Meanwhile the Islamic State for Iraq and Syria (ISIS) also took the opportunity created by the power-vacuum and by 2014 controlled a considerable portion of the country.[69]

[67] Mariam Karouny, 'Syria Intensifies Assault on Anti-Assad Protesters', *Reuters*, 3 June 2011, sec. World News, https://www.reuters.com/article/us-syria-idUSLDE73N02P20110603.

[68] Ian Black and Nour Ali, 'Syria: 100 Die in Crackdown as Assad Sends in His Tanks', *The Guardian*, 1 August 2011, sec. World news, https://www.theguardian.com/world/2011/jul/31/syria-hama-crackdown-tanks-protests.

[69] İbrahim Mazlum, 'ISIS as an Actor Controlling Water Resources in Syria and Iraq', in *Violent Non-State Actors and the Syrian Civil War: The ISIS and YPG Cases*, ed. Özden Zeynep Oktav, Emel Parlar Dal, and Ali Murat Kurşun (Cham: Springer International Publishing, 2018), 109–25.

In the spring of 2013, the Syrian government claimed that undefined terrorist groups deployed an unspecified chemical-filled rocket to target governmental forces. This triggered the establishment of the UN mission to Investigate Allegations of the Use of Chemical Weapons in the Syrian Arab Republic. In the following months, a series of allegations and counter-allegations from governmental forces and anti-governmental groups fuelled the tension over the use of prohibited chemical weapons' use, and this would become a cornerstone in the narratives of justification for an intervention in the country. The situation in Syria, at the time of writing this book, remains tragic. As Zachary Laub claims, "twelve years after protesters in Syria first demonstrated against the four-decade rule of the Assad family, hundreds of thousands of Syrians have been killed and nearly thirteen million people—more than half the country's prewar population—have been displaced. Today, the country is fractured by actors with apparently irreconcilable interests".[70]

It was in this context of atrocities that the UNSC debated the possibility of intervening in the country. As the Chapter will show, these discussions cornered around the possibility of involving the ICC in the prosecution against Assad and the prospects of an international military intervention. In this sense, they echoed debates that greatly shaped the course of the Libyan situation, discussed in the previous Chapter of this book. And the following sections will also unpack the impact that the Libyan situation had on such debates.

Box 4.2 Biographical Sketch Assad

Who Is Bashar al Assad

Bashar al Assad was born on 11 September 1965 in Damascus in a family of Alawite background. He has been the Head of the Ba'ath Party and the President of Syria since the death of his father, Hafez al Assad, for almost 25 years. His father had been in charge since 1971 so, effectively, the Assad family has been ruling the country for more than 60 years.

(*continued*)

[70] Zachary Laub, 'Syria's War and the Descent Into Horror', *Council on Foreign Relations*, 14 February 2023, https://www.cfr.org/article/syrias-civil-war.

Box 4.2 (continued)

Assad's political career started as soon as he finished his studies, (he graduated from medical school in Damascus in 1988 and specialised in ophthalmology in London in 1992) first as Army doctor and, when his older brother died, as advisor to his father. He oversaw the Syrian occupation of Lebanon in 1998 before becoming President when his father died. Despite early hopes for a democratic reform in the country, sparked by his young age and his international studies, Assad continued in his father footsteps from the very beginning. Indicative of such authoritarian tendencies is the fact the national legislature of Syria had to lower the minimum age of the President from 40 to 34 to allow Assad to become President.

Assad continued his father's conflict with Israel by giving full support to Palestinian authorities against Israel, as well as militant groups from Lebanon. Because of his stance on Israel, and particularly following Assad's accusations of neo-imperialism towards the US after the 2003 invasion of Iraq, he has always been at odds with the White House. Despite being re-elected in 2007, Assad has faced a legitimacy crisis since the beginning of the Syrian Civil War. In particular, the allegations that his government authorised the use of chemical weapons against Syrian civilians have become an incredibly heated issue at the international level. This will become the crucial point of debate both in relation to a potential ICC prosecution but also to the humanitarian intervention that is being carried out in the country.

Back to the Future: Russian and Chinese Vetoes Halt the UNSC Referral to the ICC

The first time in which the pejoration of the Syrian situation was discussed by the UNSC was 27 April 2011.[71] France, the UK, Germany, and Portugal attempted at passing a resolution to condemn and curtail the violence carried out by Syrian authorities in the crackdowns of the

[71] S/PV.6524.

protests.[72] However, despite the fact that the resolution was far milder than resolutions 1970 and 1973, which preceded the Libyan intervention, and unlike them was non-coercive in nature, Chinese and Russian authorities decided to veto it.[73] The resistance offered by the two great powers was undoubtedly exacerbated by the developments of the Western-led intervention in Libya, and re-sparked a long-standing Russian criticism of Western powers' "use of pseudo-humanitarian arguments" and China's stated opposition to "military intervention under the pretext of humanitarianism and externally imposed solutions aimed at forcing regime change".[74] Such concerns were apparently suspended when the two decided to abstain from vetoing resolutions 1970 and 1973, but resurfaced potently and as a consequence of the NATO-led bombings of 2011 that, in the eyes of Russia and China, exceeded the legitimacy that the UNSC granted to the operation and were sustained by the warrants of arrest issued against Gaddafi. This, as shown in the last Chapter, was corroborated by the fact that Western political elites referred to the arrest warrants to claim that Gaddafi was unfit to rule and welcomed his death as a success, *de facto* exploiting the efforts of the Court to legitimise regime change. For this reason, in the discussion on how to deal with the humanitarian crisis in Syria, a potential referral to the ICC became a hugely thorny issue.

Wang Min, the Chinese ambassador to the UN, declared for instance that China had some serious difficulties with the Syrian draft resolution, particularly stressing that "[...] any action seeking referral to the International Criminal Court should be based on the premise of respect for the judicial sovereignty of States and the principle of complementarity".[75] What was urgently needed was for the Government of Syria and the opposition to continue the negotiations and agree on an immediate ceasefire, Wang Min noted. The Chinese ambassador also warned that "[...] forcibly referring the situation to the Court in the current environment was neither conducive to building trust nor to the resumption of negotiations in

[72] S/2011/612.

[73] Morris, 'Libya and Syria', 1274.

[74] S/PV.6826.

[75] Ministry of Foreign Affairs of the People's Republic of China, 'Explanatory Remarks by Ambassador Wang Min after Security Council Voting on Draft Resolution on the Referral of the Situation of the Syrian Arab Republic to the International Criminal Court', 2014, accessed 26 May 2016, http://www.fmprc.gov.cn/mfa_eng/wjb_663304/zwjg_665342/zwbd_665378/t1161567.shtml.

Geneva".[76] These observations underscore the consistent utilisation of peace as a rhetorical foundation by those opposing SHoS prosecutions. Notably, the Chinese ambassador's emphasis on respecting sovereignty effectively precluded any scenario wherein Assad would be subjected to trial. On his side, Vitaly Churkin, Russia's UN ambassador, had earlier dismissed the vote as a "publicity stunt" and warned that if the resolution had passed it would hinder efforts to end the country's three-year war.[77] In a way, the issues raised by the Chinese and Russian diplomats are echoes of the peace and/or justice debate that the book unpacked in Chap. 1. It is pointless to question the veracity of these claims, but there is no doubt that the questionable results of the Libyan intervention fuelled the support for these views. In the wake of the 2013's Russian and Chinese vetoes to refer the Syrian situation to the ICC,[78] United Nations' Secretary General (UNSG) Ban Ki Moon remarked that "[…] Syria is now the biggest humanitarian and peace and security crisis facing the world, with violence reaching unthinkable levels. Syria's neighbours are bearing the increasingly unbearable humanitarian, security, political and socio-economic effects of this conflict".[79] However, in 2014 Putin reiterated that he wouldn't allow the UN to pass a resolution to intervene in Syria because "anything that the US touches turns into Iraq or Libya".[80] And in 2016, in occasion of his annual TV call-in event, he repeated that the US was ready to repeat the Libyan mistake in Syria, if Russia and China weren't there to prevent it.[81]

[76] Ministry of Foreign Affairs of the People's Republic of China, 'Explanatory Remarks by Ambassador Wang Min after Security Council Voting on Draft Resolution on the Referral of the Situation of the Syrian Arab Republic to the International Criminal Court'.

[77] Ian Black, 'Russia and China Veto UN Move to Refer Syria to International Criminal Court', *the Guardian*, 22 May 2014, http://www.theguardian.com/world/2014/may/22/russia-china-veto-un-draft-resolution-refer-syria-international-criminal-court.

[78] United Nations. 'Referral of Syria to International Criminal Court Fails as Negative Votes Prevent Security Council from Adopting Draft Resolution', 2014, accessed 8 August 2018, https://www.un.org/press/en/2014/sc11407.doc.htm.

[79] 'United Nations Secretary-General Ban Ki-Moon', accessed 2 October 2015, http://www.un.org/sg/STATEMENTS/index.asp?nid=7520.

[80] Russia Today, *Putin: Anything US Touches Turns into Libya or Iraq*, 2014, https://www.youtube.com/watch?v=qGwWD-VVBEc.

[81] Julian Robinson, 'Putin Attacks 'imperial Ambitions' of US and Takes Swipe at Obama', April 14, 2016, http://www.dailymail.co.uk/news/article-3539704/Putin-spot-12-year-old-girl-asks-save-Turkish-Ukrainian-leaders-drowning-s-not-good-news-them.html.

The vetoes, naturally, attracted criticism by many who argued that the two countries behaved as irresponsibly[82] and mimicked for only granting the government a license to kill.[83] After various public spats between Russia, the US, France, and the UK,[84] where Western powers clarified that the use of chemical weapons constituted a violation of such magnitude that could justify an international military intervention,[85] Putin decided to withdraw from the ICC in 2016, a day after the Court published a report "[...] classifying the Russian annexation of Crimea as an occupation".[86] Therefore, in the course of three years Russia, with the support of China, manifestly opposed the Court twice: first, by vetoing a referral of Syria. Second, by withdrawing from the Court altogether. This becomes even more staggering considering that in 2011, for the first time in decades, Russia abstained from vetoing a resolution that would support ICC efforts in the infringement of another state's sovereignty in Libya. While it is easy to sympathise with the blaming of Russia by the US, UK, and France, it is

[82] Ian Black, 'Russia and China Veto UN Move to Refer Syria to International Criminal Court', See for instance, 'Russia, China on Wrong Side of History: US on Syria Veto', *Rediff*, 2012, accessed 18 May 2016, http://www.rediff.com/news/report/russia-china-on-wrong-side-of-history-us-on-syria-veto/20120720.htm.

[83] The Finnish Institute of International Affairs, 'Briefing Paper - Responsibility to Protect... Itself? Russia's Strategy towards the Crisis in Syria', 9–10, 2013, accessed 11 May 2016, http://www.fiia.fi/en/publication/341/responsibility_to_protect..._itself/.

[84] Ian Black, 'Russia and China Veto UN Move to Refer Syria to International Criminal Court', *The Guardian*, 22 May 2014, sec. World news, http://www.theguardian.com/world/2014/may/22/russia-china-veto-un-draft-resolution-refer-syria-international-criminal-court; The Independent, 'France Just Called on Russia to Be Investigated for War Crimes in Syria', 10 October 2016, http://www.independent.co.uk/news/world/middle-east/russia-syria-war-crimes-investigation-france-international-court-of-justice-a7353486.html; France in the United Kingdom, 'Alain Juppé on Syria, Human Rights and French Diplomacy', 2013, accessed 8 August 2018, https://uk.ambafrance.org/Alain-Juppe-on-Syria-human-rights; Mayall Lyall Grant, 'Russia and China Will Have to Justify Their Behaviour to the Syrian People, Who Continue to Suffer under Assad's Brutal Regime. - GOV.UK', 22 May 2014, https://www.gov.uk/government/speeches/russia-and-china-will-have-to-justify-their-behaviour-to-the-syrian-people-who-continue-to-suffer-under-assads-brutal-regime.

[85] Brett Edwards and Mattia Cacciatori, 'The Politics of International Chemical Weapon Justice: The Case of Syria, 2011–2017', *Contemporary Security Policy* 39, no. 2 (3 April 2018): 286.

[86] Owen Shaun Walker Bowcott, 'Russia Withdraws Signature from International Criminal Court Statute', *The Guardian*, 16 November 2016, sec. World news, http://www.theguardian.com/world/2016/nov/16/russia-withdraws-signature-from-international-criminal-court-statute.

fundamental to remember the fact that these are the same actors that directly opposed the Court and its policies when it threatened their interests. Up to this date, the US is still not part of the ICC, the Trump administration recently threatened ICC officials,[87] the UK and France are not subject to the Kampala Amendment, and the Bilateral Immunity Agreements (BIAs) that the US signed with various South American states to shield American citizens from the Court's jurisdiction are still in place. Such intermittent support for the Court by Western members of the P-5 greatly damages narratives suggesting that the Court acts in an unbiased manner, while also reinforcing the criticism that emerges when non-Western states claim that the ICC is only a tool in the hands of expansionist Western powers that are not even subject to its rulings. This should not be read as a justification for the Russian stance, but rather highlights the double-standards that all members of the P-5 adopt when they engage with the Court and its actions.

While the motivations behind the opposition to the ICC varied among these states, a distinct thread of temporal and conceptual continuity emerges in their resistance. This alignment essentially positioned all the P-5 countries against the Court in different times. Temporally, the decisions made by China and Russia followed a trajectory of non-Western resistance that originated with increasing African discontent and allegations directed at the Court. This will be explored in detail in the next Chapter of the book. Conceptually, this underscores that such opposition isn't solely a manifestation of US hegemony or limited to the African continent; rather, it spans across all permanent members of the Security Council.

Shaming and Counter-Shaming: The Chemical Weapons' Taboo and the Limits of Western Interventionism

The Chinese and Russian decisions to veto the Syrian resolution sparked a heated debate that questioned the interests of the two great power in shielding Assad from prosecution. The leverage that great powers have on the UNSC has been a debating cornerstone since the creation of the

[87] Max Fisher, 'Trump Administration Holds Off on Issuing U.N. Funding Order', *The New York Times*, 20 January 2018, sec. World, https://www.nytimes.com/2017/01/28/world/americas/trump-un-funding-order.html.

institution, especially considering the role that UNSC referrals play in creating jurisdiction on the grounds of states non-party to the Rome Statute. Russian interests and political ties with the Assad regime have infused the debates within the UNSC with France, for instance, accusing Moscow of "[...] merely wanting to win time for the Syrian regime to crush the opposition" allowing Assad to use chemical weapons to do so.[88] A variety of treaties prohibit the use of chemical in international armed conflicts including the Hague Declaration concerning Asphyxiating Gases, the Geneva Gas Protocol, the Chemical Weapons Convention, along with the Rome Statute itself. The Rome Statute seems to have replicated the limitations of the 1925 Geneva Protocol, in the sense that the Court seems to only have jurisdiction on the use of chemical weapons in *international* armed conflicts. Such shortcomings provided the basis for an amendment to Article 8 of the Rome Statute, proposed and adopted in Kampala in 2010, in the same conference that saw the UK and French opposition to the inclusion of the crime of aggression in the crimes under the jurisdiction of the ICC. While there is no doubt that the use of chemical weapons is particularly stigmatised at the international level, it is interesting to note that on one side the UK and France contested the Kampala Amendment, and on the other the Amendment provided the legal basis for debating a referral of Assad to the ICC.

If the abstention of Russia and China from vetoing UN Resolutions 1970 and 1973, has been considered by some as the culmination of more interventionist views on justice,[89] then the vetoes in 2013 seem to indicate a retrenchment of those afflatuses. More importantly the justifications that followed the vetoes highlighted how China and Russia sought to legitimise their actions. In such discourses it is possible to identify at least two intertwined dynamics: first, by making continuous reference to Libya, Russia, and China aimed at exacerbating the limits of the liberal-institutionalist project and, consequently, challenging the Western domination of international politics. Second, appeals to sovereignty as the ultimate rational barrier of international politics to preserve its ontological diversity, indicated a hostility towards humanitarian practices that started at the end of the Cold War. In this sense, the situation in Syria can be considered as the formalisation of a moment of contraction in interna-

[88] S/PV.6627.

[89] Sun, 'Syria', 1.

tional politics, that started with the unfolding of the Libyan quagmire.[90] This, once more, suggests that the enforcement of justice paradox constitutes an almost insurmountable conceptual barrier for the ICC when prosecuting, or attempting to prosecute, SHoS. Libya, in this sense, acted as a catalyst of non-Western opposition to interventionary measures to support ICC rulings. In the formulation of this opposition, ideas of punitive and international justice, and the role of the ICC in preserving a neo-imperial and interventionist international environment have been dominant. [91] Jason Ralph and Adrian Gallagher suggested that "[t]he legitimacy deficit that accrues from excluding significant parts of the Security Council's social constituency is exacerbated by the ICC's lack of progress in ending the culture of impunity",[92] which is to be traced, once more, to the existence of a gap between legislating, institutionalising, and enforcing norms. However, the problematic unfolding of the Syrian situation didn't only bring back questions of enforcement, but "rather extended to include western interventionary practices more broadly. Debate was no longer simply about specific cases; however they might be linked; it was about a wider normative agenda".[93]

The tension between international law and states' sovereignty that *de facto* shaped both the aspirations and the limitations of the ICC was introduced in Chap. 1 of this book. And throughout each case presented, it has become remarkably clear that every investigation carried out by the Court needs to come to terms with the fact that states, especially powerful ones, have the last say when it comes to international criminal prosecutions. If necessary, the debate surrounding the potential referral of the Syrian case to the ICC, which would have triggered a prosecution against Assad, reinforces the idea that SHoS prosecutions are the apex of this tension. The international transition from Libya to Syria confirmed the centrality of states, especially great powers, in international politics. This suggests that only if they can safeguard their interests, normative aspirations, and spin

[90] Kirsten Ainley, 'The Responsibility to Protect and the International Criminal Court: Counteracting the Crisis', *International Affairs* 91, no. 1 (2015): 37.

[91] Qu Xing, 'The UN Charter, the Responsibility to Protect, and the Syria Issue', *China International Studies* 2 (2012): 15–16.

[92] Jason Ralph and Adrian Gallagher, 'Legitimacy Faultlines in International Society: The Responsibility to Protect and Prosecute after Libya', *Review of International Studies* 41, no. 03 (2015): 566.

[93] Morris, 'Libya and Syria', 1276.

an ICC investigation in their favour, they are likely to cooperate with it.[94] The exacerbation of the tension between international law and states' sovereignty that manifested in concomitance with the Syrian situation seems to indicate that the optimism that apparently pervaded international politics at the beginning of the Libyan quagmire vanquished in 2013. It also seems to reinforce the idea that, given the domestic and regional hostility that they are likely to draw, SHoS prosecutions can only happen with the complacency of the UNSC. But while it would be easy to claim that Russia and China acted the way they did to protect a useful ally, Assad, this interpretation would underestimate the fact that the two great powers became, perhaps unwillingly, champions of a broader dissatisfaction with the legalist and interventionist paradigm that underpinned the creation of the post-Cold War international community.

Protecting Criminals or Revolting Against the West?

Russian hostility towards the ICC and an intervention in Syria can be read in the context of progressive antagonistic stance that Putin adopted since the late 2010s, exemplified by the annexation of Crimea,[95] the subsequent war in Ukraine, the institutionalisation of Russian bases in the Eastern Mediterranean,[96] and the dismissal of 755 American diplomats from Russian soil.[97] On the Chinese side, the growing influence on the African continent,[98] the renewed dominion on the South China Sea,[99] and the

[94] David Kaye and Kal Raustiala, 'The Council and the Court: Law and Politics in the Rise of the International Criminal Court', SSRN Scholarly Paper (Rochester, NY: Social Science Research Network, 21 March 2016), 25, http://papers.ssrn.com/abstract=2752682.

[95] Jonathan Marcus, 'Ukraine: The Military Balance of Power', *BBC News*, 3 March 2014, sec. Europe, http://www.bbc.co.uk/news/world-europe-26421703.

[96] Alexander Mercouris: 'Russia Just Tipped the Balance of Power in the Mediterranean', *The Duran*, August 15, 2016, http://theduran.com/transforming-balance-power-eastern-mediterranean-russia-makes-syrian-base-permanent/.

[97] Neil MacFarquhar, 'Putin, Responding to Sanctions, Orders U.S. to Cut Diplomatic Staff by 755', *The New York Times*, 30 July 2017, sec. Europe, https://www.nytimes.com/2017/07/30/world/europe/russia-sanctions-us-diplomats-expelled.html.

[98] The Economist, 'China Goes to Africa', 2017, accessed 1 August 2017, https://www.economist.com/news/middle-east-and-africa/21725288-big-ways-and-small-china-making-its-presence-felt-across.

[99] Foreign Policy, 'The Week Donald Trump Lost the South China Sea', 2017, accessed 1 August 2017, http://foreignpolicy.com/2017/07/31/the-week-donald-trump-lost-the-south-china-sea/.

general extension of Chinese military across the globe[100] also seem to sustain renewed antagonistic tendencies of non-Western great powers. These are few instances but read in correlation to the hostility of Assad's prosecution, can be considered as the tip of the iceberg of a much deeper shift that aspires to challenge the Western dominance of international politics. In fact, as the book will show in the next Chapter, it is not just Russia and China contesting SHoS prosecutions and the institution tasked with their implementation. Most African states resisted the prosecutions of Al Bashir and Kenyatta, while the AU proposed to withdraw from the Court *en masse*. In a way, the two non-Western members of the P-5 are embodying a profound dissatisfaction that many non-Western states displayed towards the practice.

To offer an interpretation that is not solely based on self-interest and the desire to protect criminals from prosecution, it is necessary to reiterate the paradoxical proposition that puts in relation anti-imperialist tendencies and hostility towards international law. If international law is an instrument that can curtail the rise of new empires in international politics, then when it becomes subjugated to hegemonic powers resistance to it it's considered by some as necessary.[101] This is because hegemonic powers "[…] pose a direct challenge to the rules of co-existence and cooperation and so cannot expect to take advantage of these rules in order to satisfy [their] ambitions".[102] When this situation occurs, states recall that in the hierarchy of those norms that should facilitate international coexistence, and sovereignty and non-intervention are second to no other. This is, naturally, related to the enforcement of justice paradox that highlights that it is precisely the threat of coercive enforcement of contested norms that hampers prospects of a socialisation of those norms that underpin the Court.

Therefore, actions in contraposition with dominant political projects can be considered as dialogical manifestations of dissent, that can have poignant consequences such as the protection of alleged international criminals. This sustains conceptualisations of international politics that are

[100] The Economist, China v the Rest. 2016. https://www.economist.com/asia/2016/03/26/china-v-the-rest.

[101] Ronnie Hjorth, 'Hedley Bull's Paradox of the Balance of Power: A Philosophical Inquiry', *Review of International Studies* 33, no. 4 (2007): 602; Hedley Bull, 'The Anarchical Society: A Study of World Order', *World Politics*, 1977, 106.

[102] Richard Little, *The Balance of Power in International Relations: Metaphors, Myths and Models* (Cambridge University Press, 2007), 151.

based on the importance of intersubjective dialogue among states, especially on those norms that threaten the ability of states to rule within their boundaries.[103] Revolts against the West are moments of high intersubjectivity in which non-Western actors express dissatisfaction on some of the diktats permeating international politics, or as the negative moment in the dialectic process maintaining the primacy of sovereign statehood over contested norms.[104] As already noted, these manifestations can have tragic consequences, as happened in Syria. Just as much as the tacit compliance with international military interventionism had tragic consequences in Libya. So, while it would be easy to dismiss Russian and Chinese resistance to the prosecution of Assad as the usual protection that great powers grant to their allies, it is important to realise that SHoS prosecutions, because of their revolutionary underpinnings, shook the normative core of international politics by challenging sovereignty and non-intervention. A degree of dissatisfaction and open contestation was to be expected, and the fact that Russia and China became the banner-bearers of a widespread non-Western dissatisfaction towards the practice galvanised this antagonistic sentiment. The resisters even had the case of Libya to ethically justify their actions, which suddenly became, in line with the enforcement of justice paradox, very pragmatic and not purely ideologic.

Conclusions

Understanding the involvement of the ICC in the Libyan situation is necessary to comprehend how complex and multifaceted SHoS prosecutions are. What happened in 2011 and afterwards is indicative of the evolution of the practice in the context of a changing environment in international politics, and is also indicative of the existence of the paradox of the enforcement of justice. On one side, there is little doubt that the prosecution of Gaddafi has been the culmination of the idea that the international community, and the ICC by extension, can muster the support for prosecuting powerful individuals who stained themselves with horrendous crimes. An idea that is a funding cornerstone of the Rome Statute and has been

[103] Martin Wight, *International Theory*, 1991, 268; Hedley Bull and Adam Watson, *The Expansion of International Society* (Oxford University Press, USA, 1984), 1.

[104] Mattia Cacciatori, 'The International Criminal Court, Sitting Heads of State Prosecutions, and the Paradox of the Balance of Power', *British Journal of American Legal Studies* 8 (2019): 465.

heralded as a true revolution in international politics. On the other, the removal of the Libyan President has been criticised for encapsulating the attempt of the West to alter the internal political affairs of other states in the form of promoting regime change. The prolongation of the Libyan conflict and the impossibility of bringing Gaddafi to trial, coupled with a selective support for the ICC, are casting a looming shadow on the credibility of the ICC and the potential detrimental effects of SHoS prosecutions for the pacification of conflicts. Moreover, this unfolded under the R2P banner, and for the first time the ICC enjoyed (at least initially) the support of other organisations like NATO, and even the staunchest defenders of national sovereignty, Russia, and China, were persuaded to abstain from vetoing the resolution that, questionably, led to the intervention in Libya. This alignment re-sparked not only debates about the independence of the Court, but also questioned the legitimacy and practical viability of R2P. In fact, while authors like Weiss claimed that "Libya suggests that we can say no more Holocausts, Cambodias, and Rwandas—and occasionally mean it",[105] others, like Nuruzzaman, argued that the operations in Libya de facto "killed the R2P doctrine".[106]

It is possible to read these developments considering the peace and/or justice debate, and of the justice versus order dilemma. The prioritisation of justice over peace, at least rhetorically, sustains the idea that the creation of a domestic system based on the rule of law (and by extension on democratic values) can contribute to a minimisation of the endemic spread of violence in authoritarian contexts. However, these authoritarian manifestations are unlikely to welcome democratic reforms based on the rule of law willingly and some commentators argued that non-statist frameworks of international politics should be considered as alternatives to promote individual freedoms and rights.[107] Although these models do not wish to eliminate states, they would remove the discretion they have to make exceptions for themselves from international law.[108] Does this mean that

[105] Thomas G. Weiss, 'RtoP Alive and Well after Libya', *Ethics & International Affairs* 25, no. 03 (2011): 292.

[106] Mohammed Nuruzzaman, 'The "Responsibility to Protect" Doctrine: Revived in Libya, Buried in Syria', SSRN Scholarly Paper (Rochester, NY: Social Science Research Network, 2013), 62, http://papers.ssrn.com/abstract=2542280.

[107] Antonio Franceschet, 'Popular Sovereignty or Cosmopolitan Democracy? Liberalism, Kant and International Reform', *European Journal of International Relations* 6, no. 2 (2000): 286.

[108] Held, *Democracy and the Global Order*, 233.

the international community has the right (or even the duty) to use any means necessary, including the unilateral use of force, to promote justice? Would this mean that in these pursuits the ICC should be considered as legalising and legitimising such coercive actions? In Libya, Western political elites seemed convinced that the answer to both questions was yes. The complex nexus between these international actors and the Gaddafi regime suggested that the idea that the ICC would be more effective in shaping domestic policies if coupled with credible punitive threats was a mirage. The ICC continues to be more effective in cooperative scenarios and punitive threats do not encourage cooperation from local authorities, as outlined in the conceptualisation of the enforcement of justice paradox. If anything, SHoS know that the only way in which they can be prosecuted is if they are deposed, so clinging to power becomes their main political objective. It is clear that the ethical considerations that arise from cooperating with an alleged criminal government are many and are beyond the scope of this Chapter and this book. However, if the overall aim of the ICC is to reduce violence (through the implementation of international norms and the rule of law) the fact that such violence escalated tremendously after the issuing of the warrant of arrest is something that needs to be considered, also from an ethical perspective.

In line with the above, the Syrian case seems to be indicative of three dynamics: first, international politics is readjusting itself towards a configuration dominated by sovereign statehood after decades of international interventionist pushes; second, sovereignty remains the rhetorical barrier that non-Western actors adopt when they want to oppose interventionist practices of international law; and third, hostility towards specific injunctions of international law, like SHoS prosecutions, can signal an extension of a revolt against the West. This has been explored by reviewing the opposition that the ICC attracted in relation to the potential prosecution of Assad. While, as already stated, ethical considerations are beyond the scope of this Chapter, acknowledging that these actions and narratives can be interpreted as preserving international pluralism cannot be superficially disregarded. In normative development, there seems to be a *quasi*-consequential correspondence between the establishments of hegemonic projects; the promotion of certain norms over others; the creation of institutions tasked with the implementation of such norms; and the emergence of practices that sustain such institutions. This book showed that the transition from Libya to Syria suggests that international politics is walking this path backwards. Actors start resisting specific practices (SHoS prosecutions); then criticise secondary institutions tasked with their implementations (the ICC) to question the primacy of certain norms over others (justice over order). If this analogy is relevant, it seems legitimate to assume that resistance to the SHoS prosecutions carries an implicit criticism for the liberal-institutionalist project that should not be perceived as necessarily dismantling the society of states.

Therefore, the early 1990s "endists" that forecasted the perpetual dominion of liberalism, the end of power politics, and the potential vanquishing of superpowers are met by the notion that the resistance to international law, the return to pluralism, and the resurgence of sovereignty indicate a "return to history" after its end. This is because international politics is deeply rooted in its anti-hegemonic nature. The fact that in the space of two years the attitude towards the prosecution of a SHoS changed dramatically seems to indicate that international law has yet to gain a constitutive status in international politics. Its subservience to other constitutive elements (such as the maintenance of international anarchy through logics of sovereign statehood) makes it susceptible to rapid changes. However, the implications that this Chapter discussed are not justification of disinterest of the international community towards Syria. Nor does it suggest that Russia and China acted altruistically to preserve the independence of non-Western states around the globe. Furthermore, it does not suggest abandoning actions devoted to the solution of the Syrian conflict to respond to logics of renewed statehood nor does it justify violations of international law as an instrument to pacify international politics. It merely provides an exploration of underlying dynamics that signal a return to a situation progressively more divided between Western and non-Western actors on the normative foundations of international politics.

This Chapter, ultimately, suggests that one of the main issues that the ICC has when dealing with SHoS is the fact that punitive threats for uncooperative governments are likely to make these more dangerous and are also divisive internationally, hampering support from the UNSC. At the same time, the absence of such punitive threats makes the Court not credible in its rulings. As long as this tension is not resolved, and it might be that it can't be resolved until states remain the most important actor in international politics, the ICC is likely to face always the same enforcement issues even though the situations are different.

References

Ainley, Kirsten. 'The Responsibility to Protect and the International Criminal Court: Counteracting the Crisis'. *International Affairs* 91, no. 1 (2015a): 37–54.

Alexander Mercouris. 'Russia Just Tipped the Balance of Power in the Mediterranean'. *The Duran* (blog), 15 August 2016. http://theduran.com/transforming-balance-power-eastern-mediterranean-russia-makes-syrian-base-permanent/.

Aloklah, Wissam Aldien. 'International Efforts Against Impunity for the Use of Chemical Weapons in Syria: Is There Hope for International Justice?' *Journal of International Criminal Justice* 20, no. 3 (1 July 2022): 541–69.

BBC News. 'Libya: Obama, Cameron and Sarkozy Vow Gaddafi Must Go'. 15 April 2011, sec. Africa. http://www.bbc.co.uk/news/world-africa-13089758.

Beigi, Jamal. 'Crimes Committed in Syria and the Referral Mechanism to the International Criminal Court'. *International Criminal Law* 1, no. 1 (21 March 2023): 31–43.

Black, Ian. 'Russia and China Veto UN Move to Refer Syria to International Criminal Court'. *The Guardian*, 22 May 2014. http://www.theguardian.com/world/2014/may/22/russia-china-veto-un-draft-resolution-refer-syria-international-criminal-court.

Black, Ian and Nour Ali. 'Syria: 100 Die in Crackdown as Assad Sends in His Tanks'. *The Guardian*, 1 August 2011, sec. World news. https://www.theguardian.com/world/2011/jul/31/syria-hama-crackdown-tanks-protests.

Black, Ian. 'Russia and China Veto UN Move to Refer Syria to International Criminal Court'. *The Guardian*, 22 May 2014, sec. World news. http://www.theguardian.com/world/2014/may/22/russia-china-veto-un-draft-resolution-refer-syria-international-criminal-court.

Blake, Jillian, and Aqsa Mahmud. 'A Legal Red Line: Syria and the Use of Chemical Weapons in Civil Conflict'. *UCLA Law Review Discourse* 61 (2013): 244.

Borger, Julian. 'Libya No-Fly Resolution Reveals Global Split in UN'. *The Guardian*, 18 March 2011, sec. World news. https://www.theguardian.com/world/2011/mar/18/libya-no-fly-resolution-split.

Bosco, David. *Rough Justice: The International Criminal Court in a World of Power Politics*. Oxford University Press, 2013.

Bowcott, Shaun Walker Owen. 'Russia Withdraws Signature from International Criminal Court Statute'. *The Guardian*, 16 November 2016, sec. World news. http://www.theguardian.com/world/2016/nov/16/russia-withdraws-signature-from-international-criminal-court-statute.

Bull, Hedley. 'Natural Law and International Relations'. *Review of International Studies* 5, no. 2 (1979): 171–81.

———. 'The Anarchical Society: A Study of World Order'. *World Politics*, 1977.

Bull, Hedley, and Adam Watson. *The Expansion of International Society*. Oxford University Press, USA, 1984.

Burdeau, Cain. 'International Court Makes War of Aggression a Crime', *Courthouse News*, 17 July 2018. https://www.courthousenews.com/international-court-makes-war-of-aggression-a-crime/.

Bowcott, Shaun Walker Owen. 'ICC Crime of Aggression Comes into Effect without Key Signatories'. *The Guardian*, 17 July 2018, sec. Law. http://www.theguardian.com/law/2018/jul/17/icc-crimeof-aggression-comes-into-effect-without-key-signatories-uk-law-war.

———. 'UK Calls for "greater Clarity" on ICC's New Crime of Aggression'. *The Guardian*, 15 November 2017, sec. Law. http://www.theguardian.com/law/2017/nov/15/uk-calls-for-greater-clarity-on-iccs-new-of-aggression.

Cacciatori, Mattia. 'The International Criminal Court, Sitting Heads of State Prosecutions, and the Paradox of the Balance of Power'. *British Journal of American Legal Studies* 8 (2019): 465.

Columbia Broadcasting System/Associated Press, 'Qaddafi's Death Met with Little Sadness', October 2011. Accessed 27 March 2017. http://www.cbsnews.com/news/qaddafis-death-met-with-little-sadness/.

Çubukçu, Ayça. 'The Responsibility to Protect: Libya and the Problem of Transnational Solidarity'. *Journal of Human Rights* 12, no. 1 (1 January 2013): 40–58.

Davis, Ian. 'If NATO Cares about International Crimes of Aggression, Why Have Only 14 Member States Ratified the New ICC Statute?', *NATO Watch*, 2018. Accessed 8 August 2018. http://www.natowatch.org/default/2018/if-nato-cares-about-international-crimes-aggression-why-have-only-14-member-states.

Dib, Antoine, and Milagros Aurora Revilla Izquierdo. 'Terrorism and the Loss of Cultural Heritage: The Case of ISIS in Iraq and Syria'. In *Transcultural Diplomacy and International Law in Heritage Conservation: A Dialogue between Ethics, Law, and Culture*, edited by Olimpia Niglio and Eric Yong Joong Lee, 377–93. Singapore: Springer, 2021.

Doumit, Jessica. 'Accountability in a Time of War: Universal Jurisdiction and the Strive for Justice in Syria'. *Georgetown Journal of International Law* 52 (2021 2020): 263.

Dunne, Tim, and Jess Gifkins. 'Libya and the State of Intervention'. *Australian Journal of International Affairs* 65, no. 5 (1 November 2011): 515–29.

Edwards, Brett, and Cacciatori, Mattia. 'The Politics of International Chemical Weapon Justice: The Case of Syria, 2011–2017'. *Contemporary Security Policy* 39, no. 2 (3 April 2018): 280–97.

Fisher, Max. 'Trump Administration Holds Off on Issuing U.N. Funding Order'. *The New York Times*, 20 January 2018, sec. World. https://www.nytimes.com/2017/01/28/world/americas/trump-un-funding-order.html.

Foreign Policy. 'The Week Donald Trump Lost the South China Sea | Foreign Policy', 2017. Accessed 1 August 2017. http://foreignpolicy.com/2017/07/31/the-week-donald-trump-lost-the-south-china-sea/.

France in the United Kingdom. 'Alain Juppé on Syria, Human Rights and French Diplomacy', 2013. Accessed 8 August 2018. https://uk.ambafrance.org/Alain-Juppe-on-Syria-human-rights.

Franceschet, Antonio. 'Popular Sovereignty or Cosmopolitan Democracy? Liberalism, Kant and International Reform'. *European Journal of International Relations* 6, no. 2 (2000): 277–302.

Fung, Courtney J. 'Global South Solidarity? China, Regional Organisations and Intervention in the Libyan and Syrian Civil Wars'. *Third World Quarterly* 37, no. 1 (2 January 2016): 33–50.

Garwood-Gowers, Andrew. 'China and the "Responsibility to Protect": The Implications of the Libyan Intervention'. *Asian Journal of International Law* 2, no. 2 (July 2012): 375–93.

Gutman, Roy. 'The View from Syria: In War on Terror, Humanitarian Law Takes the Back Seat'. *Case Western Reserve Journal of International Law* 52 (2020): 9.

Harding, Luke. 'Gaddafi's Will Tells Libyans: We Chose Confrontation as a Badge of Honour'. *The Guardian*, 23 October 2011, sec. World news. https://www.theguardian.com/world/2011/oct/23/gaddafi-will-libya.

Hehir, Aidan, and Anthony Lang. 'The Impact of the Security Council on the Efficacy of the International Criminal Court and the Responsibility to Protect'. *Criminal Law Forum* 26, no. 1 (1 March 2015): 153–79.

Held, David and others. *Democracy and the Global Order*. Cambridge: Polity Press, 1995. https://www.cambridge.org/core/journals/world-politics/article/wpo-volume-49-issue-2-cover-and-back-matter/0636B44721EC5C35AAE314DB785BA59C.

Hillebrecht, Courtney. 'The Deterrent Effects of the International Criminal Court: Evidence from Libya'. *International Interactions* 42, no. 4 (2016): 616–43.

Hjorth, Ronnie. 'Hedley Bull's Paradox of the Balance of Power: A Philosophical Inquiry'. *Review of International Studies* 33, no. 4 (2007): 597–613.

Insider, U. N. 'UN Maintains Focus on Libya in NY, Geneva & D.C., Amos Briefs on Humanitarian Situation, Pascoe Wraps-up Egypt Visit and More from UN Direct'. UN Dispatch, 28 February 2011. https://www.undispatch.com/un-maintains-focus-on-libya-in-ny-geneva-d-c-amos-briefs-on-humanitarian-situation-pascoe-wraps-up-egypt-visit-and-more-from-un-direct/.

International Criminal Court. 'Review Conference'. Accessed 6 August 2018. https://asp.icc-cpi.int/en_menus/asp/reviewconference/pages/review%20conference.aspx.

Julian Robinson. 'Putin Attacks "imperial Ambitions" of US and Takes Swipe at Obama', 14 April 2016. http://www.dailymail.co.uk/news/article-3539704/Putin-spot-12-year-old-girl-asks-save-Turkish-Ukrainian-leaders-drowning-s-not-good-news-them.html.

Jurdi, Nidal Nabil. 'The Complementarity Regime of the International Criminal Court in Practice: Is It Truly Serving the Purpose? Some Lessons from Libya'. *Leiden Journal of International Law* 30, no. 1 (March 2017): 199–220.

Kaye, David, and Kal Raustiala. 'The Council and the Court: Law and Politics in the Rise of the International Criminal Court'. SSRN Scholarly Paper. Rochester, NY: Social Science Research Network, 21 March 2016. http://papers.ssrn.com/abstract=2752682.

Kuperman, Alan J. 'A Model Humanitarian Intervention? Reassessing NATO's Libya Campaign'. *International Security* 38, no. 1 (1 July 2013): 105–36.

Little, Richard. *The Balance of Power in International Relations: Metaphors, Myths and Models*. Cambridge University Press, 2007.

Lubaale, Emma Charlene, and James Carkeek. 'African Restorative Justice Approaches as Complementarity: The Case of Libya'. In *National Accountability for International Crimes in Africa*, edited by Emma Charlene Lubaale and Ntombizozuko Dyani-Mhango, 207–45. Cham: Springer International Publishing, 2022.

Lyall Grant, Mayall. 'Russia and China Will Have to Justify Their Behaviour to the Syrian People, Who Continue to Suffer under Assad's Brutal Regime.—GOV.UK', 22 May 2014. https://www.gov.uk/government/speeches/russia-and-china-will-have-to-justify-their-behaviour-to-the-syrian-people-who-continue-to-suffer-under-assads-brutal-regime.

MacFarquhar, Neil. 'Putin, Responding to Sanctions, Orders U.S. to Cut Diplomatic Staff by 755'. *The New York Times*, 30 July 2017, sec. Europe. https://www.nytimes.com/2017/07/30/world/europe/russia-sanctions-us-diplomats-expelled.html.

Marcus, Jonathan. 'Ukraine: The Military Balance of Power'. *BBC News*, 3 March 2014, sec. Europe. http://www.bbc.co.uk/news/world-europe-26421703.

Maria Golovnina and Patrick Worsnip. 'Gaddafi Orders Storm of Benghazi; U.N. Meets'. *Reuters*, 17 March 2011, sec. World News. https://www.reuters.com/article/idINIndia-55642620110317.

Mariam Karouny. 'Syria Intensifies Assault on Anti-Assad Protesters'. *Reuters*, 3 June 2011, sec. World News. https://www.reuters.com/article/us-syria-idUSLDE73N02P20110603.

Mazlum, İbrahim. 'ISIS as an Actor Controlling Water Resources in Syria and Iraq'. In *Violent Non-State Actors and the Syrian Civil War: The ISIS and YPG Cases*, edited by Özden Zeynep Oktav, Emel Parlar Dal, and Ali Murat Kurşun, 109–25. Cham: Springer International Publishing, 2018.

McMillan, Nesam, and David Mickler. 'From Sudan to Syria: Locating "Regime Change" in R2P and the ICC*'. *Global Responsibility to Protect* 5, no. 3 (1 January 2013): 283–316.

Mills, Kurt, and Alan Bloomfield. 'African Resistance to the International Criminal Court: Halting the Advance of the Anti-Impunity Norm'. *Review of International Studies* 44, no. 1 (January 2018): 101–27.

Ministère des Affaires étrangères et du Développement. 'France and the International Criminal Court (ICC)'. France Diplomatie: Ministry for Europe and Foreign Affairs. Accessed 6 August 2018. https://www.diplomatie.gouv.fr/en/french-foreign-policy/international-justice/france-and-the-international-criminal-court-icc/.

Ministry of Foreign Affairs of the People's Republic of China. 'Explanatory Remarks by Ambassador Wang Min after Security Council Voting on Draft Resolution on the Referral of the Situation of the Syrian Arab Republic to the International Criminal Court', 2014. Accessed 26 May 2016. http://www.fmprc.gov.cn/mfa_eng/wjb_663304/zwjg_665342/zwbd_665378/t1161567.shtml.

Morris, Justin. 'Libya and Syria: R2P and the Spectre of the Swinging Pendulum'. *International Affairs* 89, no. 5 (2013): 1265–83.

Nuruzzaman, Mohammed. 'The "Responsibility to Protect" Doctrine: Revived in Libya, Buried in Syria'. SSRN Scholarly Paper. Rochester, NY: Social Science Research Network, 2013. http://papers.ssrn.com/abstract=2542280.

Omar, Abdulaziz. 'Understanding and Preventing Attacks on Health Facilities During Armed Conflict in Syria'. *Risk Management and Healthcare Policy* 13 (18 March 2020): 191–203.

Peskin, Victor, and Mieczyslaw P. Boduszynski. 'The Rise and Fall of the ICC in Libya and the Politics of International Surrogate Enforcership'. *International Journal of Transitional Justice* 10, no. 2 (1 July 2016): 272–91.

Ralph, Jason. 'International Society, the International Criminal Court and American Foreign Policy'. *Review of International Studies* 31, no. 1 (2005): 27–44.

Ralph, Jason, and Adrian Gallagher. 'Legitimacy Faultlines in International Society: The Responsibility to Protect and Prosecute after Libya'. *Review of International Studies* 41, no. 03 (2015): 553–73.

Rediff News. 'Russia, China on Wrong Side of History: US on Syria Veto', 2014. Accessed 18 May 2016. http://www.rediff.com/news/report/russia-china-on-wrong-side-of-history-us-on-syria-veto/20120720.htm.

Roberts, Hugh. 'Who Said Gaddafi Had to Go?' *London Review of Books*, 17 November 2011. https://www.lrb.co.uk/the-paper/v33/n22/hugh-roberts/who-said-gaddafi-had-to-go.

Russia Today. 'Putin: Anything US Touches Turns into Libya or Iraq', 2014 https://www.youtube.com/watch?v=qGwWD-VVBEc.
Russo, Jenna B. 'R2P in Syria and Myanmar: Norm Violation and Advancement'. *Global Responsibility to Protect* 12, no. 2 (8 May 2020): 211–33.
Saba, Arif, and Shahram Akbarzadeh. 'The ICC and R2P: Complementary or Contradictory?' *International Peacekeeping* 28, no. 1 (1 January 2021): 84–109.
Scharf, Michael, and Laura Graham. 'Bridging the Divide between the ICC and UN Security Council'. *Georgetown Journal of International Law* 52 (2021 2020): 977.
Siebens, James, and Benjamin Case. 'The Libyan Civil War: Context and Consequences'. *THINK International and Human Security* 4 (2012).
'S/RES/1970' (2011) | United Nations Security Council'. Accessed 16 August 2023. https://www.un.org/securitycouncil/s/res/1970-%282011%29.
Stahn, Carsten. 'Libya, the International Criminal Court and Complementarity: A Test for "Shared Responsibility"'. *Journal of International Criminal Justice* 10, no. 2 (1 May 2012): 325–49.
Sun, Yun. 'Syria: What China Has Learned from Its Libya Experience'. Report. Washington, D.C. : *East-West Center in Washington*, 27 February 2012. http://scholarspace.manoa.hawaii.edu/handle/10125/22208.
Susan Dickson, 'The International Criminal Court's Role to Achieve Justice for Darfur Victims—GOV.UK', 2018. Accessed 6 August 2018. https://www.gov.uk/government/speeches/iccs-role-to-achieve-justice-for-victims-in-darfur.
Sweeney, Caroline. 'Accountability for Syria: Is the International Criminal Court Now a Realistic Option?' *Journal of International Criminal Justice* 17, no. 5 (1 December 2019): 1083–1115.
Teitel, Ruti G. 'Transitional Justice Genealogy'. *Harvard Human Rights Journal* 16 (2003): 69.
Thakur, Ramesh. 'R2P after Libya and Syria: Engaging Emerging Powers'. *The Washington Quarterly* 36, no. 2 (2013): 61–76.
The Economist. China v the Rest. 2016. https://www.economist.com/asia/2016/03/26/china-v-the-rest
The Economist, 'China Goes to Africa', 2017. Accessed 1 August 2017. https://www.economist.com/news/middle-east-and-africa/21725288-big-ways-and-small-china-making-its-presence-felt-across.
The Finnish institute of International Affairs. 'Briefing Paper—Responsibility to Protect ... Itself? Russia's Strategy towards the Crisis in Syria', 2013. Accessed 11 May 2016. http://www.fiia.fi/en/publication/341/responsibility_to_protect..._itself/.
The Independent. 'France Just Called on Russia to Be Investigated for War Crimes in Syria', 10 October 2016. http://www.independent.co.uk/news/world/middle-east/russia-syria-war-crimes-investigation-france-international-court-of-justice-a7353486.html.

———. 'Gaddafi Must Relinquish Power Says William Hague', *The Independent*, 26 July 2011. http://www.independent.co.uk/news/world/africa/gaddafi-must-relinquish-power-says-william-hague-2326152.html.

Tiemessen, Alana. 'The International Criminal Court and the Politics of Prosecutions'. *The International Journal of Human Rights* 18, no. 4–5 (4 July 2014): 444–61.

Tisdall, Simon. 'This Arrest Warrant Could Make Gaddafi More Dangerous | Simon Tisdall'. *The Guardian*, 27 June 2011, sec. Opinion. http://www.theguardian.com/commentisfree/2011/jun/27/gaddafi-international-criminal-court-arrest-warrant.

Ulfstein, Geir, and Hege Føsund Christiansen. 'The Legality of the Nato Bombing in Libya'. *The International and Comparative Law Quarterly* 62, no. 1 (2013): 159–71.

United Nations. 'Referral of Syria to International Criminal Court Fails as Negative Votes Prevent Security Council from Adopting Draft Resolution', 2014. Accessed 8 August 2018. https://www.un.org/press/en/2014/sc11407.doc.htm.

United Nations. 'United Nations Secretary-General Ban Ki-Moon', 2014. Accessed 2 October 2015. http://www.un.org/sg/STATEMENTS/index.asp?nid=7520.

Vilmer, Jean-Baptiste Jeangène. 'The African Union and the International Criminal Court: Counteracting the Crisis'. *International Affairs* 92, no. 6 (1 November 2016): 1319–42.

Walker, Angela. 'The Icc Versus Libya: How to End the Cycle of Impunity for Atrocity Crimes by Protecting Due Process'. *UCLA Journal of International Law and Foreign Affairs* 18, no. 2 (2014): 303–54.

Webb, Philippa. 'Deadlock or Restraint? The Security Council Veto and the Use of Force in Syria'. *Journal of Conflict and Security Law* 19, no. 3 (1 December 2014): 471–88.

Weiss, Thomas G. 'RtoP Alive and Well after Libya'. *Ethics & International Affairs* 25, no. 03 (2011): 287–92.

Whiting, Alex. 'An Investigation Mechanism for Syria: The General Assembly Steps into the Breach'. *Journal of International Criminal Justice* 15, no. 2 (1 May 2017): 231–37.

Wight, Martin. *International Theory*, 1991.

Xing, Qu. 'The UN Charter, the Responsibility to Protect, and the Syria Issue'. *China International Studies* 2 (2012): 14–36.

Zachary Laub. 'Syria's War and the Descent Into Horror'. *Council on Foreign Relations*, 14 February 2023. https://www.cfr.org/article/syrias-civil-war.

Zambakari, Christopher. 'The Misguided and Mismanaged Intervention in Libya: Consequences for Peace'. *African Security Review* 25, no. 1 (2 January 2016): 44–62.

CHAPTER 5

The ICC and the Symbolism Paradox: The Al Bashir Debacle and Putin's War

Background to the Investigation in Sudan

This Chapter deals with the third conceptual tension that arises from ICC prosecutions of SHoS that, the Chapter suggests, is underpinned by the existence of a symbolic paradox. This can be encapsulated as follows: while ICC actions globally symbolise justice and accountability, resistance against it can be construed as symbolic defiance against perceived neo-colonialism and Western interventionism. This tension has been illustrated in the introduction of this book, and recalls ideas of justice, peace, and order. The main difference between the democracy and the symbolism paradoxes is that while the first can be expected to manifest, mainly, at the intra-state level, the symbolism paradox has an international dimension to it, one in which it is not a specific investigation that is being contested, but the practice of prosecuting SHoS and its normative underpinning per se. To understand this, the Chapter starts with the ICC's efforts in Sudan, where the Court targeted President Omar Al Bashir.

Due to the fact that the ICC intervention in Sudan was the first of its kind, literature has provided with a florid debate about the rationale and implications of the Court's actions. Rapanyane et alii, for instance, suggest that international bodies, including the ICC, were ineffective in dealing with the Sudanese question because they acted too late against the

M. Cacciatori, *The International Criminal Court and the Prosecution of Sitting Heads of State*,
https://doi.org/10.1007/978-3-031-54646-4_5

Sudanese President.[1] Van der Vyver, on the other hand and very interestingly for the scope of this Chapter, suggests that among the reasons why the ICC mandate was not enforced in Africa lies in a solidarity principle that African states, and especially South Africa, prioritise over international views of justice.[2] Sluiter provides with a more legal approach to the matter, arguing that the ICC carries some of the blame for not obtaining cooperation from the Sudanese government, since certain legal disputes have remained unaddressed, including the legitimacy of UNSC resolution 1593.[3] Lubaale echoes such concerns, and adds that those currently in power in Sudan have too much to lose from handing Al Bashir to the ICC even now that he's been ousted.[4] Cwajg goes even further, and claims that even in the case that Al Bashir was facing trial at the Hague, legal questions about cooperation from governments, Heads of State immunities, and more could hamper the possibility of seeing him behind bars.[5] Rothbart et alii tried to find alternative mechanisms for the enforcement of justice, and claim that only by allowing for more participative agency of victims in Sudan the ICC could hope to achieve justice in the country and that, consequently, the difficulties are not solely legal.[6] Korostelina et alii, on similar lines, further suggest that peace and justice are not opposed

[1] Makhura Benjamin Rapanyane, Florence Ramasela Sethole, and Happy Mathew Tirivangasi, 'The United Nations, International Criminal Court and African Union's Delayed Response to the Prolonged Dictatorship in Sudan', *Journal of African Union Studies* 9, no. 3 (December 2020): 47–69.

[2] der Vyver Johan D. Van, 'Prosecuting the President of Sudan: A Dispute between the African Union and the International Criminal Court: Recent Developments', *African Human Rights Law Journal* 11, no. 2 (January 2011): 683–98.

[3] Göran Sluiter, 'Obtaining Cooperation from Sudan—Where Is the Law?', *Journal of International Criminal Justice* 6, no. 5 (1 November 2008): 871–84.

[4] Emma Charlene Lubaale, 'Now Available but Still Not Accessible to the ICC: Bashir and Africa's Politics', in *National Accountability for International Crimes in Africa*, ed. Emma Charlene Lubaale and Ntombizozuko Dyani-Mhango (Cham: Springer International Publishing, 2022), 247–85.

[5] Carolina Cwajg, 'A Wild Goose Chase? Prosecuting Al Bashir at the ICC' 1, *Rule of Law Journal (LSE)*, no. 1 (13 December 2020): 1.

[6] Daniel Rothbart, Karina Korostelina, and Beltina Gjeloshi, 'Living through War: An Oral History of Civilians in Sudan', *Conflict Resolution Quarterly* 40, no. 4 (2023): 405–27.

goal, at least for the victims, who are more inclined to see meaning in justice processes if peace is restored.[7]

This section of the Chapter evaluates these claims from the perspective of the symbolism paradox, arguing that the main issue with the enforcement of ICC rulings in Sudan lies at the systemic crux of opposing symbolic narratives that can be exploited on one side by the international community, and on the other by governments under scrutiny and its regional and international allies.

In the following sections the book explores the ICC attempt in Sudan, the ripples throughout the Sudanese society, and the regional resistance to the prosecution. There is no denying that the prosecution of Al Bashir constituted a true symbolic and revolutionary moment in international politics, one in which sovereignty is not considered as a guise under which authoritarian leaders can justify their actions and escape prosecution for their deeds. But as revolutionary as the idea might be, its actualisation in Sudan has been problematic to say the least. The Chapter focuses on how Al Bashir was able to escape international prosecution until now, while also visiting countries under the legal obligation to surrender him to the ICC. The only form of prosecution that he ever faced came after he was deposed in 2019 by an internal *coup d'état*. Meanwhile, in a process of progressive tightening of authoritarianism in the country, the warrants of arrest against the Sudanese President also coincided with a progressive marginalisation of relatively moderate political voices and a discriminate targeting of international NGOs. Both these actors, so essential for ensuring the security of citizens, have been suspected of cooperating with the ICC by the Sudanese government and as such have become primary targets of governmental retaliation.

The War in Darfur

The population of Darfur is roughly 7 million people and is home to 60–70 distinct ethnic groups.[8] The combination of scarcity of resources, and religious and inter-ethnic tensions, has plagued the area with a long

[7] Karina V. Korostelina, Daniel Rothbart, and Beltina Gjeloshi, 'Production of the Meaning of Justice in the Aftermath of War in Sudan', *Peace and Conflict: Journal of Peace Psychology* 29, no. 3 (2023): 306–16.

[8] Ola Olsson, 'After Janjaweed? Socioeconomic Impacts of the Conflict in Darfur', *The World Bank Economic Review* 24, no. 3 (1 January 2010): 388.

history of intra-state conflict.[9] In 2003, these tensions erupted forcefully. The emergence of two independentist movements, the Sudan Liberation Army (SLA) and the Justice and Equality Movement (JEM) started calling for greater autonomies for Darfur and a more sensible and equal redistribution of economic resources and political power.[10] The *casus belli* was constituted by the rebels' attack on al-Fashir airport, where the governmental army failed to protect the military supplies held at the facility. To suppress the rebellion, the Al Bashir government started to fuel tensions among different ethnic factions, while also arming and supporting local groups that opposed the SLA and the JEM. This coincided with the rise of the Janjaweed militia, a paramilitary group that was among the primary actors involved in the escalation of violence against civilians.[11] Between 2003 and 2004 it is estimated that some 300,000 were killed, with 2.7 million people becoming refugees in either Darfur or Chad.[12]

The UN described the events that started unfolding in Sudan in 2003 as "the world's worst humanitarian crisis" with the US government echoing international calls to label it a genocide. In 2003 the Sudanese government and the SPLA engaged in Peace Negotiations that would eventually lead to the signing of the Comprehensive Peace Agreement (CPA) in 2005 in Kenya. Members of the National Congress Party (NCP) and of the Sudan People's Liberation Movement (SPLM), signed the CPA to settle the dispute over Darfur. The plan, among other things, called for the withdrawal of northern troops from the south, national elections, a census, and the sharing of oil revenues. It also included provisions for power-sharing, and it set a timetable for a referendum on independence for southern Sudan. The signing of the peace agreement in 2005 signalled a potential for the Sudanese society to normalise intra-state relationships. However, it also posed a practical question on what to do to deal with the crimes that were perpetrated before 2005. Commentators often look at prosecutions as impediments to peaceful transitions from violence—and the opening of the investigation in June 2005 certainly fuelled similar doubts. Especially considering what

[9] Julie Flint and Alex de Waal, *Darfur: A Short History of a Long War* (Bloomsbury Publishing, 2008), 77–78.

[10] Ahmad Sikainga, '"The World's Worst Humanitarian Crisis": Understanding the Darfur Conflict', *Origins*, accessed 22 March 2023, https://origins.osu.edu/article/worlds-worst-humanitarian-crisis-understanding-darfur-conflict?language_content_entity=en.

[11] Olsson, 'After Janjaweed?', 390.

[12] Olsson, 390.

happened in Uganda, observers wondered if the Sudanese investigation was to follow in the footsteps of the Ugandan one. However, the two situations unfolded in starkly different manners.

Box 5.1 Biographical Sketch Al Bashir

Who Is Omar Al Bashir

Omar al Bashir (Omar Hassan Ahmad Al Bashir) was born on 7 January 1944. Of humble origins, he joined the army after moving to Khartoum from the countryside with his family. His military career started in the early 1970s, when he fought alongside the Egyptian army in the Arab Israeli War. In the mid-1980s he was already leading the Sudanese army against the SPLA.[13] In 1989 he led a successful *coup d'état* against the leadership of President Ahmed al-Mirghani. In those initial years, Al Bashir already showed the traits of its ruling, banning political parties, censoring the press, and ensuring the collaboration of the National Islamic Front (NIF), which led to a progressive islamisation of the country, that culminated with the introduction of the Shariah law in 1991.[14] In October 1993 Al Bashir was appointed President of Sudan, with the leader of the NIF, Hasan Al Turabi, elected President of the National Assembly. In 1998 he introduced a new constitution that nominally opened to political contestation. However, later that year, Al Bashir deposed Al Turabi (accused of conspiring against the President) by means of military force. In March 2000 Al Bashir declared a short state of emergency, that would become permanent after the December 2000 elections.

Al Bashir became one of the primary actors in the governmental response against the Darfurian rebels and has been considered one of the major culprits of the horrors that unfolded after 2003, for which he was the first ever SHoS indicted by the ICC. He was deposed after an internal coup in 2019, after 30 years of undisputed control over Sudan.

[13] 'Profile: Omar al-Bashir, Sudan's Longtime Ruler', accessed 22 March 2023, https://www.aljazeera.com/news/2019/4/11/profile-omar-al-bashir-sudans-longtime-ruler.

[14] Sergey Kostelyanets, 'Sudan's December Revolution and the Demise of the Al Bashir Regime', in New Wave of Revolutions in the MENA Region: A Comparative Perspective, ed. Leonid Issaev and Andrey Korotayev, Perspectives on Development in the Middle East and North Africa (MENA) Region (Cham: Springer International Publishing, 2022), 37–39.

The ICC and the Issuing of Two Warrants of Arrest for Al Bashir

On 25 January 2005, the UN-mandated International Commission of Inquiry on Darfur submitted its final report, urging Sudanese authorities and the international community to hold accountable those allegedly responsible for violating international humanitarian law and human rights law in the context of the Darfur War. On 31 March 2005 the UNSC adopted Resolution 1593 regardless of four abstentions (Algeria, Brazil, China, and the US), to refer the situation to the ICC. Following this, Prosecutor Moreno Ocampo obtained two warrants for the arrest of Ahmad Harun (formed Minister of the Interior and head of the Darfur Security Desk) and Ali Kushayb (leader of the Janjaweed militia in West Darfur) for the crimes committed between 2003 and 2004.[15] Meanwhile, the UN was facing severe difficulties in establishing a peacekeeping force to mitigate the spill-over effects of the Darfur War, also because of the indictments of senior officials of the Sudanese government. A UNSC Resolution in 2007 decided on a UN/African Union (AU) peacekeeping mission (UNAMID). The government's hostility towards the Court, but towards the international community itself, naturally further solidified when Moreno-Ocampo obtained two arrest warrants against the President itself in 2009 and 2010, on charges of war crimes, crimes against humanity, and genocide.[16] Before 2009, no SHoS had been ever prosecuted by the Court, so it was unclear how serious and credible the threat was.

While Chap. 3 highlighted how the ICC felt it was necessary to negotiate its operations with a local government, and that eventually led to the tacit agreement between the Court and Ugandan President Museveni, in Sudan the ICC was true to the Rome Statute and went after President Al Bashir himself. If international politics is dominated by the Westphalian idea of sovereign statehood, where no actor is superior to states, then ICC actions in Sudan are truly revolutionary. Legitimised by the UN, the ICC launched a direct attack on traditional conceptualisations of sovereignty,

[15] Luigi Condorelli and Annalisa Ciampi, 'Comments on the Security Council Referral of the Situation in Darfur to the ICC', *Journal of International Criminal Justice* 3, no. 3 (1 July 2005): 591–594.

[16] Allard Duursma and Tanja R. Müller, 'The ICC Indictment against Al-Bashir and Its Repercussions for Peacekeeping and Humanitarian Operations in Darfur', *Third World Quarterly* 40, no. 5 (4 May 2019): 894–95.

by actualising the moral imperative that claims that there are crimes so heinous and repulsive, that they should be prosecuted regardless of the status of the alleged criminals. However, the Chapter indicates, this was to cause ripples in Sudan and in international politics, representing the idea that some might morally and ethically feel that there is a need to surpass notions of traditional sovereignty in instances as grave as genocides, but this is likely to be opposed to retain the primacy of states as the most important actors in international politics.[17] This, in turn, corroborates the existence of a symbolic paradox that opposes two apparently irreconcilable rhetorical spaces: one that suggests that the ICC, and the international community, should prioritise the development and enforcement of global values. The other that justifies opposition to the Court and its underpinning normative dimension by galvanising anti-colonial sentiments in the non-Western world. Such inferences are explored in the following sections by focusing on both the domestic and regional implications of ICC actions against Al Bashir.

The Aftermath of the Arrest Warrants: Al Bashir Against Taha

Sudan's recent history is one of entrenched authoritarianism. The state has been labelled Worst of the Worst by Freedom House throughout the time of the ICC investigation,[18] which means that the absence of political contestation was already a problematic feature in the country even before the Court stepped in. However, this section will highlight how after the release of the warrants of arrest continuous attacks on political opponents and international actors shaped governmental narratives to justify a harshening of these measures against political contestation. The tightening of authoritarian practices in Sudan was arguably influenced by two international dynamics that raised the stakes for Al Bashir to remain President, as well as setting the basis for him to blame moderate forces within the NCP for cooperating with international aggressors. These are the expiring of the CPA and, as noted, the release of the warrants of arrest against him by

[17] Nicholas J. Wheeler and Timothy Dunne, 'Hedley Bull's Pluralism of the Intellect and Solidarism of the Will', *International Affairs* 72, no. 1 (1 January 1996): 91–107.

[18] *Freedom House*, 'Sudan', accessed 23 May 2016, https://freedomhouse.org/country/sudan.

the ICC. In a context in which any foreign meddling with Sudanese affairs has been effectively depicted as neo-imperialism, Al Bashir adopted an effective rhetorical strategy in which he was not to be considered a criminal anymore, but rather a Sudanese martyr under the threat of Western powers.

This martyrisation coincided with the progressive marginalisation of Ali Osman Taha, considered by many the champion of the moderate forces within the NCP, who apparently represented the only visible internal party opposition to the dominance of Al Bashir.[19] Taha has been described as a statesman "with a distinguished history in the NIF, [...] good communication skills and rapport with international actors",[20] and was particularly popular after the signing of the CPA agreement, having being described by many observers as the true mind behind it.[21] The New Sudan that he envisioned would have opened to democratisation processes, as well as requiring a deep transformation in the structure of the NCP to allow for more internal contestation.[22] Taha's moderate contestation of the Al Bashir presidency manifested in several occasions when he criticised the President publicly for not cooperating with international forces to solve the Darfur crisis.[23] In the context of Sudan, this is no small feat, to the point that Sudan Tribune commented that Taha's openness to international actors is what lied at the heart of the differences between him and the President. These differences also led to evident frictions with the government, with Taha attempting to appoint governmental representatives tasked to facilitate international solutions to the Darfur crisis, while Al Bashir appointed ministers openly hostile to any international solution like the CPA and the ICC.[24] Because of his international profile and his political leanings, Taha became the perfect scapegoat for Al Bashir.

[19] It must be noted that political moderation is here considered as a relational concept. So Taha's political standing is not to be considered moderate in absolute, but moderate in relation to Sudanese authoritarianism.

[20] Giorgio Musso, 'Sudan Divided: Continuing Conflict in a Contested State Ed. by Gunnar M. Sørbø, Abdel Ghaffar M. Ahmed (Review)', *African Conflict & Peacebuilding Review* 5, no. 2 (2015): 82–83.

[21] Alex De Waal, 'Darfur, the Court and Khartoum: The Politics of State Non-Cooperation', *Courting Conflict? Justice, Peace and the ICC in Africa*, 2008, 34.

[22] Watts Roba Gibia Nyirigwa, 'Why All These Dispute between Bashir and Taha?', *Sudan Tribune*, 30 March 2006.

[23] Sudan Tribune, 'Sudan's Taha Criticises al-Bashir Rejection of Darfur UN Force', 25 July 2006, http://www.sudantribune.com/spip.php?article16801.

[24] 'Sudan's Taha Criticises al-Bashir Rejection of Darfur UN Force'.

In fact, with the expiration of the CPA in 2010, and the release of the second warrant of arrest,[25] Al Bashir revived anti-imperialist narratives that can be traced back to 2008. At the time, for example, a presidential advisor of Al Bashir said that "the Western media campaign around the Darfur conflict served to cover up the US failure in Iraq". According to Al Bashir himself "crusaders and zionists were targeting Muslims all over the world".[26] In this anti-Western climate, a public figure like Taha was abruptly removed from any position in which he could exert influence on governmental practices. He eventually resigned from his role of Vice-President in 2013 (being left for the first time without any institutional role since the mid-1990s) and, while the official position is that he stepped down "voluntarily because he supported the change to open more opportunities to the new generations",[27] many have speculated that in fact he was forced out of office for its involvement with the CPA and the ICC.[28] The resignation of Taha sustained an ominous prediction made by the Sudanese President, who claimed that: "the decision of the ICC prosecutor is already solidifying our internal front, the internal front of our Sudanese people, and that is the source of our power and we will fight their actions".[29] In case there was any doubt about the reasons why Taha was excluded from the country's political life, the fact that Sudan's former Vice-President was substituted by two of his historical rivals, Dr. Nafie Ali Nafie and by Lieutenant General Bakri Hassan Salih[30] should be taken as an indication of the progressive deterioration of authoritarianism in Sudan. The two were both loyalists of the Al Bashir regime, and both supporters of the President's hardline against international actors, and embodied all that Taha fought against.[31] This was noted by de Waal, who claimed that "[...] the rally effect for al Bashir can be measured in the loss of influence

[25] International Criminal Court. 'Al Bashir Case', accessed 20 May 2016, https://www.icc-cpi.int/darfur/albashir.

[26] Patrick S. Wegner, *The International Criminal Court in Ongoing Intrastate Conflicts: Navigating the Peace-Justice Divide* (Cambridge University Press, 2015), 140–41.

[27] Muhammed Amin, 'Sudan's First VP Ali Osman Taha Resigns to Allow for "Change"', *Africa Review*, 2013, http://www.africareview.com/News/Sudans-First-VP-Ali-Osman-Taha-resigns-to-allow-for-change/-/979180/2101906/-/ve3sdxz/-/index.html.

[28] Muhammed Amin, 'Sudan's First VP Ali Osman Taha Resigns to Allow for "Change"'.

[29] Musso, 'Sudan Divided', 84.

[30] Muftah, 'Omar Al-Bashir's Cabinet Reshuffle & Absolute Rule in Sudan', 2014, accessed 3 December 2015, http://muftah.org/bashirs-cabinet-reshuffle-and-absolute-rule-in-sudan/.

[31] *Sudan Tribune* 'Plural News and Views on Sudan', accessed 27 May 2016, http://www.sudantribune.com/spip.php?mot1386.

of the comparatively moderate Vice President [...], who was very powerful between 2005 and 2007 after the CPA agreement".[32] Mohammed Elshabik noted that this signified that "[...] the NCP gradually shifted away from permitting small degrees of openness to adopting the tyranny of absolutism".[33] Hopes for a democratic opening inside the Sudanese society and within the NCP were shattered months after Al Bashir's indictment by the Court.

These events might be systemic signals to understand what is likely to happen when the ICC unseals warrants of arrest against SHoS. Under the threat of trial, jail, and international condemnation, authoritarian leaders are likely to cling to power with all the means at their disposal. After all, historically examples of SHoS being effectively put to trial are close to none. So, SHoS know that their best option to avoid prosecution is to retain their seat. This echoes evidence from Chaps. 3 and 4 of this book, and sustain the idea of two paradoxes (democracy and enforcement of justice) that influence the ability of the ICC to deliver on the mandate of SHoS prosecutions. But, as will be shown in the remainder of the Chapter, the situation in Sudan also confirms the existence of a symbolism paradox, according to which resistance against ICC actions against a SHoS can signal the emergence of normative patterns in non-Western contexts that challenge not only the Court, but the practice per se and its underpinning normative fabric.

Alex Arieff sustains this by claiming that "[...] the warrants of arrest increased al Bashir motivation to remain President of Sudan and defend his position to protect himself from ICC indictments".[34] This book shows that SHoS have various ways to ensure this. In Sudan and in terms of internal political contestation, Al Bashir opted for marginalising perhaps the most important political voice that brought international attention to his role in the 2003–2004 violence.[35] By claiming that his political opponents were concocting his demise and conspiring against him and, by extension, against the people of Sudan in general, Al Bashir was surprisingly able to ensure that more and more people started supporting him after the

[32] De Waal, 'Darfur, the Court and Khartoum', 34.

[33] Muftah, 'Omar Al-Bashir's Cabinet Reshuffle & Absolute Rule in Sudan'.

[34] Alexis Arieff, 'Sexual Violence in African Conflicts', *Congressional Research Service*, Library of Congress, 2011, http://digital.library.unt.edu/ark:/67531/metadc491381/m1/1/high_res_d/R40956_2010Nov30.pdf.

[35] Krishanu Sengupta, 'Peace or Justice?: The Dilemma of the International Criminal Court', 2008, https://www.uleth.ca/dspace/handle/10133/1202.

warrants of arrest.[36] As a testimony, huge demonstrations with thousands rallying in Khartoum followed the announcement by the ICC of the indictment of the President,[37] with the army and members of several tribes swearing oaths of allegiance to the Sudanese President.[38] It is always difficult to gauge how genuine these manifestations are in a context of closed authoritarianism—but it remains important to note that the army closed its ranks against their President and any hope for popular manifestations of dissent was postponed for at least a decade. It is important to recall that, as outlined in Chap. 1, the three paradoxes that underpin the conceptual architecture of the book are not to be perceived as practically distinct. They can manifest simultaneously when the ICC prosecutes a SHoS, and their ramifications can overlap.

The Prosecution and the NGO Dilemma

The marginalisation of political contestation in Sudan was not limited to the ostracisation of Taha, but extended to international actors in the form of an attack against NGOs that the Al Bashir government depicted as collaborators of a neo-imperial international justice system. This dynamic has been explored in Chap. 3 in relation to what happened in Kenya. The fact that few years prior a similar phenomenon occurred in Sudan testifies to the systemic nature of these reactions. In fact, hours after the warrant of arrest against Al Bashir was issued, the government of Sudan expelled 14 international aid agencies.[39] In the following weeks Al Bashir additionally closed three more human rights groups[40] and intensified the "[…] surveillance of opposition and human rights organisations".[41] The International Rescue Committee (IRC) was one of the initial foreign humanitarian NGOs organisations expelled by Sudan's government for allegedly cooperating

[36] Richard Cockett, *Sudan* (Yale University Press, 2010), 268.

[37] Al Arabiya, 'Thousands Protest for Bashir in Khartoum', 2009, http://www.alarabiya.net/articles/2009/03/06/67859.html.

[38] BBC, 'Warrant Issued for Sudan's Leader', *BBC*, 4 March 2009, sec. Africa, http://news.bbc.co.uk/1/hi/world/africa/7923102.stm.

[39] Alex De Waal and Gregory H. Stanton, 'Should President Omar Al-Bashir of Sudan Be Charged and Arrested by the International Criminal Court? An Exchange of Views', *Genocide Studies and Prevention* 4, no. 3 (2009): 309.

[40] Julie Flint, *Rhetoric and Reality: The Failure to Resolve the Darfur Conflict* (Citeseer, 2010), 26, http://citeseerx.ist.psu.edu/viewdoc/download?doi=10.1.1.180.522&rep=rep1&type=pdf.

[41] Wegner, *The International Criminal Court in Ongoing Intrastate Conflicts*, 140.

with the ICC. Despite the advice of UN's humanitarian affairs chief John Holmes who encouraged aid groups to be impartial and independent, in July 2005 Reuters reported that IRC's protection programme coordinator Joseph Aguettant, circulated a memorandum that outlined the guidelines for IRC's cooperation with the ICC. He outlined that this "[...] would help Sudan's people and bring criminals to justice". IRC spokeswoman Melissa Winkler firstly acknowledged this, but eventually denied that the memorandum was given any serious consideration. An official IRC communication outlined that "[t]he policy that was later adopted specifically directs IRC staff members not to communicate in any way with the ICC and not to support ICC investigations".[42] Other well-known NGOs expelled from Darfur included the French aid organisation Medicins Sans Frontieres (Doctors without Borders) (MSF), and Oxfam. Accusations against them by Sudan's UN envoy Abdalmahmood Abdalhaleem ranged from assisting the ICC investigation to "first-class espionage".[43] Al Bashir declared that all foreign aid groups would have halted activities in Sudan within a year beginning in 2009, year of the release of the first arrest warrant.

Something that is often lost in abstract peace and/or justice discussions is the practical repercussions of such events on everyday life. In the case of NGO expulsions, the consequences are not just political by signalling a progressive tightening of authoritarianism, but impact those who need international assistance the most. The IRIN centre of humanitarian news and analysis claimed on 9 March 2009 that halting NGOs operations left 1.1 million Sudanese without food, 1.5 million without healthcare, and at least one million without drinking water.[44] Reactions from NGO workers at the time of the expulsion, all remark the fact that "we feared restrictions ... but not this—not that all the biggest [agencies] should go at once".[45] The UN, that described the situation in Sudan as part of the biggest humanitarian intervention in history, depicted a bleak situation by saying: "[...] if the life-saving assistance these agencies were providing is not restored shortly, it will have immediate, lasting and profound impacts

[42] Louis Charbonneau, 'NGO Expelled from Darfur Considered ICC Cooperation', *Reuters*, 2009, http://www.reuters.com/article/2009/03/16/us-sudan-warcrimes-ngo-idUSTRE52F6SX20090316.

[43] Louis Charbonneau.

[44] IRIN News, 'SUDAN: NGO Expulsion to Hit Darfur's Displaced', 2009, http://www.irinnews.org/report/83370/sudan-ngo-expulsion-to-hit-darfur-s-displaced.

[45] IRIN News, 'SUDAN: NGO Expulsion to Hit Darfur's Displaced'.

on the wellbeing of millions of Sudanese citizens", and added "it is not possible, in any reasonable timeframe, to replace the capacity and expertise these agencies have provided over an extended period of time".[46] Many noted that the opposition of the Al Bashir government to NGOs is not something that emerged in 2009 but escalated dramatically after the opening of the investigation and the issuing of the warrants of arrest. As early as 28 October 2004, when the possibility of an ICC investigation was already very much on the table, the President described Western aid agencies as "enemies of Sudan"[47] and in March 2005 the government accused Oxfam, MSF and the Norwegian Refugee Council of conducting a political campaign on rape in Darfur and arrested MSF staff members.[48] After the opening of the investigation, governmental hostility towards NGOs reached its zenith. On 21 February 2006, the Al Bashir government passed the Organisation of Humanitarian and Voluntary Work Act that required NGOs to register with the Humanitarian Aid Commission (HAC), which started obstructing the work of the agencies by different bureaucratic means.[49] This resulted in the issuing of a report in which it was argued that "[...] President Al Bashir started to encourage attacks on humanitarian aid workers".[50]

There is little doubt that the escalation of hostility towards NGOs developed in concomitance with the ICC operations, and the expulsion of NGOs after the release of the warrants of arrest was a pivotal moment in Sudan's recent history. Even by assuming that the warrants of arrest just provided a justification for Al Bashir to harshen a long-standing policy towards NGOs,[51] it seems legitimate to ask if the governmental stance towards NGOs would have developed in the same way without the ICC's involvement—especially considering Al Bashir's growing popularity. *Ipso facto*, the prosecution of Al Bashir made it possible for the government to take a course of action that might have been planned for a long time, but

[46] UNICEF, 'Statement on the Humanitarian Situation in Darfur', 2015, accessed 3 December 2015, http://www2.unicef.org:60090/spanish/media/media_48507.html.

[47] Wegner, *The International Criminal Court in Ongoing Intrastate Conflicts*, 184.

[48] Frank Chalk and Danielle Kelton, *Mass-Atrocity Crimes in Darfur and the Response of Government of Sudan Media to International Pressure* (na, 2009), 115, https://migs.concordia.ca/Media_Monitoring/documents/Chapter_5_SudanRadio.pdf.

[49] Wegner, *The International Criminal Court in Ongoing Intrastate Conflicts*, 185.

[50] Julie Flint and Alex De Waal, *Darfur: A New History of a Long War* (Zed Books, 2008), 197, http://eprints.lse.ac.uk/id/eprint/42072.

[51] Wegner, *The International Criminal Court in Ongoing Intrastate Conflicts*, 186.

before the release of the warrants of arrest would have been very unpopular. As already noted, these events were echoed a few years later in Kenya.

African Contestation for the ICC After 2009

Something that often emerges when discussing the impact of warrants of arrest on SHoS is that they should, at least, restrict the possibility of travelling and entertaining diplomatic efforts by the accused. However, the three paradoxical dynamics that underpin this book suggest that this might be an ill-placed hope. Especially in relation to the symbolism paradox, not arresting an individual with an ICC warrant pending on his head might symbolically bolster regional resistance to the Court, the practice of prosecuting SHoS, and the values that it propagates.

With ICC member-states being under legal obligation to surrender criminals to the Court, this should greatly inhibit the influence of someone like Al Bashir at least at the regional level, considering how many African states are party to the Rome Statute. In the words of ICC's Judge Cuno Tarfusser "[…] there exists no ambiguity or uncertainty with respect to the obligation to immediately arrest and surrender Omar Al Bashir to the Court, and that the competent authorities […] are already aware of this obligation".[52] However, as remainder of this section will show, not only this didn't happen, but the warrants of arrest seem to have sparked the diffusion of an African anti-ICC sentiment that would put the legitimacy of the Court at stake.

Since the release of the warrant of arrest in 2009, Al Bashir has visited several African members of the Rome Statute, like Chad, Kenya, Malawi, and South Africa. None of these has complied with the warrants, and Al Bashir remained a free man even before the ICC's dropping of charges in 2016. Waves of outrage have characterised Western narratives on these failures to comply with the rulings of the ICC. For instance, Elise Keppler, head of HRW's international justice programme, insisted that "[a] political deal between Chad and Sudan is no justification for shielding alleged war criminals".[53] This stance echoes many episodes in which Western

[52] Judge Cuno Tarfusser, 'Decision Following the Prosecutor's Request for an Order Further Clarifying That the Republic of South Africa Is under the Obligation to Immediately Arrest and Surrender Omar Al Bashir', 13 June 2015.

[53] The Guardian, 'Chad Refuses to Arrest Omar Al-Bashir on Genocide Charges', 22 July 2010.

political elites have oversimplified the debate around the ICC in a Manichean manner, burying debates about the complexities of dealing with such cases in abstract discussions of moral imperatives. This is not limited to the situation in Sudan. For instance, during Museveni's inauguration ceremony in May 2016, when the Ugandan President criticised the Court for only targeting African leaders, American, Canadian, and European representatives "abruptly left the room".[54]

As noted in Chap. 1, international laws are reflections of international politics and, as such, the normative pillars on which they rest, can and should be discussed. It is easy to sympathise with the idea that African leaders should arrest Al Bashir because he is a criminal. However, claiming that resistance to the arrest is merely grounded on the desire of African leaders to shield criminals from prosecution, is not taking resistance seriously. Before exploring these African resistance narratives however, it is important to acknowledge that the Darfur crisis was a major political upheaval in sub-Saharan Africa. The spill-over effects of the crisis not only reshaped Sudan domestically, leading to the creation of South Sudan, but also escalated the conflict on the borders,[55] exacerbating the necessity of normalising state relationships in the continent.

Both Chad and Kenya are neighbours of Sudan and, as noted by Al Bashir himself, the relationship between these countries has historically been based on conflict.[56] In 2010 a peace deal was signed by Idriss Deby, the Chadian President, and Al-Bashir, which coincided with a lowering of the fights and casualties on the border of the two countries.[57] Furthermore, many of the key protocols of the CPA that were signed between 2003 and 2007 to put an end to the civil war were signed in Kenya. In short, after years of continuous atrocities committed within Sudan, and along Sudanese borders, the countries found a precarious equilibrium that helped the

[54] Al Jazeera, 'Western Officials Walk Museveni Inauguration', 2016, http://www.aljazeera.com/news/2016/05/Western-officials-walk-museveni-inauguration-160513093336340.html.

[55] Idean Salehyan, 'No Shelter Here: Rebel Sanctuaries and International Conflict', *The Journal of Politics* 70, no. 01 (January 2008): 54; Gérard Prunier, 'Africa's World War', *Congo, the Rwandan Genocide and The Making of a Continental Catastrophe*, 2009, 862, http://www.jstor.org/stable/pdf/40542212.pdf.

[56] Moumine Ngarmbassa, 'Sudan's Bashir Defies Court with Chad Trip', *Reuters*, 21 July 2010, http://af.reuters.com/article/worldNews/idAFTRE66K2V720100721.

[57] Thomson Reuter Foundation, 'Darfur Conflict', 2015, accessed 7 August 2015, http://www.trust.org/spotlight/Darfur-conflict.

de-escalation of casualties, and Al-Bashir was a crucial part of these peace deals. This is what Chad's Foreign Minister Moussa Faki Mahamat advanced when, in the wake of Al Bashir's visit to Chad in the July of 2010,[58] declared that "Omar al-Bashir was invited to the summit in his capacity as President of a CEN-SAD member and he has nothing to worry about, [because] everybody is working for the resolution of the Darfur crisis. It is not the moment to add other charges to complicate the situation. Our priority is peace in Sudan".[59] The Chadian ambassador to the UN was even clearer when he stated that "[w]hen you normalise relations with a country you are not going to arrest the head of state".[60] Similar concerns emerged from the Kenyan political elite, after the visit that Al Bashir paid to the country in the September of 2010 in occasion of the signing of the new Kenyan constitution. Richard Onyonka, an assistant foreign minister, advocated that arresting Al Bashir would have hampered the prospects of a peaceful resolution of the Sudanese conflict. The foreign minister was quoted saying "[a]part from being an immediate neighbour, Sudan's stability is vitally linked to Kenya's continued peace and well-being" and "we must have a peaceful resolution to the issues of Sudan and Kenya is going to make sure that we achieve the results". Onyonka concluded his speech by clearly stating that peace was the only thing that mattered and, "[i]f it means negotiating with both parties we shall".[61]

While Chad and Kenya, by being neighbours of Sudan, are expected to be more vocal about the prosecution of the former Sudanese President, the resistance to it was not limited to them. When Al Bashir visited the Malawian capital Lilongwe, Malawian politicians reacted similarly.[62] Information Minister Patricia Kaliati told the BBC's Network Africa programme that detaining Al Bashir was beyond question, explicitly saying that "[…] he's coming for business and we don't have any business to do with the arrest of President Omar". Malawi's foreign minister furthermore told Reuters that the country would not arrest Al Bashir because of

[58] The Guardian, 'Chad Refuses to Arrest Omar Al-Bashir on Genocide Charges'.

[59] Sudan Tribune, 'Chad Rolls Red Carpet for Sudanese President, Says Bashir Is Safe from Arrest', 2010, http://www.sudantribune.com/spip.php?article35732.

[60] James Copnall, 'Bashir Warrant: Chad Accuses ICC of Anti-African Bias', *BBC News*, accessed 31 May 2016, http://www.bbc.co.uk/news/world-africa-10723869.

[61] The Guardian, 'Kenya Defends Failure to Arrest Sudan's President Omar al-Bashir in Nairobi', 29 August 2010.

[62] BBC News, 'Sudan's Omar al-Bashir in Malawi: ICC Wants Answers', accessed 31 July 2015, http://www.bbc.co.uk/news/world-africa-15384163.

the "brotherly coexistence" between member-states of the Common Market for Eastern and Southern Africa.[63] Al Bashir's most publicised visit to a country member of the Rome Statute took place on 14 June 2015, to attend an AU summit held by Zimbabwean President Robert Mugabe in South Africa. John Jeffery, Deputy Minister of Justice and Constitutional Development in South Africa, defused Judge Tarfusser's remarks on the obligation to comply with the Rome Statute by saying that "[w]e perceive it as tending to act as a proxy instrument for these [Western] states, who see no need to subject themselves to its discipline, to persecute African leaders and affect regime change on the continent".[64] In the same statement he hinted at the fact that if South Africa was to actively prevent Al Bashir from leaving the country, this would have been a declaration of war against Sudan.[65] The regional consensus building against the prosecution of Al Bashir reached its zenith when the AU declared in a press release that Chad, being neighbour of Sudan and considered the recent warring past of the two countries, "[...] must do what it can to promote peace and encourage the government and elected leaders, including Al Bashir".[66] Conforming to the instrumental value of not complying with the ICC, the Head of the AU, Dr. Nkosazana Dlamini-Zuma, declared in 2012 that "it is important to get peace in Sudan, especially in Darfur, President al-Bashir has to be part of that"[67] adding that "[i]t is more important to get peace in Sudan than to rush for an arrest".[68]

The four cases above signal that a regional consensus is building on the necessity of discussing the saliency of antagonising ICC prosecutions of SHoS as an ordering principle. This consensus has manifested on every occasion in which a member-state to the Rome Statute hosted Al Bashir on official visits and failed to arrest him, and has apparently gained traction

[63] Reuters, 'Hague Court Questions Bashir's Visit to Malawi', 19 October 2011, http://af.reuters.com/article/topNews/idAFJOE79I0K520111019.

[64] Deputy Minister of Justice and Constitutional Development, the Hon JH Jeffery, MP, *Debate in Terms of Rule 103: The Implications of the Attendance and Departure of President Omar al-Bashir from the African Union Summit in South Africa*, 2015, http://www.justice.gov.za/m_speeches/2015/20150623_PresidentBashir.html#sthash.5Kj5j3G1.dpu.

[65] Deputy Minister of Justice and Constitutional Development, the Hon JH Jeffery, MP.

[66] Gwen P. Barnes, 'International Criminal Court's Ineffective Enforcement Mechanisms: The Indictment of President Omar Al Bashir, The', *Fordham Int'l LJ* 34 (2010): 1611.

[67] Africa Review, 'Sudan Peace More Important than Bashir Arrest: AU Boss', accessed 14 December 2015, http://www.africareview.com/News/Sudan-peace-more-important-than--Bashir-arrest/-/979180/1469100/-/kqhgsq/-/index.html.

[68] 'Sudan Peace More Important than Bashir Arrest'.

also because of what this resistance symbolises. The narratives of justification that emerged after the non-compliance with the warrants of arrest signal that African political elites are rejecting the idea that Westernised justice should be prioritised over practical considerations that involve the de-escalation of conflicts in Africa. This sustains the idea that non-prosecution is seen as an ordering principle that effectively helped normalising relationships among African states after the crisis in Darfur. This is consistent with pluralist interpretations of international politics that, as already shown in Chap. 1, warned about the dangers of enforcing contested norms. Doing so, in the eyes of African leaders, would mean sacrificing something extremely tangible (order) for something abstract (justice). This also reinforces the idea of a symbolic space that is harnessing non-Western support to challenge the ICC, the practice of prosecuting SHoS, and the normative architecture that sustains them.

The AU Threatens to Leave the ICC

In the previous section the book already noted that some African countries started questioning the legitimacy of the practice of prosecuting SHoS by the ICC when Al Bashir visited state parties to the Rome Statute, which refused to comply with the warrants for the arrest of the Sudanese President. The major concern for these states was that complying with the Court's decision would mean harshening the relationship with Sudan, hampering diplomatic, economic, and security prospects. Temporally, when the ICC went after a second SHoS, Kenyatta, African states would radicalise their position. The Kenyatta case is unpacked in Chap. 3 of this book, but it is necessary to recall here that when Kenyatta was elected with summons to appear by the ICC pending on his head, this scepticism was reorientated to question the legitimacy and impartiality of the ICC, its neo-imperial tendencies, and its associations with regime change. In a famous document released in concomitance with the opening of the Kenyan investigation, the AU resolved that "[t]he abuse and misuse of indictments against African leaders have a destabilizing effect that will negatively impact on the political, social and economic development of States and their ability to conduct international relations [...]".[69] The link

[69] African Union, 'Decision on the Report of the Commission on the Abuse of the Principle of Universal Jurisdiction', 25 December 2010, Doc. Assembly/AU/14(XI), http://www.minec.gov.mz/index2.php?option=com_docman&task=doc_view&gid=12&Itemid=48. Ext/Assembly/AU/Dec.1.

between ICC prosecutions and regime change has constituted a thorny issue for the Court since its inception, which would become a particularly prominent theme with the situations in Libya and Syria. However, during the prosecutions of Al Bashir and Kenyatta, the discussion was underpinned by regional undertones that would eventually become global concerns. In this sense, when the Kenyatta case was opened by the ICC in 2013, African leaders speaking at the AU made it clear that the AU was united in the resistance, and that the hostility towards the ICC was not limited to the Al Bashir case. Since the opening of the Kenyatta case, AU narratives on the necessity of leaving the Court became more prominent. Hailemariam Desalegn, the Ethiopian Prime Minister, was cautious in addressing the 2013 annual AU meeting by stating that "[i]t should be underscored that our goal is not and should not be a crusade against the ICC, but a solemn call for the organisation to take Africa's concerns seriously".[70]

By examining AU reports from 2002, the year in which the Rome Statute was ratified by most African countries, and 2015 it is easy to note that ICC matters have been constantly subjects of discussion during the meetings. But while until 2008 the Court received relatively little attention, and mostly positive, the prosecutions of Al Bashir and Kenyatta (and afterwards Gaddafi), sparked an anti-ICC sentiment that invested all the AU. AU annual reports indicate a growing dissatisfaction that many African states expressed towards the Court, a dissatisfaction that started emerging in 2009, in concomitance with the unsealing of the two warrants of arrest against Al Bashir and reached its peak in 2011—when the Court issued a warrant of arrest against Libyan President Muammar Gaddafi. During this time several African states refused to arrest and hand over Al Bashir to the ICC. In contrast, before 2009, the African stance towards the ICC can be considered as largely positive and this is not only evident by looking at AU narratives, but also by understanding that during the preparatory stages that led to the creation of the Court African states constantly expressed support for this institution. It is therefore natural to assume that SHoS prosecutions played a significant role in the harshening of this relationship. In 2016 it was precisely Kenya that formalised a

[70] The Telegraph, 'African Union Agrees on ICC Immunity for Heads of State', accessed 11 July 2017, http://www.telegraph.co.uk/news/worldnews/africaandindianocean/10374538/African-Union-agrees-on-ICC-immunity-for-heads-of-state.html.

proposal for all members of the AU to leave the ICC. This proposal received widespread backing within the organisation and, even though no binding decision was made, it indicated the next step of the African resistance to the ICC, from opposing a specific practice to opposing the Court as a whole. In the words of a Kenyan spokesperson at the 2016 AU summit, the "[…] proposal [was put forward] to develop a roadmap for the withdrawal of all African nations".[71] After the summit the idea of African states leaving the ICC took physical form when South Africa, Burundi, and the Gambia announced their decision to withdraw from it.[72] This decision was eventually not formalised, and actually retracted in the case of South Africa and the Gambia. In South Africa the High Court ruled the decision to leave the ICC unconstitutional. In the Gambia, newly installed President Adama Barrow allegedly changed his mind after in open defiance of the previous government's decision to leave the Court.[73] Burundi, on the other hand, became the first country to leave the ICC in October 2017.[74] Despite the fact that two withdrawals didn't formally manifest, African unrest towards the Court has been, and continues to be, palpable and is exemplified not only by statements made within the AU but also by these practical actions that members are taking or threatening to take. Meanwhile, in an interesting turn of events, in occasion of the signing of the new Kenyan constitution, US President Barack Obama said "I am disappointed that Kenya hosted Sudanese President Omar al-Bashir in defiance of International Criminal Court arrest warrants for war crimes, crimes against humanity, and genocide".[75] This statement echoed many calls (especially European) for the cooperation of Sudan in ensuring that

[71] Dixon, Robin. 'African Union Members Back Kenyan Plan to Leave ICC', *The Guardian*, 2016, accessed 11 July 2017, https://www.theguardian.com/world/2016/feb/01/african-union-kenyan-plan-leave-international-criminal-court.

[72] Dixon, Robyn. 'African Leaders Amp up Pressure on the International Criminal Court, with a Plan for Mass Exit', *Los Angeles Times*, 1 February 2017, http://www.latimes.com/world/africa/la-fg-southafrica-icc-massexit-20170201-story.html.

[73] BBC News, 'South Africa Revokes ICC Withdrawal after Court Ruling', 8 March 2017, sec. Africa, https://www.bbc.com/news/world-africa-39204035.

[74] BBC News, 'Burundi Leaves International Criminal Court amid Row', 27 October 2017, sec. Africa, https://www.bbc.com/news/world-africa-41775951.

[75] Egypt Independent, 'Obama "disappointed" Kenya Hosted Sudan's Bashir', 28 August 2010, https://www.egyptindependent.com/obama-disappointed-kenya-hosted-sudans-bashir/.

Al Bashir would face justice at the ICC.[76] Even more explicitly the US Ambassador to the UN, Samantha Power, faced with a possible visit of the Sudanese President to the 2013 meeting of the General Assembly in New York, stated that

> President Bashir, as you know, stands accused of genocide, war crimes and crimes against humanity by the International Criminal Court. Such a trip would be deplorable, cynical and hugely inappropriate. We would suggest that given that he is under those charges, and that the ICC has indicted him, again, on genocide, war crimes, and crimes against humanity charges that it would be more appropriate for him to present himself to the ICC and travel to The Hague.[77]

While it is easy to be sympathetic with such calls for justice, the history of the ICC shows that they are hypocritical at best. In fact, African hostility against the ICC enacted in practice what the US had been advocating for itself since the very establishment of the Court: non-extradition. Many African states have proven to be unwilling to accept the idea that an international body can decide the fate of SHoS, often advocating in favour of immunities that jar with the Rome Statute. This stance is heightened by the fact that most prosecutions happened in Africa and that, until Putin, only African SHoS have been targeted by the Court. This attitude, coupled with growing allegations of neo-imperialism leveraged against the ICC, is one of the major developments in the Court's entire existence and consistent with the existence of a symbolism paradox.

Background to the Investigation in Russia

The latest development in the practice of prosecuting SHoS at the time of writing this book is the release of the warrant of arrest against Russian President Vladimir Putin for the crimes allegedly committed during the 2022 escalation of the Ukraine War. After more than ten years since the last warrant of arrest against a SHoS was released for former Libyan President Muammar Gaddafi, the ICC was requested to act against one of

[76] BBC News, 'In Quotes: ICC Accuses Bashir', 14 July 2008, http://news.bbc.co.uk/1/hi/world/europe/7505937.stm.

[77] Lynch, Colum. 'Samantha Power's Problem from Hell', *Foreign Policy*, 2013, accessed 8 August 2018, https://foreignpolicy.com/2013/09/23/samantha-powers-problem-from-hell/.

the most powerful men in international politics. Not only that, but the ICC is investigating a situation that involves a permanent member of the UNSC, which has withdrawn from the ICC in 2016, and this makes the context of the investigation extremely complicated. This move was welcomed by many as an indication that the ICC was not afraid of prosecuting powerful states, attempting to dismantle a common feeling that threats against these states are often not credible,[78] or that "international law is an instrument through which the powerful punish the weak".[79]

Due to the novelty of the case, literature is still reacting heterogeneously to these developments. Shevchuk, for instance, notes that the ICC intervention in Ukraine requires more pragmatic approaches to the application of international law in domestic contexts than purely legalistic ones[80] considering the position of those under investigation. Nagy, acknowledging this points out that any possibility for future trials will be determined by whether or not Putin wins this war.[81] Imoedemhe suggests that the ICC might be aided in its quest by more local expressions of justice instead of purely international ones,[82] and this is worth mentioning especially considering the difficulties of dealing with great powers. Marchuk sustains this view by arguing that cooperation between international and local mechanisms of justice is essential to close the impunity gap in Ukraine.[83] Echoing this Kelly warns that international law, especially when dealing with great powers, is subservient to realpolitik calculations

[78] Vittorio Bufacchi, 'War Crimes in Ukraine: Is Putin Responsible?', *Journal of Political Power* 16, no. 1 (2 January 2023): 5.

[79] Daniele Archibugi and Alice Pease, *Crime and Global Justice: The Dynamics of International Punishment*, Wiley, 2018.

[80] Viktor Shevchuk, 'Problems of Criminalistic Support of the Practice of the International Criminal Court in Ukraine', *Збірник наукових праць ΛΌΓΟΣ*, 12 October 2020, 14–19.

[81] Noémi Nagy, 'The Case of David vs. Goliath?', in *Threats to Peace and International Security: Asia versus West: Current Challenges in a New Geopolitical Situation*, ed. Juan Cayón Peña and J. Martín Ramírez, Advanced Sciences and Technologies for Security Applications (Cham: Springer Nature Switzerland, 2023), 47–61.

[82] Ovo Imoedemhe, 'The International Criminal Court: Whether the Crime of Aggression in Ukraine', *International and Comparative Law Review* 23, no. 1 (1 August 2023): 27–52.

[83] Iryna Marchuk, 'Domestic Accountability Efforts in Response to the Russia–Ukraine War: An Appraisal of the First War Crimes Trials in Ukraine', *Journal of International Criminal Justice* 20, no. 4 (1 September 2022): 787–803.

and as such prosecuting Putin might be extremely complex.[84] Masol, however, suggests that the tainted information environment is giving birth to seemingly contradictory understandings of the role of the Court in the conflict.[85] Geneuss and Jessberger offer an alternative viewpoint, considering the criticism that the Court has faced since its inception. They highlight that the situation in Russia has re-vitalised prospects for the ICC after decades of accusations of bias and prosecutorial discrimination.[86] Pinzauti and Pizzutti, like others, focused on the actual legal groundings for an ICC investigation into the situation, suggesting that Russian actions merit international scrutiny for a breach of the self-determination principle.[87] The above highlights that the fact that Russian President occupies a pre-eminent position in international politics exacerbates the issues that this book deals with. This seems already to corroborate the idea of a symbolic tension that underpins SHoS prosecutions, as per the introduction of this Chapter. The following sections highlight not only that the investigation in Russia is complicated by international political pressures and leverages, but also that it has the potential to bolster non-Western opposition to the Court from a symbolic perspective.

The Court already partially signalled its intentions to move beyond Africa when it decided to open an investigation on the crimes allegedly committed by British forces in Iraq,[88] making the situation in Ukraine the second time in which the Court attempted such a move. Despite Prosecutor Fatou Bensouda claiming that there was "[...] a reasonable basis to believe that members of the British armed forces committed the war crimes of wilful killing, torture, inhuman/cruel treatment, outrages upon personal dignity, and rape and/or other forms of sexual violence", the Court

[84] Michael J. Kelly, 'The Role of International Law in the Russia-Ukraine War', *Case Western Reserve Journal of International Law* 55 (2023): 61.

[85] Sergii Masol, 'Ukraine and the International Criminal Court: Between Realpolitik and Post-Truth Politics', *Journal of International Criminal Justice* 20, no. 1 (1 March 2022): 167–90.

[86] Julia Geneuss and Florian Jeßberger, 'Russian Aggression and the War in Ukraine: An Introduction', *Journal of International Criminal Justice* 20, no. 4 (1 September 2022): 783–86.

[87] Giulia Pinzauti and Alessandro Pizzuti, 'Prosecuting Aggression against Ukraine as an "Other Inhumane Act" before the ICC', *Journal of International Criminal Justice* 20, no. 5 (1 November 2022): 1061–83.

[88] Mattia Cacciatori, 'How Investigating Britain for Crimes in Iraq Can Save the International Criminal Court', 27 October 2014, https://researchportal.bath.ac.uk/en/publications/how-investigating-britain-for-crimes-in-iraq-can-save-the-interna.

decided to conclude the preliminary examination and not open a formal investigation in 2020.[89] This decision was criticised by many, who signalled that the UK (and the US) had been effective in derailing the ICC's accountability efforts.[90] The preliminary investigation for British abuses in Iraq already signalled how difficult it is for the ICC to investigate a member of the P-5, even one that is party to the Rome Statute. And even in cases that involved low and mid-level offenders.

The difference between the British and the Russian investigations is, naturally, that the Court's actions regarding the former didn't lead to any issuing of arrest warrants, while two warrants of arrest were issued for Russian President Putin and Maria Alekseyevna Lvova-Belova, Commissioner for Children's Rights of the Russian Federation. The case is extremely novel at the time of writing this book and, as such, it is hard to predict how it will unfold. However, because of the discussions and debates that this book has examined and introduced, it is possible to highlight certain systemic issues that are characterising the situation. The section first focuses on the issue of double-standards, which has gained particular prominence since the issuing of the warrants of arrest. Second, the section turns to examine the credibility of the threat posed by the arrest warrant, and its meaning for the Russian President and the international community. Lastly, the Chapter explores the idea that the warrant might undermine the political status of the Russian President, both internally and internationally, while also indicating that the investigation might have a detrimental effect for the notion of universal jurisdiction, one of the main features of the ICC. The combination of these three elements suggests that the reading offered by the symbolism paradox becomes particularly pertinent now that, seemingly, the normative dissonance between Western and non-Western actors over the practice of prosecuting SHoS has reached its zenith because of the attempted prosecution of Putin.

It must be noted that this Chapter deals with the Russian invasion of Ukraine that started in 2022. While acknowledging that the roots of this conflict are to be traced back, at least, to the 2014 invasion of Ukraine, the remit of the Chapter and the book is to investigate the 2023 ICC issuing

[89] International Criminal Court, 'Statement of the Prosecutor, Fatou Bensouda, on the Conclusion of the Preliminary Examination of the Situation in Iraq/United Kingdom', 2020 accessed 30 June 2023, https://www.icc-cpi.int/news/statement-prosecutor-fatou-bensouda-conclusion-preliminary-examination-situation-iraq/united.

[90] Human Rights Watch, 'United Kingdom: ICC Prosecutor Ends Scrutiny of Iraq Abuses', 10 December 2020, https://www.hrw.org/news/2020/12/10/united-kingdom-icc-prosecutor-ends-scrutiny-iraq-abuses.

of the warrant for the arrest of Putin, which happened in the context of, and in relation to the crimes allegedly committed during the 2022 escalation. Nonetheless, there is little doubt that the international condemnation for the 2014 annexation of Ukraine played a crucial part in spreading a sentiment of distrust, fear, and repulsion that would unite the international community to support the efforts of the ICC.

The Russian Invasion of Ukraine

On 24 February 2022 Russia re-sparked the Russia-Ukraine war that started in 2014 and that had momentarily de-escalated also because of the global pandemic caused by COVID-19. In the early months of this renewed violence, which followed a concentration of Russian forces on the Ukrainian border, the conflict resulted in tens of thousands of deaths and caused more than 8 million people to be internally displaced within the borders of the country. President Putin allegedly acted to support Russian forces that were involved in the Donbas conflict.

Russian troops attacked Ukraine with renewed violence in the spring of 2022, capturing the cities of Kherson and Mariupol, while simultaneously bombing civilian infrastructures. The bombing of the Ukrainian power grid in the middle of the Ukrainian winter contributed immensely to the displacement of millions of Ukrainian citizens who fled the cold towards Europe, instigating what has been called the largest refugee crisis in Europe since WWII. The war saw in 2023 continuous attacks and counter-attacks between Russian and Ukrainian forces. A considerable part of the international community reacted mainly by sending humanitarian aids to Ukrainian citizens and logistic and military support to the Ukrainian army. At the moment of writing this book, the escalation of the Ukrainian conflict is in its second year of development, with no real sign of it ending anytime soon.

Box 5.2 Biographical Sketch Putin

Who Is Vladimir Putin

Vladimir Vladimirovich Putin, born on 7 October 1952, began his military career in 1975 by joining the Committee for State Security, the KGB. He served as an undercover agent in Dresden in Germany since 1985. He allegedly left the KGB after the deposition of Mikhail Gorbachev, expressing dissent over the military coup.

(*continued*)

Box 5.2 (continued)

After retiring from the KGB, he occupied important local positions in Saint Petersburg before being appointed by Boris Yeltsin as deputy chief of the Presidential Staff in 1997 and, in 1998, as director of the Federal Security Service. In 1999 Yeltsin promoted Putin as Acting Prime Minister, indicating him as his ideal successor. So, when Yeltsin resigned in 1999, Putin became acting President of the Russian Federation. When presidential elections were held in March 2000, Putin won with 53% of the votes, formally becoming President-elect. In 2004 he was re-elected with 74% of the votes. In the first two terms of his presidency Putin faced several internal issues, among which were several terrorist attacks led by Chechen rebels that were met with decisive violence by the Putin government. Meanwhile in the late 2000s Putin also started publicly complaining about NATO expansionism in Eastern Europe.

Due to constitutional constraints, Putin could not be re-elected President for a third consecutive time. So, in 2008, he became Prime Minister, with his former First Deputy Prime Minister, Dmitry Medvedev, elected as President of the Russian Federation. Protests in Russia sparked after this move, calling for more transparent electoral processes and more freedom to run for elections. Unsurprisingly, newly elected President Medvedev, suggested that Putin would be the perfect successor as presidential candidate. Despite accusations of electoral fraud, Putin was re-elected President for a third time in 2012. During his third presidency the President continued to face internal protests, the most internationally recognised one is the famous "Pussy Riot", while also initiating the Russo-Ukrainian war with the annexation of Crimea in 2014. Putin was also very active in supporting the Assad regime against Western humanitarian interventionism that started in 2013, as discussed in Chap. 4. In 2018 Putin was elected President for a fourth time with 63% of the votes and continues to be President of the Russian Federation at the time of writing this book. The fourth mandate was characterised by the spreading of the COVID-19 pandemic and the escalation of the Ukrainian conflict that caused international condemnation and, eventually, led to the issuing of the warrant for his arrest.

Humanitarian Outcries and Double-Standards

The escalation of the Ukraine War caused immense turmoil in the international community. Allegations of war crimes being committed by Russian forces led to a multiplication of official declarations in which various representatives of Western political elites called for the ICC, and other international organisations, to step in and prosecute Putin. However, this situation perhaps more than any other really questions the existing relationship between the UNSC and the ICC.[91] This book has already outlined how the link between the two has been complex from the beginning. By being formally detached from the UN, the Court was seeking an impartiality that would allow it to carry out its investigations even if they were hostile towards the most potent states in the world. However, the Court also needed the cooperation of the UNSC to examine and potentially investigate situations in states that didn't ratify the Rome Statute, as happened in Sudan and Libya. So, those situations in which at least one of the member-states doesn't want the ICC to get involved, would not be examined because of the veto power that the P-5 are granted in the UNSC, as happened in Syria. Lastly, the UNSC is also vital for pressuring compliance by UN state parties with the rulings of the Court. It is evident that the situation in Ukraine is to test the potential and limits of the cooperation between the ICC and the UNSC like no other situation has done before.

Humanitarian outcries started proliferating as early as the Russian invasion of Crimea in 2014, however it was in the early 2020s that such outcries have been formalised in the form of calling for a direct criminal investigation of Putin and his forces. These emerged in concomitance within the borders of Ukraine[92] and in Europe.[93] Initially, commentators

[91] Milena Sterio, 'The International Criminal Court: Current Challenges and Prospect of Future Success', *Case Western Reserve Journal of International Law*, 2020, 473–74.

[92] Public Broadcasting Service Newshour, 'Ukraine's Top Prosecutor Builds War Crimes Case against Russia as Invasion Grinds On', 2 February 2023, https://www.pbs.org/newshour/show/ukraines-top-prosecutor-builds-war-crimes-case-against-russia-as-invasion-grinds-on.

[93] Eurojust, 'International Centre for the Prosecution of the Crime of Aggression Made Official at United for Justice Conference in Ukraine', 2023, accessed 28 June 2023, https://www.eurojust.europa.eu/news/international-centre-prosecution-crime-aggression-made-official-united-justice-conference; Johannes Block, 'Committed in Ukraine, Prosecuted in Germany?: War Crimes and Crimes against Humanity in the Russian Invasion of Ukraine', *Völkerrechtsblog*, 7 April 2022.

and politicians were questioning the legitimacy of the ICC to prosecute this case given the jurisdictional constraints of the Court, with Ukrainian President Volodymyr Zelenskyy floating the idea of creating a European *ad-hoc* Court to prosecute the Russian President.[94] Such calls have been dismissed by the ICC, which argued that doing so would be detrimental for the prosecutorial process as they would fragment international efforts of accountability.[95]

Beyond Ukrainian officials, three Western actors emerged as particularly vocal in calling for an international prosecution of Putin: the US, the UK, and France. In March 2022 the US Senate urged the ICC to investigate the abuses related to the Russian invasion of Ukraine.[96] This was supported by Ukrainian American Congresswoman Victoria Spartz, who directly asked the Court to investigate Putin and his officials.[97] Anthony Blinken, US Secretary of State, reinforced this view on several occasions. For instance, he publicly stated: "[…] Russian President Vladimir Putin has unleashed unrelenting violence that has caused death and destruction across Ukraine. We've seen numerous credible reports of indiscriminate attacks and attacks deliberately targeting civilians, as well as other atrocities".[98] Blinken, in occasion of a UNSC meeting on 17 February 2022, added: "[b]ecause the basic principles that sustain peace and security—principles that were enshrined in the wake of two world wars and a Cold War—are under threat. The principle that one country cannot change the borders of another by force. The principle that one country cannot dictate another's choices or policies, or with whom it will associate. The principle of national sovereignty. This is the exact kind of crisis that

[94] Noémi Nagy, 'The Case of David vs. Goliath?', in *Threats to Peace and International Security: Asia versus West: Current Challenges in a New Geopolitical Situation*, ed. Juan Cayón Peña and J. Martín Ramírez, Advanced Sciences and Technologies for Security Applications (Cham: Springer Nature Switzerland, 2023), 57.

[95] Euronews, 'War Crimes Prosecutor: ICC Should Prosecute Aggression, Can Try Heads of State', 6 December 2022, https://www.euronews.com/2022/12/06/ukraine-crisis-war-crimes-eu.

[96] Moira Warburton and Viktor Chernii, 'U.S. Senate Unanimously Condemns Putin as War Criminal', *Reuters*, 16 March 2022.

[97] Patricia Zengerle and Patricia Zengerle, 'U.S. Lawmakers Join Calls for War Crimes Probe of Russia', *Reuters*, 2 March 2022, sec. United States, https://www.reuters.com/world/us/us-lawmakers-join-calls-war-crimes-probe-russia-2022-03-02/.

[98] United States Department of State, 'War Crimes by Russia's Forces in Ukraine', 2022, accessed 28 June 2023, https://www.state.gov/war-crimes-by-russias-forces-in-ukraine/.

the United Nations—and specifically this Security Council—was created to prevent".[99] American cries for a criminal investigation reached their zenith when US President Joe Biden openly called Putin "a butcher", while also labelling him a "war criminal" and an inhuman "murderous dictator, a pure thug who is waging an immoral war against the people of Ukraine".[100]

In a similar vein, former UK Prime Minister Boris Johnson, addressing his Parliament in 2022, declared: "[w]hat we have seen already from Vladimir Putin's regime in the use of the munitions that they have already been dropping on innocent civilians, in my view, already fully qualifies as a war crime and I know that the ICC prosecutor is already investigating, and I am sure the whole House will support that".[101] Ian Blackford (leader of the Scottish National Party) asked the ICC "[t]o prosecute Putin and his regime the full range of war crime charges need to be used including the crime of aggression by a state", however he rightly pointed out that "the UK's always refused to sign up to the prosecution of this crime in international law".[102] Meanwhile France initially backed the creation of a European Tribunal to prosecute Putin for the crime of aggression, to overcome the jurisdictional complications arising from Russia's withdrawal from the Rome Statute.[103] However, in February 2023 French Foreign Minister Catherine Colonna, reoriented the French position by declaring: "[w]e are working with the ICC and the entire international community so that there is no impunity for the authors and those responsible for the

[99] United States Department of State, 'Secretary Antony J. Blinken on Russia's Threat to Peace and Security at the UN Security Council', 2022, accessed 28 June 2023, https://www.state.gov/secretary-antony-j-blinken-on-russias-threat-to-peace-and-security-at-the-un-security-council/.

[100] CNN, 'Biden Calls Putin "a Butcher" after Meeting with Refugees in Poland', 2022, accessed 28 June 2023, https://edition.cnn.com/2022/03/26/politics/joe-biden-vladimir-putin-butcher/index.html.

[101] POLITICO, 'Boris Johnson: Vladimir Putin Guilty of War Crimes', 2 March 2022, https://www.politico.eu/article/boris-johnson-accuse-vladimir-putin-war-crime/.

[102] Richard Vaughan Singh Arj, 'Boris Johnson Accuses Putin of War Crimes Following Use of Cluster Bombs in Ukraine Invasion', *INews*, 2 March 2022, https://inews.co.uk/news/boris-johnson-accuses-vladimir-putin-war-crimes-ukraine-russia-cluster-bombs-1493822.

[103] Isobel Koshiw and Jennifer Rankin, 'France Backs Plans for Tribunal for Russian Officials over Ukraine War', *The Guardian*, 1 December 2022, sec. World news, https://www.theguardian.com/world/2022/dec/01/france-backs-plans-for-tribunal-for-russian-officials-over-ukraine-war.

war" and added "[t]he International Criminal Court is investigating and will follow the law".[104]

While there is no doubt that the crimes committed by Putin and his forces amount to the most heinous ones conceivable by humankind, it must be recalled that the Western members of the P-5, which are now supportive of the ICC's involvement in the Russian case, have not always been that aligned with the remits of the Court. The US support for it has been intermittent at best. This book has already shown how in the last 20 years or so the US has proven to be hostile to the ICC in more than one instance, like signing BIAs with Latin American states in the early days of the Court,[105] or when, as late as 2020 under the Trump Administration, the American government launched "an economic and legal offensive on the ICC" in occasion of the opening of an investigation into war crimes in Afghanistan.[106] Even the UK and France, that are now extremely vocal about the necessity of prosecuting Putin for crimes related to the Russian aggression of Ukraine, have not always been so intransigent in supporting the Court. As we have already seen in Chap. 4, France while publicly supporting the Court never ratified the 2010 Kampala amendment to include the crime of aggression in the crimes covered by the ICC. In occasion of the 20th anniversary of the Court, the French Ministry for Europe and Foreign Affairs reaffirmed that France "does not accept the jurisdiction of the Court [in these matters]".[107] Similarly, a British Foreign Office spokesperson declared in 2017 that "[t]he UK has no plans to ratify the crime of aggression amendments. We believe that the UN security council bears the main responsibility for maintaining international peace and security and should be the primary body to determine when an act of aggression

[104] France 24, 'Putin Trial for War Crimes "a Possibility" - French Minister', 23 February 2023. https://www.france24.com/en/live-news/20230223-putin-trial-for-war-crimes-a-possibility-french-minister.

[105] Silal Khan, 'Status of the U.S. Bilateral Immunity Agreements under the Rome Statute', *Cambridge International Law Journal* (blog), 9 December 2020, http://cilj.co.uk/2020/12/09/status-of-the-u-s-bilateral-immunity-agreements-under-the-rome-statute/.

[106] Julian Borger, 'Trump Targets ICC with Sanctions after Court Opens War Crimes Investigation', *The Guardian*, 11 June 2020, sec. US news, https://www.theguardian.com/us-news/2020/jun/11/trump-icc-us-war-crimes-investigation-sanctions.

[107] France in the UK, 'France Reaffirms Backing for International Criminal Court', accessed 29 June 2023, https://uk.ambafrance.org/France-reaffirms-backing-for-International-Criminal-Court.

has occurred".[108] Subjecting this decision to the veto power of the two countries, it must be noted. This stance led Gegout to rightly observe that "[y]ou'd think that, of all people, the nations which sat in judgment at Nuremberg would be embarrassed, if not ashamed, by the utter hypocrisy of failing to lead by example in accepting the court's aggression jurisdiction".[109]

The selective support that US, UK, and French political elites have manifested towards the ICC and its investigations is a quintessential factor to consider when debating the current international calls for the prosecution of the Russian President. It is already hard enough for the Court to launch an investigation against one of the most powerful men on Earth, and if the support the ICC enjoys by these countries is perceived to be subjugated to their political goals, then the legitimacy of the Court is at risk because it is very complicated right now to sustain solidarist pushes that come from actors that have openly antagonised the ICC in the past. Questions about double-standards, selective prosecutions, and neo-imperialism have been ever present since the Court launched its first investigation against a SHoS in 2009, and they are bound to multiply now that Putin is under ICC scrutiny. This, as already noted, is not only for purely pragmatic reasons, but also because of the growth of an anti-ICC symbolic space that is gaining momentum among non-Western opposers to the practice of prosecuting SHoS.

An Empty Threat? The Warrant for Putin's Arrest

On 15 February 2023 the US Conflict Observatory reported that *at least* 6000 children from Ukraine were deported to 43 camps in Russia.[110] The National Information Bureau of the Ukrainian government supplemented this information claiming, in May, that said that the number of Ukrainian

[108] Owen Shaul Walker Bowcott, 'ICC Crime of Aggression Comes into Effect without Key Signatories', *The Guardian*, 17 July 2018, sec. Law, https://www.theguardian.com/law/2018/jul/17/icc-crimeof-aggression-comes-into-effect-without-key-signatories-uk-law-war.

[109] Catherine Gegout, 'The Crime of Aggression, the UK and France: Time to Show Leadership on the Principles of International Law at the International Criminal Court', openDemocracy, 2 May 2018, https://www.opendemocracy.net/en/can-europe-make-it/crime-of-aggression-uk-and-france-time-to-show-leadership-on-pri/.

[110] Amanda Macias, 'Russian Forces Have Relocated at Least 6,000 Ukrainian Children to Camps since Start of War, New Report Says', *CNBC*, 14 February 2023, https://www.cnbc.com/2023/02/14/ukraine-war-news-russia-has-relocated-more-than-6000-children.html.

citizens who disappeared, were captured, deported, or forced to mobilise could be as high as 19000.[111] Zelenskyy urged all allies to cooperate to liberate all Ukrainians from Russian captivity.[112] Some argued that, along with prosecuting Russian forces for the illegitimate attacks on civilians and civilian infrastructures, which amounts to war crimes,[113] it is the quality of the crime of deporting children that fuelled such a potent reaction by the international community.[114] ICC Prosecutor Karim Khan, as early as 28 February 2022 and amid war crimes allegations, declared that he was seeking approval for opening an investigation, calling for all member-states to materially contribute to the funding of the operation. He declared "[t]he importance and urgency of our mission [in Ukraine] is too serious to be held hostage to lack of means".[115] This followed the efforts, among others, of Canadian Foreign Minister Melanie Joly, who during a speech held in a session of the UNHRC, decided to refer the situation to the Court. She claimed "[w]e are working with other ICC member-states to take this significant action as a result of numerous allegations of the commission of serious international crimes in Ukraine by Russian forces", and added "[t]he ICC has our full support and confidence. We call on Russia to cooperate with the Court".[116]

[111] Ukrinform, 'National Information Bureau Received Almost 19,000 Capture and Deportation Reports in April', 8 May 2023, https://www.ukrinform.net/rubric-society/3705814-national-information-bureau-received-almost-19000-capture-and-deportation-reports-in-april.html.

[112] Ukrinform, 'President Zelenskyy: We Must Return and Will Return All Our People from Russian Captivity', 6 May 2023, https://www.ukrinform.net/rubric-ato/3705755-president-Zelensky-we-must-return-and-will-return-all-our-people-from-russian-captivity.html.

[113] Marlise Simons, 'The International Criminal Court Prosecutor Fast-Tracks an Investigation of Possible War Crimes in Ukraine.', *The New York Times*, 3 March 2022, sec. World, https://www.nytimes.com/2022/03/03/world/europe/war-crimes-russia-ukraine-icc.html.

[114] Del Monte Micaela, 'Russia's War on Ukraine: Forcibly Displaced Ukrainian Children', 14 April 2023, https://policycommons.net/artifacts/3681370/russias-war-on-ukraine/4487250/.

[115] Anthony Deutsch and Toby Sterling, 'ICC Prosecutor to Proceed with Investigation into Alleged War Crimes in Ukraine', *Reuters*, 28 February 2022, sec. Europe, https://www.reuters.com/world/europe/icc-prosecutor-proceed-with-investigation-into-alleged-war-crimes-ukraine-2022-02-28/.

[116] Reuters, 'Canada to Refer ICC to Probe Alleged Russian War Crimes in Ukraine', 2 March 2022, sec. World, https://www.reuters.com/world/canada-petition-icc-probe-alleged-russian-war-crimes-foreign-minister-2022-03-01/.

On 17 March 2023 the ICC issued two warrants of arrest for Putin and Alekseyevna Lvova-Belova. The crimes for which the arrest warrants were released were indeed the unlawful deportation and transfer of population from occupied areas of Ukraine to the Russian Federation, starting at least from 24 February 2022.[117] This suggests that, as commentators argued, it was the report that highlighted the deportation of children that pushed the ball over the line. Russia has, naturally, denied allegations of atrocities by its soldiers in Ukraine. Dmitri Peskov, Kremlin spokesman called them lies without any evidence to support them.[118] As highlighted by Yaman, however, the warrants carried specific implications that have been introduced in this book. Namely, the fact that the Court is more effective when it cooperates with local authorities, the political meaning of the arrest warrants, and the cooperation required by state parties to the Rome Statute to comply with the warrants.[119] On these notes, it must be acknowledged that virtually no commentator or policy-maker suggested that the warrants would lead to a conviction of Putin. Considering this, some argued that the purpose of the arrest warrant was not practical but rather that "the symbolism of charging [Putin and Lvova-Belova] for war crimes is historic".[120] Others, referring to the deterrent effect of prosecutions, argued that "[...] public awareness of the warrants may contribute to the prevention of the further commission of crimes".[121] However, for this to be the case, the Russian investigation would need full cooperation from states in international politics,[122] otherwise rifts among supporters and

[117] International Criminal Court, 'Situation in Ukraine: ICC Judges Issue Arrest Warrants against Vladimir Vladimirovich Putin and Maria Alekseyevna Lvova-Belova', accessed 28 June 2023, https://www.icc-cpi.int/news/situation-ukraine-icc-judges-issue-arrest-warrants-against-vladimir-vladimirovich-putin-and.

[118] Lawrence J. Trautman and Maia McFarlin, 'Putin, Russia and Ukraine: International Human Rights Violations, War Crimes, & Future Implications', SSRN Scholarly Paper (Rochester, NY, 20 March 2023), 33–34.

[119] Dilara Karmen Yaman, 'Heads of States Before the ICC: On the Arrest Warrant against Putin and Its Consequences', *Völkerrechtsblog*, 5 April 2023.

[120] Abhinav Mehrotra and Biswanth Gupta, 'Vladimir Putin, the War Criminal Explained', *International Policy Digest*, 4 April 2023, https://intpolicydigest.org/the-platform/vladimir-putin-the-war-criminal-explained/.

[121] International Criminal Court, 'Situation in Ukraine'.

[122] Aghem Hanson Ekori and Paul S. Masumbe, 'Putin on Trial: The Reality of Heads of State Immunity before International Criminal Courts', *Polit Journal* 2, no. 1 (5 April 2022): 32.

opposers of the Court are not only likely to hamper any practical effect of ICC operations, but also question the alleged symbolism that underpins them. As already noted however, these events are taking place in a context already plagued with the infusion of anti-ICC symbolic meanings in non-Western contexts.

The contours of this international cooperation are blurred. On one side Hamilton, argues that "[…] all member states of the ICC are under a legal obligation to arrest Putin should he come onto their territory",[123] suggesting that the warrant of arrest might reduce significantly Putin's ability to travel. If he does travel to a Rome Statute member-state's territory, then said member-state would be under the legal obligation to arrest him and send him to The Hague. But legal obligations, as this book has shown in several instances, are often subjugated to the political will of the actors that are responsible for enforcing them. First, there are several Russian allies that are not party to the ICC that would welcome a visit from the Russian President.[124] Second, even some member-states have proven to be unwilling to enforce warrant of arrest against SHoS in the past. An emblematic case is South Africa, often referred to as the zenith of human rights' development in Africa, that refused to arrest Al Bashir in occasion of an official visit in 2015.[125] This followed several other instances in which the Sudanese President visited African party members to the Rome Statute.[126] Al Bashir's willingness to travel posed a diplomatic challenge even for the US, when Al Bashir threatened a visit to New York in occasion of a UNGA summit on sustainable development, given that the US is not a signatory of the Rome Statute.[127] So on one side, not only it would be

[123] Rebecca Hamilton, 'The ICC Goes Straight to the Top: Arrest Warrant Issued for Putin', *Just Security*, 17 March 2023, https://www.justsecurity.org/85529/the-icc-goes-straight-to-the-top-arrest-warrant-issued-for-putin/.

[124] Deborah Pearlstein, 'Should We Worry That the President Called Putin a "War Criminal" Out Loud?', 8 April 2022, https://larc.cardozo.yu.edu/faculty-online-pubs/9.

[125] Allan Ngari, 'The Real Problem behind South Africa's Refusal to Arrest al-Bashir', *ISS Africa*, 10 July 2017, https://issafrica.org/iss-today/the-real-problem-behind-south-africas-refusal-to-arrest-al-bashir.

[126] Mattia Cacciatori, 'Rectifying the Society of States: The International Criminal Court and the Paradox of International Law', *British Journal of American Legal Studies*, 2019, 479, https://researchportal.bath.ac.uk/en/publications/rectifying-the-society-of-states-the-international-criminal-court.

[127] Hennie Strydom, 'Why Al-Bashir's Visit to the UN Presents the US with a Diplomatic Challenge', *The Conversation*, 1 September 2015, http://theconversation.com/why-al-bashirs-visit-to-the-un-presents-the-us-with-a-diplomatic-challenge-46898.

naïve to think that the warrant could be enforced domestically, but also international cooperation with it seems to rest on shaky grounds. After all, it seems, Putin can freely travel to all those states that are not party to the Rome Statute and could also be potentially welcome in those states that have previously challenged ICC's warrants of arrest for other SHoS. The resistance could also come from those Western states that are currently challenging the *status quo* of international politics, aligning themselves more and more with Russia. For instance, NATO's ally Hungary has already clarified that even if Putin travels to the country the government led by Victor Orban won't enforce the warrant despite being a member of the ICC.[128] Turkey's Tayyip Erdogan has also confirmed that he is more than willing to welcome Putin in occasion of a Russo-Turkish summit in August 2023.[129]

The other dimension of international cooperation might be even more worrying for the Court, and that is that the warrant could justify an escalation of Western unilateral military operations in Ukraine. Although an international military action has been debated several times since the beginning of the Ukraine war,[130] so far these talks have not produced a concrete political will to engage actively in the war beyond EU and some NATO member countries contributing financially[131] and militarily[132] to the Ukrainian resistance. In a way, this indecisiveness suggests that the warrant of arrest for Putin is not likely to change the Western stance dramatically. However, it is important to point out that the warrants of arrest

[128] Luke McGee, 'Hungary Says It Would Not Arrest Putin If He Entered the Country', *CNN*, 23 March 2023, https://www.cnn.com/2023/03/23/europe/hungary-icc-warrant-putin-intl/index.html.

[129] Daniel Binns, 'Vladimir Putin Plans Rare Overseas Trip to Visit NATO Member Turkey', *Sky News*, 8 July 2023, https://news.sky.com/story/vladimir-putin-plans-rare-overseas-trip-to-visit-nato-member-turkey-12917197.

[130] Rahel Philipose, 'Explained: Why NATO Isn't Sending Troops to Ukraine', *The Indian Express* (blog), 3 March 2022, https://indianexpress.com/article/explained/russia-ukraine-war-nato-troops-deployment-article-5-7798588/; Patrick Wintour, 'Nato Members May Send Troops to Ukraine, Warns Former Alliance Chief', *The Guardian*, 7 June 2023, sec. World news, https://www.theguardian.com/world/2023/jun/07/nato-members-may-send-troops-to-ukraine-warns-former-alliance-chief.

[131] POLITICO, 'EU Plans up to €72 Billion in Aid for Ukraine', 14 June 2023, https://www.politico.eu/article/eu-plans-e72-billion-of-new-common-debt-to-aid-ukraine/.

[132] European Union Military Assistance Mission of Ukraine, 'About EU Military Assistance Mission in Support of Ukraine', 2022, accessed 29 June 2023, https://www.eeas.europa.eu/eumam-ukraine/about-eu-military-assistance-mission-support-ukraine-eumam-ukraine_en?s=410260.

against Gaddafi have been perceived as justifying the military campaign that eventually led to the death of the Libyan President. With the UNSC currently frozen in an unsurmountable deadlock because of Russian (and Chinese) veto power, the risk is that Western actors will use the arrest warrants as justifications for launching an international military operation in Ukraine. This would be reminiscent of the 1999 NATO bombing of Serbia to force Slobodan Milosevic to retreat from Kosovo, Operation Allied Force, which was not blessed by the UNSC.[133] While this, as said, remains unlikely, the ICC has already been subject to widespread criticism for aligning with international regime-change operations in the cases of Libya and Syria. If international cooperation with the arrest warrant turns out to mean justifying a unilateral military action in Ukraine, it would become nearly impossible to defend the Court from allegations of being a tool in the hands of powerful Western states. And these, unsurprisingly, have already started to permeate from Russia. Medvedev threatened to fire missiles at the ICC headquarters,[134] while a Parliamentary Deputy told the Moscow Times that ICC actions are "essentially a call to overthrow the government in Russia".[135]

In this context, the issuing of the arrest warrant might have a detrimental effect on the peace negotiations between Russia and Ukraine, since "[t]he Western democracies would have to worry about public opinion costs if they made the morally questionable decision to trade justice for peace in such an explicit fashion".[136] This seems to be sustained by some Russian allies, like Orban, Erdogan, and Serbian Aleksandar Vucic, who claimed "[...] issuing an arrest warrant for Putin, not to go into legal matters, will have bad political consequences and it says that there is a great reluctance to talk about peace (and) about truce".[137] Even US Senator

[133] NATO, 'Kosovo Air Campaign (1999)', 17 May 2022, https://www.nato.int/cps/en/natohq/topics_49602.htm.

[134] Isabel van Brugen, 'Russia Threatens to Blow up ICC with Hypersonic Missile', *Newsweek*, 20 March 2023, https://www.newsweek.com/russia-medvedev-icc-hypersonic-missile-putin-arrest-warrant-1788805.

[135] Pyotr Kozlov, 'ICC Arrest Warrant for Putin Sparks Nervousness in Russian Elite', *The Moscow Times*, 24 April 2023, https://www.themoscowtimes.com/2023/04/24/icc-arrest-warrant-for-putin-sparks-nervousness-in-russian-elite-a80903.

[136] Mike Corder, 'War-Crimes Warrant for Putin Could Complicate Ukraine Peace', *Associated Press News*, 2 April 2023, https://apnews.com/article/putin-arrest-warrant-ukraine-war-crimes-court-93bfa0eb81dd2abe5edb008b78df568d.

[137] Associated Press News, 'Serbian President Criticizes ICC Arrest Warrant for Putin', 19 March 2023, https://apnews.com/article/serbia-vucic-putin-ukraine-russia-838fb97cde73440a6dd135dc76eddec6.

Rand Paul publicly stated his doubts about this, arguing that "[…] someone who is fighting a war is less likely to prosecute a peace or to engage in peace talks if he thinks, Hmmm, if there is peace, we're going to The Hague",[138] and this was echoed by acknowledged by French President Macron.[139] This relates, once more, to the peace versus justice dilemma introduced in Chap. 1 of this book. Although, as Bosco rightly points out, it seems unlikely that the warrant will be considered as a crucial component driving the negotiations for Putin,[140] it is very likely that it could be used as a rhetorical tool by the Russian President to threaten the ICC and, by extension, the international community—as happened in Uganda and Kenya, for instance. This, in turn, is likely to bolster that symbolic space that contraposes the allegedly universal values upheld by the ICC, and non-Western interpretations of what these values mean.

Undermining Putin or Weakening the ICC?

Another debate that the warrant of arrest has spurred relates to the consequence that this might have for Putin as a political figure, both internally and internationally, given that the likelihood of Putin being tried at The Hague seems extremely slim. Commentators noted that "[…] the symbolic aspect of an ICC arrest warrant against Putin matters first and foremost to Ukrainians, who seek acknowledgement of the harms they have faced and want Putin's leadership to be delegitimized in the eyes of the international community".[141] Allegedly, former and current Russian officials claimed that the warrant of arrest created concerns about the internal

[138] Masood Farivar, 'Calls Grow for Tribunal for Russia's "Crime of Aggression"', *Voice Of America*, 21 February 2023, https://www.voanews.com/a/calls-grow-for-tribunal-for-russia-s-crime-of-aggression-/6968489.html.

[139] Daniel DePetris, 'Macron Has a Point about Russian War Crimes', *The Spectator*, 2 June 2023, https://www.spectator.co.uk/article/macron-has-a-point-about-russian-war-crimes/; Patrick Wintour and Patrick Wintour Diplomatic editor, 'West May Have to Negotiate with Putin as Well as Pursue War Crimes Trial, Macron Says', *The Guardian*, 31 May 2023, sec. World news, https://www.theguardian.com/world/2023/may/31/macron-to-call-for-european-strategic-awakening-after-ukraine-invasion.

[140] David Bosco, 'Why Putin Isn't Likely Worried about a Warrant for His Arrest', *MSNBC*, 21 March 2023, https://www.msnbc.com/opinion/msnbc-opinion/putin-arrest-warrant-icc-ukraine-war-crimes-rcna75529.

[141] Hamilton, 'The ICC Goes Straight to the Top'.

stability of Russia.[142] Some argued that the arrest warrant could damage Putin's reputation.[143] Hamilton explicitly argued that "for opponents of Putin's regime however, be they vocal dissidents or those currently silent, the arrest warrant has the potential to invigorate the space for imagining a post-Putin Russia".[144] The idea that arrest warrants could legitimise internal opposition to an authoritarian regime has been ingrained in ICC operations, at least, since the opening of the investigation in Sudan. However, this never fully manifested. Al Bashir, for instance, retained full power over the country until the military coup ousted him, years after the release of the arrest warrants. In fact, as discussed in Chap. 3, many reported that in the days following the issuing of the warrant, thousands rallied in Khartoum to express their support for the President.[145] Even more emblematic perhaps, Kenyatta was elected as President of Kenya in 2013, two years after the Court accused him of human rights violations.[146] In Libya, the newly installed NTC that followed the downfall of Gaddafi openly opposed the ICC, and even detained ICC personnel for a month.[147] So, the idea that an arrest warrant would ultimately galvanise and legitimise internal political contestation in authoritarian contexts seems to be extremely dependent on the ability of the accused SHoS to manipulate the narrative to portray himself as a martyr of international actors. And this leads to a symbolic dimension that is less evident.

Kundert claimed that "[…] the reality is that Russia, and other states, did not join the ICC for a reason. To try them under it would smack of victor's justice which would only transform Russian leaders into martyrs and in turn stunt the peacebuilding process in Russia".[148] This seems to be sustained by a multiplicity of comments made by Russian officials, and by

[142] Shannon Vavra, 'Leakers Reveal Kremlin Secretly Panicking Over Putin's Arrest Warrant', *Yahoo News*, 24 April 2023, https://uk.news.yahoo.com/leakers-reveal-kremlin-secretly-panicking-204529897.html.

[143] Emerald Expert Briefings, 'ICC Accusation of War Crimes Will Damage Putin', 1 January 2023.

[144] Hamilton, 'The ICC Goes Straight to the Top'.

[145] BBC, 'Warrant Issued for Sudan's Leader'.

[146] International Crisis Group, 'Kenya's 2013 Elections', 2013, http://www.crisisgroup.org/en/regions/africa/horn-of-africa/kenya/197-kenyas-2013-elections.aspx.

[147] James Siebens and Benjamin Case, 'The Libyan Civil War: Context and Consequences', *THINK International and Human Security* 4 (2012): 36.

[148] Braden Kundert, 'Justice Today, Peace Tomorrow: Reinventing the Crime of Aggression in the Age of Putin', SSRN Scholarly Paper (Rochester, NY, 6 June 2023).

the fact that the Russian Investigative Committee announced, days after the issuing of the arrest warrant, that Prosecutor Karim Khan was on the government's wanted list.[149] However, the rallying around Putin might not be contained to Russia. We have already seen, throughout the book when discussing the Revolt against the West, a growing dissatisfaction is currently characterising the relationship between certain non-Western states, mainly African, and the ICC. Russia, in this sense, might fortify its role as champion of those who are resisting the ICC and, more specifically, the practice of prosecuting SHoS, in line with the reasoning of the symbolism paradox.

To add another problematic layer of complexity, one of the revolutionary features of the ICC is the ability to be granted jurisdiction over every state in the world if the UNSC refers a case to the Court. This manifested, for instance, in Sudan and Libya. Both states are not parties to the Rome Statute, but the cases were referred to the ICC by UNSC resolutions and, as such, the Court was able to exercise its jurisdiction on Al Bashir and Gaddafi. Less successful is the case of Syria, where cross-vetoes by Russia and China prevented the ICC from acting against Assad. If the relationship between the UNSC has always been strained, and all the P-5 expressed in one time or the other, hostility towards the Court, investigating Putin might be the death-toll of one of the mechanisms through which the ICC can open an investigation. It is complicated, in fact, to imagine a near future in which Russian representatives to the UN would agree in passing a resolution to allow the ICC to investigate a non-member of the Rome Statute. Considering that Medvedev threatened to blow up the ICC, and that ICC officials are on the Kremlin's wanted lists, cooperation between the two seems unlikely. This means that the Court is likely to come out from this investigation materially weakened by being deprived of the possibility of investigating serious crimes via a blessing of the UN.

Conclusions

The Al Bashir case should have been a pivotal moment in the history of the ICC, of international law, and of international politics in general. For once, the idea that SHoS can get away with everything if they have the

[149] Rebekah Yeager-Malkin, 'Russia Indicts ICC Prosecutor and Judge That Issued Putin Arrest Warrant', *Jurist,* 22 May 2023, https://www.jurist.org/news/2023/05/russia-indicts-icc-prosecutor-and-judge-that-issued-putin-arrest-warrant/.

right connections was contested at the international level and was welcomed with a great sense of achievement and hope for a future where heinous dictators would fear jail if they threatened the security of their citizens. However, the situation unfolded very differently. The warrants of arrest didn't produce any trial, Al Bashir never faced international justice, and eventually became the cornerstone of African resistance against a Court that African states themselves so passionately supported. In the process, any hope for a more democratic Sudan—where Darfurians would effectively have a voice in the management of intranational politics—were shattered after the unsealing of the warrants of arrest with the marginalisation of figures of more moderate leanings like Taha. In concomitance with this, the progressively hostile attitude towards international NGOs also had tremendous repercussions on the everyday life of millions of Sudanese people. The combination of such high expectations and these results led to an almost immediate disenchantment towards what the ICC stands for, and what it can produce. But because the investigation against Al Bashir was only possible after a UNSC referral, and because of the friction between ICC operations and the establishment of a UN peacekeeping force, the ripples of the Sudanese case also created a certain degree of animosity between the Court itself and the UN. Recent studies showed an increase of local violence against UNAMID personnel that followed the indictment of Al Bashir, suggesting that ICC investigations can complicate peacekeeping attempts.[150]

Meanwhile, when the case against Al Bashir turned into a stalemate, the ICC pleaded for stronger support from the UN, and specifically from the UNSC. In 2012, the then President Judge Sang-Hyun stated "[f]or the ICC to effectively deal with situations referred by the council ... it needs to be able to count on the full and continuing cooperation of all U.N. members, whether they are parties to (the court) or not" and added "[i]n making any future referrals, it would be very helpful if the Security Council could underline this obligation of full cooperation, without which it is very difficult for the ICC to discharge the mandate the council has given it".[151] While it is clear that Song's complaints were directed at those states,

[150] Duursma and Müller, 'The ICC Indictment against Al-Bashir and Its Repercussions for Peacekeeping and Humanitarian Operations in Darfur', 902.

[151] Michelle Nichols, 'ICC Complains of Lack of Cooperation, Wants More U.N. Support', *Reuters*, 17 October 2012, sec. World News, https://www.reuters.com/article/us-crime-un-icc-idUSBRE89G1M720121017.

party to the UN, that refused to surrender Al Bashir to the ICC when they had the chance to do so, these statements also signal an issue of cooperation between the two IOs. The ICC doesn't have an enforcement mechanism, and it must rely on the cooperation of member-states to deliver when it unseals a warrant of arrest. Because of the role of the UN in referring the Sudanese case, the Court seemed to assume this kind of cooperation. So, on one side UN concerns about ICC actions hampering successful peacekeeping missions signal a first instance of friction between the two institutions. On the other, the idea that UN member-states will unquestionably aid the ICC in bringing alleged criminals to justice seems also to put a strain between the UNSC and the Court, a strain that would become ever more evident in subsequent cases such as Libya and Syria. The latest development on the Al Bashir case occurred in 2019, when an internal coup deposed the President after 30 years of reign. The warrants of arrest could have still been enforced when the coup took place, and in theory the new government could have sent Al Bashir directly to The Hague. At the time of writing of this book, this is yet to happen. Al Bashir is facing internal trials for fraud and corruption, but the current government seems to be lukewarm to the possibility of sending him to fact trial at the ICC. This can be the case for a multiplicity of reasons. Regardless, even if the new government was in fact to hand Al Bashir over to the ICC, this wouldn't still count as a success story. First, the revolutionary practice that this book treats is prosecutions of SHoS, prosecuting someone who has been deposed is commendable, but something that has already happened several times in the past. Second, tying the success of the ICC to regime change (even more evidently) might be a dangerous game to play, and feed into the neo-imperialist narratives that are already so dominant in ICC-related debates in Africa and elsewhere. This would only amplify the existence and implications of the symbolic paradox that is currently hampering the prospects of the practice of prosecuting SHoS.

The very recent issuing of the arrest warrant against Putin is showing some of the limitations, but also prospects, of other cases investigated in this book. To start with, the idea that the warrant would lead to the conviction of the Russian President was met with scepticism. These doubts are fuelled by two considerations: first, the ICC has not been able to convict any SHoS it investigated—from Al Bashir, to Kenyatta, to Gaddafi. At this stage, it is legitimate to ask if the aim of the ICC is indeed to convict these alleged criminals, or to more simply turn the attention of the international community to specific cases. Second, this time the Court went after the

President of one of the P-5. This not only makes the cooperation between the ICC and the Russian government unlikely, but even hampers the possibility of the UNSC being decisive in this matter. Further to this, the situation is also questioning the future relationship between the UNSC and the Court, which has often been heralded as one of the most revolutionary features of the ICC. The situation in Ukraine also exposed some of the double-standards that certain Western states, namely the US, the UK, and France, have been adopting in only supporting the Court in certain instances, while hampering its remit and operations when they seemed to threaten them. This book highlighted this on several occasions, but it is worth noticing that in 2023 issues that first emerged in 2009 are yet to be solved. This is problematic because defending the ICC against accusations of bias becomes more complicated every time it acts upon the calls of states that seem to resort to it only when it's beneficial to them. This issue could become even more pressing if some Western states will exploit the warrant of arrest to justify a unilateral military intervention. When the ICC operates in conjunction with international military operations that aim, explicitly or implicitly, at overthrowing a regime, the risk of being accused of complicity in one of the taboo practices in international politics is extremely high—as happened in Libya.

Some argued that Putin's ability to travel could be restricted, and that this will have an impact on his international reputation. But there are doubts even about this. First, many allies of the Russian Federation are not party to the Rome Statute. And even if they were, there would be no guarantee that they would execute the warrant of arrest. The Russian President might become unwillingly the champion of all those states that are dissatisfied with the ICC and its attempts to hold SHoS accountable for their deeds. Many argued that this could have an impact on the internal support for Putin. While most focus on the potential diminished support that Putin might enjoy after the issuing, certain cases like Sudan and Kenya show that this depends on the ability of the Russian President to spin the narrative in his favour—and on the capillarity of his control over the media. There have been situations in which SHoS with a warrant of arrest pending on their heads have enjoyed boosts in popularity by claiming, in various forms, that they were persecuted by a neo-imperial institution. This martyrisation seems to have been effective for Al Bashir and Kenyatta at least. Along with these considerations, this Chapter highlighted the existence of a symbolism paradox that contraposes Western and non-Western actors in terms of what ICC SHoS prosecutions *mean*. It seems that this tension lies at the basis for the progressive non-Western resistance towards the Court, which is in turn interpreted by Western actors as an assault to global ideas of justice.

References

Africa Review 'Sudan Peace More Important than Bashir Arrest: AU Boss', 2012. Accessed 14 December 2015. http://www.africareview.com/News/Sudan-peace-more-important-than-Bashir-arrest/-/979180/1469100/-/kqhgsq//index.html.

African Union. 'Decision on the Report of the Commission on the Abuse of the Principle of Universal Jurisdiction', 25 December 2010. Doc. Assembly/AU/14(XI). http://www.minec.gov.mz/index2.php?option=com_docman&task=doc_view&gid=12&Itemid=48. Ext/Assembly/AU/Dec.1.

Ahmad Sikainga. '"The World's Worst Humanitarian Crisis": Understanding the Darfur Conflict'. *Origins*, 2009. Accessed 22 March 2023. https://origins.osu.edu/article/worlds-worst-humanitarian-crisis-understanding-darfur-conflict?language_content_entity=en.

Al Arabiya. 'Thousands Protest for Bashir in Khartoum', 2009. http://www.alarabiya.net/articles/2009/03/06/67859.html.

Al Jazeera. 'Profile: Omar al-Bashir, Sudan's Longtime Ruler', 2019, accessed 22 March 2023. https://www.aljazeera.com/news/2019/4/11/profile-omar-al-bashir-sudans-longtime-ruler.

Arieff, Alexis. 'Sexual Violence in African Conflicts'. *Congressional Research Service*, Library of Congress, 2011. http://digital.library.unt.edu/ark:/67531/metadc491381/m1/1/high_res_d/R40956_2010Nov30.pdf.

Associated Press News. 'Serbian President Criticizes ICC Arrest Warrant for Putin', 19 March 2023. https://apnews.com/article/serbia-vucic-putin-ukraine-russia-838fb97cde73440a6dd135dc76eddec6.

Barnes, Gwen P. 'International Criminal Court's Ineffective Enforcement Mechanisms: The Indictment of President Omar Al Bashir, The'. *Fordham Int'l LJ* 34 (2010): 1584.

BBC News. 'In Quotes: ICC Accuses Bashir'. 14 July 2008. http://news.bbc.co.uk/1/hi/world/europe/7505937.stm.

———. 'Warrant Issued for Sudan's Leader'. *BBC*, 4 March 2009, sec. Africa. http://news.bbc.co.uk/1/hi/world/africa/7923102.stm.

———. 'Burundi Leaves International Criminal Court amid Row'. 27 October 2017a, sec. Africa. https://www.bbc.com/news/world-africa-41775951.

———. 'South Africa Revokes ICC Withdrawal after Court Ruling'. 8 March 2017b, sec. Africa. https://www.bbc.com/news/world-africa-39204035.

———. 'Sudan's Omar al-Bashir in Malawi: ICC Wants Answers'. Accessed 31 July 2015. http://www.bbc.co.uk/news/world-africa-15384163.

Block, Johannes. 'Committed in Ukraine, Prosecuted in Germany?: War Crimes and Crimes against Humanity in the Russian Invasion of Ukraine'. *Völkerrechtsblog*, 7 April 2022.

Borger, Julian. 'Trump Targets ICC with Sanctions after Court Opens War Crimes Investigation'. *The Guardian*, 11 June 2020, sec. US news. https://www.theguardian.com/us-news/2020/jun/11/trump-icc-us-war-crimes-investigation-sanctions.

Bowcott, Shaun Walker Owen. 'ICC Crime of Aggression Comes into Effect without Key Signatories'. *The Guardian*, 17 July 2018, sec. Law. https://www.theguardian.com/law/2018/jul/17/icc-crimeof-aggression-comes-into-effect-without-key-signatories-uk-law-war.

Brugen, Isabel van. 'Russia Threatens to Blow up ICC with Hypersonic Missile'. *Newsweek*, 20 March 2023. https://www.newsweek.com/russia-medvedev-icc-hypersonic-missile-putin-arrest-warrant-1788805.

Bufacchi, Vittorio. 'War Crimes in Ukraine: Is Putin Responsible?' *Journal of Political Power* 16, no. 1 (2 January 2023): 1–6.

Cacciatori, Mattia. 'How Investigating Britain for Crimes in Iraq Can Save the International Criminal Court', 27 October 2014. https://researchportal.bath.ac.uk/en/publications/how-investigating-britain-for-crimes-in-iraq-can-save-the-interna.

———. 'Rectifying the Society of States: The International Criminal Court and the Paradox of International Law'. *British Journal of American Legal Studies*, 2019. https://researchportal.bath.ac.uk/en/publications/rectifying-the-society-of-states-the-international-criminal-court.

Catherine Gegout. 'The Crime of Aggression, the UK and France: Time to Show Leadership on the Principles of International Law at the International Criminal Court'. *Open Democracy*, 2 May 2018. https://www.opendemocracy.net/en/can-europe-make-it/crime-of-aggression-uk-and-france-time-to-show-leadership-on-pri/.

Chalk, Frank, and Danielle Kelton. *Mass-Atrocity Crimes in Darfur and the Response of Government of Sudan Media to International Pressure*. na, 2009. https://migs.concordia.ca/Media_Monitoring/documents/Chapter_5_SudanRadio.pdf.

CNN. 'Biden Calls Putin "a Butcher" after Meeting with Refugees in Poland', 2022. Accessed 28 June 2023. https://edition.cnn.com/2022/03/26/politics/joe-biden-vladimir-putin-butcher/index.html.

Cockett, Richard. *Sudan*. Yale University Press, 2010.

Condorelli, Luigi, and Annalisa Ciampi. 'Comments on the Security Council Referral of the Situation in Darfur to the ICC'. *Journal of International Criminal Justice* 3, no. 3 (1 July 2005): 590–99.

Cwajg, Carolina. 'A Wild Goose Chase? Prosecuting Al Bashir at the ICC' 1, *Rule of Law Journal (LSE)*, no. 1 (13 December 2020): 1.

Daniel Binns. 'Vladimir Putin Plans Rare Overseas Trip to Visit NATO Member Turkey'. *Sky News*, 8 July 2023. https://news.sky.com/story/vladimir-putin-plans-rare-overseas-trip-to-visit-nato-member-turkey-12917197.

Daniele Archibugi and Alice Pease. *Crime and Global Justice: The Dynamics of International Punishment*. Wiley, 2018. https://www.wiley.com/en-us/Crime+and+Global+Justice%3A+The+Dynamics+of+International+Punishment-p-9781509512652.

David Bosco. 'Why Putin Isn't Likely Worried about a Warrant for His Arrest', *MSNBC News*, 21 March 2023. https://www.msnbc.com/opinion/msnbc-opinion/putin-arrest-warrant-icc-ukraine-war-crimes-rcna75529.

De Waal, Alex. 'Darfur, the Court and Khartoum: The Politics of State Non-Cooperation'. *Courting Conflict? Justice, Peace and the ICC in Africa*, 2008, 29–35.

De Waal, Alex, and Gregory H. Stanton. 'Should President Omar Al-Bashir of Sudan Be Charged and Arrested by the International Criminal Court? An Exchange of Views'. *Genocide Studies and Prevention* 4, no. 3 (2009): 329–53.

DePetris, Daniel. 'Macron Has a Point about Russian War Crimes'. *The Spectator*, 2 June 2023. https://www.spectator.co.uk/article/macron-has-a-point-about-russian-war-crimes/.

Deputy Minister of Justice and Constitutional Development, the Hon JH Jeffery, MP. *Debate in Terms of Rule 103: The Implications of the Attendance and Departure of President Omar al-Bashir from the African Union Summit in SouthAfrica*,2015.http://www.justice.gov.za/m_speeches/2015/20150623_PresidentBashir.html#sthash.5Kj5j3G1.dpu.

Deutsch, Anthony, and Toby Sterling. 'ICC Prosecutor to Proceed with Investigation into Alleged War Crimes in Ukraine'. *Reuters*, 28 February 2022, sec. Europe. https://www.reuters.com/world/europe/icc-prosecutor-proceed-with-investigation-into-alleged-war-crimes-ukraine-2022-02-28/.

Dixon, Robyn. 'African Leaders Amp up Pressure on the International Criminal Court, with a Plan for Mass Exit'. *Los Angeles Times*, 1 February 2017. http://www.latimes.com/world/africa/la-fg-southafrica-icc-massexit-20170201-story.html.

Duursma, Allard, and Tanja R. Müller. 'The ICC Indictment against Al-Bashir and Its Repercussions for Peacekeeping and Humanitarian Operations in Darfur'. *Third World Quarterly* 40, no. 5 (4 May 2019): 890–907.

Egypt Independent. 'Obama "disappointed" Kenya Hosted Sudan's Bashir', 28 August 2010. https://www.egyptindependent.com/obama-disappointed-kenya-hosted-sudans-bashir/.
Ekori, Aghem Hanson, and Paul S. Masumbe. 'Putin on Trial: The Reality of Heads of State Immunity before International Criminal Courts'. *Polit Journal* 2, no. 1 (5 April 2022): 29–36.
Emerald Expert Briefings, 'ICC Accusation of War Crimes Will Damage Putin', 1 January 2023.
Eurojust. 'International Centre for the Prosecution of the Crime of Aggression Made Official at United for Justice Conference in Ukraine', 2023. Accessed 28 June 2023. https://www.eurojust.europa.eu/news/international-centre-prosecution-crime-aggression-made-official-united-justice-conference.
European Union Military Assistance Mission of Ukraine. 'About EU Military Assistance Mission in Support of Ukraine', 2022. Accessed 29 June 2023. https://www.eeas.europa.eu/eumam-ukraine/about-eu-military-assistance-mission-support-ukraine-eumam-ukraine_en?s=410260.
Farivar, Masood. 'Calls Grow for Tribunal for Russia's "Crime of Aggression"'. *Voice Of America*, 21 February 2023. https://www.voanews.com/a/calls-grow-for-tribunal-for-russia-s-crime-of-aggression-/6968489.html.
Flint, Julie. *Rhetoric and Reality: The Failure to Resolve the Darfur Conflict*. Citeseer, 2010. http://citeseerx.ist.psu.edu/viewdoc/download?doi=10.1.1.180.522&rep=rep1&type=pdf.
Flint, Julie, and Alex De Waal. *Darfur: A New History of a Long War*. Zed Books, 2008a. http://eprints.lse.ac.uk/id/eprint/42072.
Fluehr-Lobban, Carolyn, and Richard Lobban. 'The Sudan Since 1989: National Islamic Front Rule'. *Arab Studies Quarterly* 23, no. 2 (2001): 1–9.
France 24. 'Putin Trial for War Crimes "a Possibility"'. France 24, 23 February 2023. https://www.france24.com/en/live-news/20230223-putin-trial-for-war-crimes-a-possibility-french-minister.
France in the UK, 'France Reaffirms Backing for International Criminal Court', 2023, accessed 29 June 2023. https://uk.ambafrance.org/France-reaffirms-backing-for-International-Criminal-Court.
Freedom House, 'Sudan'. Accessed 23 May 2016. https://freedomhouse.org/country/sudan.
Geneuss, Julia, and Florian Jeßberger. 'Russian Aggression and the War in Ukraine: An Introduction'. *Journal of International Criminal Justice* 20, no. 4 (1 September 2022): 783–86.
Hamilton, Rebecca. 'The ICC Goes Straight to the Top: Arrest Warrant Issued for Putin'. *Just Security*, 17 March 2023. https://www.justsecurity.org/85529/the-icc-goes-straight-to-the-top-arrest-warrant-issued-for-putin/.

Human Rights Watch. 'United Kingdom: ICC Prosecutor Ends Scrutiny of Iraq Abuses', 10 December 2020. https://www.hrw.org/news/2020/12/10/united-kingdom-icc-prosecutor-ends-scrutiny-iraq-abuses.

Imoedemhe, Ovo. 'The International Criminal Court: Whether the Crime of Aggression in Ukraine'. *International and Comparative Law Review* 23, no. 1 (1 August 2023): 27–52.

International Criminal Court. 'Al Bashir Case'. Accessed 20 May 2016. https://www.icc-cpi.int/darfur/albashir.

———. 'Situation in Ukraine: ICC Judges Issue Arrest Warrants against Vladimir Vladimirovich Putin and Maria Alekseyevna Lvova-Belova', 2023. Accessed 28 June 2023. https://www.icc-cpi.int/news/situation-ukraine-icc-judges-issue-arrest-warrants-against-vladimir-vladimirovich-putin-and.

———. 'Statement of the Prosecutor, Fatou Bensouda, on the Conclusion of the Preliminary Examination of the Situation in Iraq/United Kingdom', 2020. Accessed 30 June 2023. https://www.icc-cpi.int/news/statement-prosecutor-fatou-bensouda-conclusion-preliminary-examination-situation-iraq/united.

International Crisis Group. 'Kenya's 2013 Elections', 2013. http://www.crisisgroup.org/en/regions/africa/horn-of-africa/kenya/197-kenyas-2013-elections.aspx.

IRIN News. 'SUDAN: NGO Expulsion to Hit Darfur's Displaced', 2009. http://www.irinnews.org/report/83370/sudan-ngo-expulsion-to-hit-darfur-s-displaced.

James Copnall. 'Bashir Warrant: Chad Accuses ICC of Anti-African Bias', 2010. *BBC News*. Accessed 31 May 2016. http://www.bbc.co.uk/news/world-africa-10723869.

Judge Cuno Tarfusser. 'Decision Following the Prosecutor's Request for an Order Further Clarifying That the Republic of South Africa Is under the Obligation to Immediately Arrest and Surrender Omar Al Bashir', 13 June 2015.

Kelly, Michael J. 'The Role of International Law in the Russia-Ukraine War'. *Case Western Reserve Journal of International Law* 55 (2023): 61.

Korostelina, Karina V., Daniel Rothbart, and Beltina Gjeloshi. 'Production of the Meaning of Justice in the Aftermath of War in Sudan'. *Peace and Conflict: Journal of Peace Psychology* 29, no. 3 (2023): 306–16.

Koshiw, Isobel, and Jennifer Rankin. 'France Backs Plans for Tribunal for Russian Officials over Ukraine War'. *The Guardian*, 1 December 2022, sec. World news. https://www.theguardian.com/world/2022/dec/01/france-backs-plans-for-tribunal-for-russian-officials-over-ukraine-war.

Kostelyanets, Sergey. 'Sudan's December Revolution and the Demise of the Al Bashir Regime'. In *New Wave of Revolutions in the MENA Region: A Comparative Perspective*, edited by Leonid Issaev and Andrey Korotayev,

33–56. Perspectives on Development in the Middle East and North Africa (MENA) Region. Cham: Springer International Publishing, 2022.

Kozlov, Pyotr. 'ICC Arrest Warrant for Putin Sparks Nervousness in Russian Elite'. *The Moscow Times*, 24 April 2023. https://www.themoscowtimes.com/2023/04/24/icc-arrest-warrant-for-putin-sparks-nervousness-in-russian-elite-a80903.

Kundert, Braden. 'Justice Today, Peace Tomorrow: Reinventing the Crime of Aggression in the Age of Putin'. SSRN Scholarly Paper. Rochester, NY, 6 June 2023.

Louis Charbonneau. 'NGO Expelled from Darfur Considered ICC Cooperation'. *Reuters*, 2009. http://www.reuters.com/article/2009/03/16/us-sudan-warcrimes-ngo-idUSTRE52F6SX20090316.

Lubaale, Emma Charlene. 'Now Available but Still Not Accessible to the ICC: Bashir and Africa's Politics'. In *National Accountability for International Crimes in Africa*, edited by Emma Charlene Lubaale and Ntombizozuko Dyani-Mhango, 247–85. Cham: Springer International Publishing, 2022.

Lynch, Colum. 'Samantha Power's Problem from Hell', *Foreign Policy*, 2013. Accessed 8 August 2018. https://foreignpolicy.com/2013/09/23/samantha-powers-problem-from-hell/.

Macias, Amanda. 'Russian Forces Have Relocated at Least 6,000 Ukrainian Children to Camps since Start of War, New Report Says'. *CNBC*, 14 February 2023. https://www.cnbc.com/2023/02/14/ukraine-war-news-russia-has-relocated-more-than-6000-children.html.

Marchuk, Iryna. 'Domestic Accountability Efforts in Response to the Russia–Ukraine War: An Appraisal of the First War Crimes Trials in Ukraine'. *Journal of International Criminal Justice* 20, no. 4 (1 September 2022): 787–803.

Masol, Sergii. 'Ukraine and the International Criminal Court: Between Realpolitik and Post-Truth Politics'. *Journal of International Criminal Justice* 20, no. 1 (1 March 2022): 167–90.

McGee, Luke. 'Hungary Says It Would Not Arrest Putin If He Entered the Country', *CNN*, 23 March 2023. https://www.cnn.com/2023/03/23/europe/hungary-icc-warrant-putin-intl/index.html.

Mehrotra, Abhinav, and Biswanth Gupta. 'Vladimir Putin, the War Criminal Explained'. *International Policy Digest*, 4 April 2023. https://intpolicydigest.org/the-platform/vladimir-putin-the-war-criminal-explained/.

Micaela, Del Monte. 'Russia's War on Ukraine: Forcibly Displaced Ukrainian Children', 14 April 2023. https://policycommons.net/artifacts/3681370/russias-war-on-ukraine/4487250/.

Michelle Nichols. 'ICC Complains of Lack of Cooperation, Wants More U.N. Support'. *Reuters*, 17 October 2012, sec. World News. https://www.reuters.com/article/us-crime-un-icc-idUSBRE89G1M720121017.

Mike Corder. 'War-Crimes Warrant for Putin Could Complicate Ukraine Peace', *Associated Press News*, 2 April 2023. https://apnews.com/article/putin-arrest-warrant-ukraine-war-crimes-court-93bfa0eb81dd2abe5edb008b78df568d.

Moumine Ngarmbassa. 'Sudan's Bashir Defies Court with Chad Trip', *Reuters*, 21 July 2010. http://af.reuters.com/article/worldNews/idAFTRE66K2V7 20100721.

Muftah. 'Omar Al-Bashir's Cabinet Reshuffle & Absolute Rule in Sudan', 2014. Accessed 3 December 2015. http://muftah.org/bashirs-cabinet-reshuffle-and-absolute-rule-in-sudan/.

Muhammed Amin. 'Sudan's First VP Ali Osman Taha Resigns to Allow for "Change"', *Africa Review*, 2013. http://www.africareview.com/News/Sudans-First-VP-Ali-Osman-Taha-resigns-to-allow-for-change/-/979180/2101906/-/ve3sdxz/-/index.html.

Musso, Giorgio. 'Sudan Divided: Continuing Conflict in a Contested State Ed. by Gunnar M. Sørbø, Abdel Ghaffar M. Ahmed (Review)'. *African Conflict & Peacebuilding Review* 5, no. 2 (2015): 166–69.

Nagy, Noémi. 'The Case of David vs. Goliath?' In *Threats to Peace and International Security: Asia versus West: Current Challenges in a New Geopolitical Situation*, edited by Juan Cayón Peña and J. Martín Ramírez, 47–61. Advanced Sciences and Technologies for Security Applications. Cham: Springer Nature Switzerland, 2023.

NATO. 'Kosovo Air Campaign (1999)'. NATO, 17 May 2022. https://www.nato.int/cps/en/natohq/topics_49602.htm.

Ngari, Allan. 'The Real Problem behind South Africa's Refusal to Arrest al-Bashir'. *ISS Africa*, 10 July 2017. https://issafrica.org/iss-today/the-real-problem-behind-south-africas-refusal-to-arrest-al-bashir.

Olsson, Ola. 'After Janjaweed? Socioeconomic Impacts of the Conflict in Darfur'. *The World Bank Economic Review* 24, no. 3 (1 January 2010): 386–411.

Pearlstein, Deborah. 'Should We Worry That the President Called Putin a "War Criminal" Out Loud?' *Online Publications*, 8 April 2022. https://larc.cardozo.yu.edu/faculty-online-pubs/9.

Pinzauti, Giulia, and Alessandro Pizzuti. 'Prosecuting Aggression against Ukraine as an "Other Inhumane Act" before the ICC'. *Journal of International Criminal Justice* 20, no. 5 (1 November 2022): 1061–83.

POLITICO. 'Boris Johnson: Vladimir Putin Guilty of War Crimes', 2 March 2022. https://www.politico.eu/article/boris-johnson-accuse-vladimir-putin-war-crime/.

———. 'EU Plans up to €72 Billion in Aid for Ukraine', 14 June 2023. https://www.politico.eu/article/eu-plans-e72-billion-of-new-common-debt-to-aid-ukraine/.

Prunier, Gérard. 'Africa's World War'. *Congo, the Rwandan Genocide and The Making of a Continental Catastrophe*, 2009. http://www.jstor.org/stable/pdf/40542212.pdf.

Public Broadcasting Service NewsHour. 'Ukraine's Top Prosecutor Builds War Crimes Case against Russia as Invasion Grinds On', 2 February 2023. https://www.pbs.org/newshour/show/ukraines-top-prosecutor-builds-war-crimes-case-against-russia-as-invasion-grinds-on.

Rahel Philipose. 'Explained: Why NATO Isn't Sending Troops to Ukraine'. *The Indian Express* (blog), 3 March 2022. https://indianexpress.com/article/explained/russia-ukraine-war-nato-troops-deployment-article-5-7798588/.

Rapanyane, Makhura Benjamin, Florence Ramasela Sethole, and Happy Mathew Tirivangasi. 'The United Nations, International Criminal Court and African Union's Delayed Response to the Prolonged Dictatorship in Sudan'. *Journal of African Union Studies* 9, no. 3 (December 2020): 47–69.

Rebekah Yeager-Malkin. 'Russia Indicts ICC Prosecutor and Judge That Issued Putin Arrest Warrant', 22 May 2023. https://www.jurist.org/news/2023/05/russia-indicts-icc-prosecutor-and-judge-that-issued-putin-arrest-warrant/.

Reuters. 'Canada to Refer ICC to Probe Alleged Russian War Crimes in Ukraine', 2 March 2022, sec. World. https://www.reuters.com/world/canada-petition-icc-probe-alleged-russian-war-crimes-foreign-minister-2022-03-01/.

———. 'Hague Court Questions Bashir's Visit to Malawi'. 19 October 2011. http://af.reuters.com/article/topNews/idAFJOE79I0K520111019.

Rothbart, Daniel, Karina Korostelina, and Beltina Gjeloshi. 'Living through War: An Oral History of Civilians in Sudan'. *Conflict Resolution Quarterly* 40, no. 4 (2023): 405–27.

Salehyan, Idean. 'No Shelter Here: Rebel Sanctuaries and International Conflict'. *The Journal of Politics* 70, no. 01 (January 2008): 54–66.

Sengupta, Krishanu. 'Peace or Justice?: The Dilemma of the International Criminal Court', 2008. https://www.uleth.ca/dspace/handle/10133/1202.

Shannon Vavra. 'Leakers Reveal Kremlin Secretly Panicking Over Putin's Arrest Warrant'. *Yahoo News*, 24 April 2023. https://uk.news.yahoo.com/leakers-reveal-kremlin-secretly-panicking-204529897.html.

Shevchuk, Viktor. 'Problems of Criminalistic Suppot of the Practice of the International Criminal Court in Ukraine'. *Збірник наукових праць ΛΌГОΣ*, 12 October 2020, 14–19.

Siebens, James, and Benjamin Case. 'The Libyan Civil War: Context and Consequences'. *THINK International and Human Security* 4 (2012).

Silal Khan. 'Status of the U.S. Bilateral Immunity Agreements under the Rome Statute'. *Cambridge International Law Journal* (blog), 9 December 2020. http://cilj.co.uk/2020/12/09/status-of-the-u-s-bilateral-immunity-agreements-under-the-rome-statute/.

Simons, Marlise. 'The International Criminal Court Prosecutor Fast-Tracks an Investigation of Possible War Crimes in Ukraine'. *The New York Times*, 3 March 2022, sec. World. https://www.nytimes.com/2022/03/03/world/europe/war-crimes-russia-ukraine-icc.html.

Singh, Richard Vaughan, Arj. 'Boris Johnson Accuses Putin of War Crimes Following Use of Cluster Bombs in Ukraine Invasion', *INews*, 2 March 2022. https://inews.co.uk/news/boris-johnson-accuses-vladimir-putin-war-crimes-ukraine-russia-cluster-bombs-1493822.

Sluiter, Göran. 'Obtaining Cooperation from Sudan — Where Is the Law?' *Journal of International Criminal Justice* 6, no. 5 (1 November 2008): 871–84.

Sterio, Milena. 'The International Criminal Court: Current Challenges and Prospect of Future Success'. *Case Western Reserve Journal of International Law*, 2020.

Strydom, Hennie. 'Why Al-Bashir's Visit to the UN Presents the US with a Diplomatic Challenge'. *The Conversation*, 1 September 2015. http://theconversation.com/why-al-bashirs-visit-to-the-un-presents-the-us-with-a-diplomatic-challenge-46898.

Sudan Tribune. 'Chad Rolls Red Carpet for Sudanese President, Says Bashir Is Safe from Arrest'. 2010. http://www.sudantribune.com/spip.php?article35732.

———. 'Sudan's Taha Criticises al-Bashir Rejection of Darfur UN Force'. 25 July 2006. http://www.sudantribune.com/spip.php?article16801.

———. 'Plural News and Views on Sudan'. Accessed 27 May 2016. http://www.sudantribune.com/spip.php?mot1386.

The Guardian. 'Chad Refuses to Arrest Omar Al-Bashir on Genocide Charges'. 22 July 2010a.

———. 'Kenya Defends Failure to Arrest Sudan's President Omar al-Bashir in Nairobi'. 29 August 2010b.

———. 'African Union Members Back Kenyan Plan to Leave ICC'. Accessed 11 July 2017. https://www.theguardian.com/world/2016/feb/01/african-union-kenyan-plan-leave-international-criminal-court.

The Telegraph. 'African Union Agrees on ICC Immunity for Heads of State'. Accessed 11 July 2017. http://www.telegraph.co.uk/news/worldnews/africaandindianocean/10374538/African-Union-agrees-on-ICC-immunity-for-heads-of-state.html.

Thomson Reuter Foundation. 'Darfur Conflict', 2015, accessed 7 August 2015. http://www.trust.org/spotlight/Darfur-conflict.

Trautman, Lawrence J., and Maia McFarlin. 'Putin, Russia and Ukraine: International Human Rights Violations, War Crimes, & Future Implications'. SSRN Scholarly Paper. Rochester, NY, 20 March 2023.

Ukrinform. 'President Zelenskyy: We Must Return and Will Return All Our People from Russian Captivity', 6 May 2023. https://www.ukrinform.net/rubric-ato/3705755-president-Zelensky-we-must-return-and-will-return-all-our-people-from-russian-captivity.html.

———. 'National Information Bureau Received Almost 19,000 Capture and Deportation Reports in April', 8 May 2023. https://www.ukrinform.net/rubric-society/3705814-national-information-bureau-received-almost-19000-capture-and-deportation-reports-in-april.html.

UNICEF. 'Statement on the Humanitarian Situation in Darfur' 2015, accessed 3 December 2015. http://www2.unicef.org:60090/spanish/media/media_48507.html.

United States Department of State. 'Secretary Antony J. Blinken on Russia's Threat to Peace and Security at the UN Security Council', 2022, accessed 28 June 2023a. https://www.state.gov/secretary-antony-j-blinken-on-russias-threat-to-peace-and-security-at-the-un-security-council/.

———. 'War Crimes by Russia's Forces in Ukraine', 2022, accessed 28 June 2023b. https://www.state.gov/war-crimes-by-russias-forces-in-ukraine/.

Van, der Vyver Johan D. 'Prosecuting the President of Sudan : A Dispute between the African Union and the International Criminal Court: Recent Developments'. *African Human Rights Law Journal* 11, no. 2 (January 2011): 683–98.

Warburton, Moira, and Viktor Chernii. 'U.S. Senate Unanimously Condemns Putin as War Criminal', *Reuters,* 16 March 2022.

Watts Roba Gibia Nyirigwa. 'Why All These Dispute between Bashir and Taha?' *Sudan Tribune*, 30 March 2006.

Wegner, Patrick S. *The International Criminal Court in Ongoing Intrastate Conflicts: Navigating the Peace-Justice Divide.* Cambridge University Press, 2015.

Wheeler, Nicholas J., and Timothy Dunne. 'Hedley Bull's Pluralism of the Intellect and Solidarism of the Will'. *International Affairs* 72, no. 1 (1 January 1996): 91–107.

Wintour, Patrick, and Patrick Wintour Diplomatic editor. 'Nato Members May Send Troops to Ukraine, Warns Former Alliance Chief'. *The Guardian*, 7 June 2023a, sec. World news. https://www.theguardian.com/world/2023/jun/07/nato-members-may-send-troops-to-ukraine-warns-former-alliance-chief.

———. 'West May Have to Negotiate with Putin as Well as Pursue War Crimes Trial, Macron Says'. *The Guardian*, 31 May 2023b, sec. World news. https://www.theguardian.com/world/2023/may/31/macron-to-call-for-european-strategic-awakening-after-ukraine-invasion.

Yaman, Dilara Karmen. 'Heads of States Before the ICC: On the Arrest Warrant against Putin and Its Consequences'. *Völkerrechtsblog*, 5 April 2023.
Zengerle, Patricia, and Patricia Zengerle. 'U.S. Lawmakers Join Calls for War Crimes Probe of Russia'. *Reuters*, 2 March 2022, sec. United States. https://www.reuters.com/world/us/us-lawmakers-join-calls-war-crimes-probe-russia-2022-03-02/.

CHAPTER 6

Conclusions

The 1648 Treaty of Westphalia has been considered by many as the historical event on which contemporary international politics was founded. Among other provisions, the Treaty sanctified the existence of states, and the notion that in international politics no actor can undermine their authority. A variety of subsequent treaties, from Utrecht (1713) to the UN Charter (1945), glorified such a notion, fuelling the idea that international politics is based on two basic rules: sovereignty and non-intervention. This book explored the implications associated with the attempts at eroding these fundamental normative pillars of international politics, by investigating the limitations, obstacles, and prospects of the practice of prosecuting SHoS. The book started with a discussion on how revolutionary this practice is, considering the normative fabric of international politics, and the ramifications that this might have for international law. It is tempting to consider international law as a constitutive element of international politics, claiming that international laws shape the behaviour of actors encouraging them to restrain from criminal behaviour which includes the four crimes that the ICC has jurisdiction on: genocides, war crimes, human rights' violations, and the crime of aggression. This consideration however must come to terms with the idea that the role of the state envisioned by Thomas Hobbes, a state whose primary function is to preserve the security of its citizens by establishing rules that prevent the escalation of intra-state conflicts, is challenged precisely by the existence of

M. Cacciatori, *The International Criminal Court and the Prosecution of Sitting Heads of State*,
https://doi.org/10.1007/978-3-031-54646-4_6

those four crimes that the ICC is tasked with prosecuting. In some of the instances explored in this book, the state is allegedly the primary culprit, or at least complicit in, the creation of an environment that threatens the security of its citizens. The question then becomes, *quis custodiet ipsos custodes*? Who protects citizens from their protectors?

After more than 20 years of operations, the ICC has scrutinised 31 cases, its judges have issued 40 arrest warrants and 9 summonses to appear; 21 people have appeared before the Court—resulting for the time being in 10 convictions and 4 acquittals. Among these, no trial involving a SHoS has ever been completed. It is important to now recall that the purpose of this book is not to scrutinise the ICC as a whole institution, nor is it to say that more convictions necessarily mean more effectiveness. The ICC is a Court of last resort and only deals with situations that are immensely problematic so, in a way, the fact that the Court was able to finish proceedings for 14 individuals in 20 years is an impressive feat *per se*. However, in the domain of prosecuting SHoS, the Court has not been effective so far, and three systemic characteristics have emerged from the dissection of the situations presented in this book:

1. Domestic resistance to SHoS prosecutions has to be assumed, as no government would willingly cooperate in its own prosecution;
2. The likelihood of regional opposition to such actions is significant when states are tasked with executing warrants of arrest against the SHoS of another sovereign nation, as the fear of potential conflict can be exploited as a justification, even by members of the Rome Statute, not to comply with the ICC's mandate;
3. International resistance is possible, as long as the practice of prosecuting SHoS is perceived as an imposition of Western ideas of justice and a tool for Western states to justify their imperial aspirations.

This book has explored six cases in which, directly or indirectly, the ICC was involved in a situation potentially involving a SHoS. Below, is a brief summary of each case presented in a chronological rather than thematic manner.

Summary of the Cases

The case of **Uganda** has been included in this book, despite not involving a prosecution of a SHoS, to illustrate how power-dynamics between the ICC and the host-state of an investigation can shape the efforts of the

Court towards accountability. In Chap. 3 the book explored such dynamics, and namely how the fact that the Museveni government self-referred the situation to the ICC, and the subsequent decision of the Prosecutor only to indict LRA commanders shielding, *de facto*, governmental actors has spurred considerable debate among academics, commentators, and practitioners. The case of Uganda shows that the fact that the ICC often requires the cooperation from local authorities can be a severe hindrance in the Court's quest for legitimacy and transparency. Furthermore, the intermittent support that Museveni and his government granted to the Court throughout the years hints at the fact that the cooperation between the ICC and local authorities is likely to be always subjugated to time and context-specific domestic political goals. A full ICC investigation takes years to complete, and, in the meantime, a government can decide to withdraw its support if the Court is suddenly perceived to be acting in opposition to domestic interests. This is indicative of the fact that states are often going to have a good leverage on a cooperative relationship between them and the Court.

The trajectory of the ICC in **Sudan** has been dramatically different to what happened in Uganda. For the first time the Court issued, in 2009, two warrants for the arrest of a SHoS, Omar al Bashir. In Chap. 5 it is shown how the situation remained static for years, with the former President attacking openly the Court for being a neo-imperialist tool while visiting state members to the Rome Statute, which didn't comply with their obligation of surrendering Al Bashir to the Court. These developments coincided with a progressive harshening of the authoritarian conditions of the country, including cabinet reshuffles to replace more moderate voices with hardliner loyalists of the Al Bashir government, and the tightening of the governmental grip on international NGOs. The case of Sudan is in many ways the diametric counterpart to the Museveni case in Uganda. By directly acting against a SHoS, the ICC implicitly acknowledged the impossibility of any form of cooperation between the Court's efforts and domestic authorities. In the absence of this cooperation, and by not receiving any direct support from the UN towards an accountability mechanism for Al Bashir aside from the UNSC referring the case to the Court, the investigation was derailed. Even after the 2019 *coup d'état*, the debate about sending Al Bashir to face trial permeated domestic dynamics in the country, without ever amounting to the former President being present in front of the judges at The Hague at the time of writing this book.

The question of prosecuting SHoS re-emerged potently when the ICC decided to act *propio motu* to investigate the escalation of post-electoral violence in **Kenya** in 2010. Uhuru Kenyatta, one of the main suspects in this escalation, was not President of the country when the investigation started. However, by skillfully exploiting the Court's investigation to boost his internal support via a mixture of anti-imperialist claims and allegations of international meddling in Kenyan internal affairs, he was able to secure the Presidency. Chapter 3 has shown how the ICC efforts have been one of the crucial components of the Presidential campaign, also contributing to the creation of an unlikely alliance between Kenyatta and Ruto, another suspect summoned to appear in front of the ICC in 2014. This political strategy paid off, and not only Kenyatta became President while being formally investigated by the Court, but he was also able to derail the ICC's investigation as soon as he was elected President. The situation in Kenya also echoed what happened in Sudan in terms of governmental backlash against NGOs. More than 500 were exiled from the country as soon as Kenyatta was elected. So, the ICC seems to have contributed to the creation of the Jubilee Alliance between Kenyatta and Ruto, giving the duo a powerful rhetorical strategy that aided them in their quest for power. This suggests that ICC investigations can become strategic tools in the hands of local politicians who, on one side, know that accessing positions of power will implicitly make a prosecution impossible.

The above are situations in which the international community was not particularly proactive in aiding the Court's efforts towards accountability. In many ways, the ICC was left alone to investigate incredibly complex circumstances, without an active aid by the international community. To a certain extent, and in the eyes of some commentators, the contours of the investigation in **Libya** were quite different, and they are explored in Chap. 4. In 2011 the Court released a warrant for the arrest of former Libyan President Gaddafi. Meanwhile, following various threats that Gaddafi made towards Libyan citizens, the UNSC, acknowledging the historical Russian and Chinese abstentions, passed a resolution that has been perceived as paving the way for a military intervention under the NATO umbrella. This was led by the UK and France, with the US in the background. The Court has constantly been criticised for lacking the coercive power to enforce its rulings. In Libya this coercive power was granted by the NATO military intervention. In October 2011 Gaddafi was killed and his regime was toppled. However, the dubious results of these combined efforts, that led to a significant increase in civilian fatalities and the overall disintegration of Libya, questioned not only the effectiveness of foreign military interventions to restore peace in conflict situations, but also sparked a heated debate about the role of the ICC in legitimising the use of force in such contexts. After all, if an individual on whose head a warrant of the arrest is pending refuses to give up power, what other choice does the international community have? Answering this question would provide with an insight on the moral compromises that the international community is willing to make to ensure that alleged criminals are removed from positions of power.

These doubts infused the entire debate about prosecuting Bashar al Assad for the escalation of governmental violence against the citizens of **Syria**, also addressed in Chap. 4. This is the second scenario in which the book doesn't discuss an actual prosecution of a SHoS, and was included to show how these are inherently shaped by great power-dynamics that not only determine the support that the ICC receives once a prosecution started, but also that this can be halted by the UNSC when the alleged crimes are committed on the ground of states that are not party to the Rome Statute. In other terms, if in Uganda the Court decided not to prosecute Museveni and governmental forces, in Syria such a decision resulted from a deadlock of the UNSC, with Russia and China vetoing the resolution to refer the case to the Court. Naturally, the way in which the events unfolded in Libya had a crucial impact on the Syrian case, as did the political inclinations that tied Damascus to Moscow. However, it is fundamental to highlight that the practice of prosecuting SHoS is not only inextricably linked with the idea that the Court must operate against the will of local authorities but, in many cases, also in the context of a fragmented international community in which great powers fight their battles within the UNSC. And given the recent turn of events, this is only likely to get progressively more acute in the coming years.

Chapter 5 dealt with the very recent involvement of the ICC in **Russia**. Because of the novelty of the issue, it is impossible to predict if and how the release of the arrest warrant against Putin will influence the Russia-Ukraine war. This difficulty is further exacerbated by the fact that the Court for the first time openly moved against one of the most powerful men in international politics and a permanent member of the UNSC. Even though any prediction would be incredibly speculative, certain specific issues have already emerged in the Russian context. First, some of the most vocal actors demanding for the prosecution of the Russian President, namely the US, the UK, and France, have openly antagonised the ICC in the past, exposing a certain degree of hypocrisy by doing so. This, naturally, galvanises anti-ICC narratives emerging from Russia and its allies. Only supporting the Court when it seems profitable for the political goals of these states is likely to reinforce anti-imperialist rhetoric that has plagued the ICC since it went after its first SHoS. Second, it is necessary to reflect on the fact that the idea of universal jurisdiction is bound, for the ICC, to the cooperation between the Court and the UNSC. Now that one of the P-5 is under scrutiny, the likelihood of any case being referred via the UNSC seems utopic—at least for the foreseeable future. Admittedly some of the cracks in the relationship already emerged with the discussion on the potential prosecution of Assad, but they are certainly aggravated by the situation in Russia.

SHoS Prosecutions, the Dilemma of Local Cooperation, and the Democracy Paradox

One of the issues that emerges more potently when looking at all six cases presented in the book is the fact that the ICC often necessitates the cooperation of local authorities to deliver on its mandate. This is recognised in the Rome Statute's Principle of Complementarity and is what lies behind the definition of the Court as an instrument of last resort for states that are incapable or unwilling to prosecute criminals. This, the book argues, is linked with the democracy paradox that postulates that while ICC actions should promote democracy locally by establishing the rule of law, they can also be exploited by local authorities to consolidate their (often authoritarian) grip on the country under investigation. Naturally, the reasons why a state might decide to cooperate with the Court, to the point of referring itself to its scrutiny, are varied and heterogeneous. Sometimes, like the case of Uganda, even questionable. When the Museveni government started its profitable relationship with the ICC many suggested that this was done to prevail on the LRA rebel group, which had escaped governmental retaliation for more than 15 years. The fact that allegedly to ensure the longevity of this cooperation the ICC only focused on LRA commanders excluding Museveni and his colleagues from prosecution raised doubts about how impartial a proceeding can be if the ICC strikes a deal with one of the parties involved in the crimes under investigation. The case of Uganda has also shown a variety of local practices that focus more on restorative approaches that do not envisage punishment in the same manner that the ICC conceptualises it. This is undoubtedly an obstacle that the Court needs to consider carefully in the future, because there seems to be a discrepancy between the fact that states adhered to the Rome Statute, but local communities might reject international notions of criminal accountability. Overall, this case exemplified all the practical difficulties that the Court has when it becomes entangled in contexts in which the government is allegedly among the culprits of an escalation of intra-state violence and poses an important dilemma: can the ICC sacrifice impartiality to ensure an effective prosecution of some of the perpetrators of the crimes it was set up to prosecute?

An alternative approach is to refute any cooperation with local authorities when these are accused of heinous crimes. And this encapsulates all the cases in which the ICC attempts at prosecuting a SHoS. Such cases, perhaps more importantly, create situations in which states are manifestly unwilling to carry out prosecutions for the crimes covered by the Rome Statute. It can be safely assumed that in these instances states are going to oppose the Court. In other words, it seems unquestionable that a government whose Head is being prosecuted by the ICC will not be cooperative. This was evident in the Kenyan case, where the ICC acted *proprio motu* and ended up summoning to appear Kenyatta—who became President of the country in 2013. Initially Kenyatta cooperated with the Court and even faced travelled to The Hague. However, through an inflammatory rhetorical strategy that depicted the ICC and its supporters as neo-imperialist forces and international spies, he was able to derail the prosecution and remained solidly President. The cases of Uganda and Kenya, if anything, suggest that the support that the host of an investigation is granting the Court is conditional on the specific circumstances that define the prosecution, and this support is not perennial but subject to constant governmental consideration and, as such, cannot be assumed. The other side of the coin of these considerations is that the inability of the ICC to enforce its provisions against SHoS might send a dangerous message to SHoS involved in an internal struggle of power. In fact, if a SHoS knows that the only way in which he or she will face prosecution is by losing power, is there anything off the table to maintain it? Or to access it? In Kenya the investigation against Kenyatta and Ruto was a crucial consideration why the two felt the imperative to win the 2013 elections—so it doesn't seem far-fetched to suggest that SHoS will use anything at their disposal to win an internal conflict to avoid international prosecution. The cases of Uganda and Kenya seem to sustain that the existence of the democracy paradox has profound implications for the formation of domestic policies. In some cases, it can be argued, ICC actions can shape the outcomes of intra-state political processes. In Uganda this has happened through an implicit legitimisation of the Museveni government. In Kenya, ICC actions have favoured and perhaps encouraged the formation of the Jubilee Alliance that was to dominate the Kenyan political sphere for more than ten years.

SHoS Prosecutions, Coercion, and the Enforcement of Justice Paradox

Cooperation with authorities that are hosts to ICC investigations is only one piece of the mosaic. Cooperation with the Court can, and in specific cases should, be granted also by other signatories to the Rome State and the international community. Nonetheless, as already noted in Chap. 1, there seems to exist a legal and political tension between the idea of prosecuting SHoS and this form of cooperation. While Art.27 of the Rome Statute suggests that nobody is exempt from ICC prosecution for genocide, war crimes, and gross human rights violations, Art.98 requires the Court not to issue requests for cooperation that would result in member-states violating pre-existing obligations to provide immunities under customary international law, and international humanitarian law. This issue resurfaced potently both in Libya and Syria.

The Libyan situation was referred to the ICC by the UNSC, triggering legal compliance with the arrest warrant by all members of the UN, not just states that ratified the Rome Statute. In the events that characterised the Western intervention against the Gaddafi regime, the ICC became inextricably linked with the military intervention led by the UK and France under the NATO umbrella. The disastrous consequences of international efforts in Libya, and the way in which they constituted a benchmark for the non-Western refusal of a similar approach to Syria, indicate that the enforcement of justice paradox can be used as a conceptual lens to understand the complications of linking ICC actions with the threat of punishment for non-cooperative governments. The escalation of violence in Libya after the release of the warrant for the arrest of Muammar Gaddafi does indicate, in fact, that the threat of coercive force doesn't encourage governments under scrutiny to abandon their criminal ways, but rather galvanises their willingness to remain in power whatever the cost. This is because remaining in power is the easiest way to avoid the punishment that they are threatened with. Because the ICC often has to operate in the context of non-signatories to the Rome Statute, and because any form of credible international punishment has to be UNSC authorised, it is not surprising that the enforcement of justice paradox reaches its zenith when the Council is involved in either referring a situation to the Court, or legitimising the use of force against non-compliant governments. And this is what happened in Syria. The attempts to authorise an ICC investigation into the crimes allegedly committed by Syrian President Assad was vetoed by Russia and China that, two years prior, abstained from impeding a similar strategy in Libya. On one side, it is clear that Russia and China acted out of political opportunism to defend an international ally. On the other, the outcomes in Libya made the creation of a rhetorical space to justify the vetoes much easier. The bottom line seems to be that not only the threat of punitive action makes governments even less willing to cooperate with the Court, but also carries the potential of deadlocking the UNSC.

This also raised questions about the role that the warrant of arrest played in justifying this coercive strategy and *de facto* linked the Court with the taboo notion of regime change, in an international environment in which allegations of neo-imperialism leveraged towards the ICC by African states were already paramount. The question therefore is: how much is the international community willing to sacrifice to promote the idea that SHoS must face trial for their deeds? So, it seems that international support for SHoS prosecutions is either regionally subjugated to political considerations that make compliance unlikely, or internationally connected to contested practices of military enforcement that can amount to serious accusations of neo-imperialism. *Tertium non datur*. The ICC, however, cannot be faulted for doing what it was set up to do. It is up to states to ensure cooperation with an institution that they signed up for or, alternatively, that they do not exploit the ICC's mandate to justify military interventions that rest on questionable grounds.

SHoS Prosecutions, Normative Dissonance, and the Symbolism Paradox

The situations in Sudan and Russia seem to indicate that very few policymakers actually believes that issuing a warrant of arrest necessarily leads to a trial and a conviction of the investigated SHoS. So, what is the point? Some argue that it is to shine light on what's happening in a situation, hoping that this international attention would encourage the SHoS to abandon allegedly criminal practices. Others claim that this is done to restrict SHoS' ability to travel to certain countries, damaging their international reputation. It has also been argued that warrants of arrest could galvanise internal opposition to the SHoS and recognise the validity of internal demands for more freedoms and democracy. Finally, certain commentators argued that the warrants of arrest legitimise (and maybe legalise) international military actions to remove an allegedly criminal SHoS from power. These aims could lie at the heart of the issuing of international warrants of arrest but, as the book has shown, they carry some problematics. In the sense that while all these interpretations are valid, the book has shown, they are valid if the citizens of a country under scrutiny and states in the international community perceive the ICC as a global symbol of justice that should be normatively accepted. The symbolism paradox, however, suggests that while the Court strives to be perceived as such, its actions can be exploited by intra- and inter-state actors to challenge the Western domination of international politics.

The cases presented here, taken in their complexity, are illustrative of such a paradoxical interpretation, and indicate that there might be an underlying normative dissonance between established practices in international politics and the institutions tasked with their implementation. In other words, institutions like the ICC might operate in a context in which states' support for the norms that underpin them is contested. This is especially true for a practice like prosecuting SHoS—which aims at revolutionising the normative fabric of international politics by altering the value that states attribute to sovereignty and non-intervention, historically regarded as fundamental rules for appropriate inter-state behaviour. International institutions (laws, courts, etc.) are *reflexive* features of international politics. In the sense that they are derivations formalising the existence of normative patterns of behaviour that shape inter-state relationships. They are not, strictly speaking, *constitutive* elements of it. The polarisation of the debate on the erosion of sovereignty in favour of international criminal accountability for SHoS, is a manifestation of the divide between those who support this erosion and those who oppose it. Since the ICC relies mostly on the cooperation of those states under investigation to be effective, this normative resistance is severely damaging the efficacy (and reputation) of the Court. A deeper understanding of the relationship between norms and institutions is essential to grasp the role of these regimes in international politics, but also to sustain the identification of the value that states attribute to norms and how this is subject to alterations in the context of ever-changing international dynamics of war, peace, and diplomacy. This relationship is deeply related to a dialectic proposition that relates those norms that are perceived as prioritising order among states (sovereignty and non-intervention) and those that aim at establishing novel practices to ensure that states do not enjoy unquestioned freedom on how they deal with their citizens—like the practice of prosecuting SHoS. This proposition suggests that the need for order in ontological conditions of ethical diversity and anarchy might be undermined in the pursuance of universal ideals and norms. And this, in turn, confirms the existence of a symbolism paradox that seems to be unsolvable for the Court.

This book has indicated that institutions like the ICC galvanise dissent over the supremacy of certain revolutionary norms over historically established ones. In other terms, where the normative friction between two norms is particularly pronounced, institutions become *fora* to express dissatisfaction over the imposition of non-agreed-upon norms. Institutions like the ICC give dissatisfied actors a venue to express hostility towards the prioritisation of norms like the prosecution of SHoS. This manifested in several of the cases explored in this book, most notably in Sudan and Russia. It has been indicated that the resistance offered to SHoS prosecutions by non-Western actors can be indicative of the prolongation of the Revolt against the West. This is not to dismiss the fact that often these states act out of self-interest in opposing the ICC, but given the critical mass that composes the camp, this can't be taken lightly. When the self-interests of a multiplicity of states align in contraposition to the establishment of new normative patterns, they cease to pertain to single states or single situations and become issues that need to be debated for the conduct of inter-state relationships. Resisting SHoS prosecutions, in other terms, symbolically can mean resisting Western imperialistic tendencies that prioritise international quests of accountability over local and regional concerns.

The manifestation of such tensions emerged as soon as 2009, when Al Bashir visited several states that are party to the Rome Statute, and has been formalised by various international legal scholars, as well as regional organisations such as the AU. When the ICC reminded the governments of Chad and Malawi to comply with the cooperation requests with respect to surrender Al Bashir in 2012, the AU responded formally that such requests would contradict Art. 98 of the Rome Statute. Subsequently, when Al Bashir visited South Africa and left without being arrested, even though South Africa is a member of the ICC, local authorities justified themselves by resorting to pre-existing obligations that the government of

Cape Town had with Sudan. Various legal interpretations have been advanced to disprove the legal validity of this justification, mainly suggesting that the gravity of the crimes that the Court is set to investigate prevails on any agreement that states might have in place. Regardless, Al Bashir remained a free man until the military government that led the Sudanese coup jailed him for tax evasion. This suggests that if the legal aspect of the tension can be minimised, its political dimension seems unsurmountable for the time being. If states have cooperative relationships with the wanted SHoS they are not likely to arrest him if he visits on an official occasion. As such, claims that international arrest warrants restrict the ability of the accused to travel have to always be evaluated considering the attitude of specific states towards them. It might be that states act as safe havens where the accused can travel without fear of being arrested. Several African states have proven to be willing to play this role. In addition to this, the ICC has been involved in several situations that occurred in concomitance with peace-processes among warring parties. While the idea that ICC investigations might trigger an escalation of violence doesn't seem substantiated by current research (with the notable exception of Libya), it is also possible that SHoS prosecutions might persuade governmental actors not to engage or not to commit fully in peace talks. As exemplified by the Al Bashir case, sometimes the ICC is involved in very unstable areas of the world. The inter-state relationships in these regions are complex, and often rest on very shaky diplomatic agreements to promote and maintain peace between two or more countries. When the ICC asked countries neighbouring to Sudan to arrest Al Bashir these refused, adducing the justification that this would have compromised a very precarious peace deal.

On the idea that international attention might restrain a SHoS from his criminal behaviour, it has been shown how a warrant of arrest could have the opposite effect. By now SHoS know that the only way in which such warrants can be enforced in the absence of an international military action is if they lose power. This suggests, as happened in Kenya, that they might do whatever it takes to cling to power—making them even more dangerous. As for restricting the SHoS' ability to travel—it has been shown how this had limited effects in Sudan. While it is true that a SHoS is unlikely to travel, for instance, to Europe, it has also been highlighted how several countries are more than welcoming to host SHoS that are being investigated by the Court. This on one side symbolically signals a widespread non-Western resistance to the ICC and the specific practice of prosecuting SHoS. On the other it can be used by the SHoS to demonstrate the ineffectiveness of the Court and to legitimise claims of neo-imperialism—as happened with Al Bashir in Sudan. As for fuelling and legitimising internal support against authoritarian rule, the cases of Kenya and Sudan seem to show that this is more complex than issuing an arrest warrant. While it is difficult to understand if internal support for Al Bashir and Kenyatta was genuine given the context in which it emerged, the construction of a siege mentality underpinned by anti-imperialist narratives, the capillary hold that SHoS in these situations have on local media, and the disproportionate access to resources that governments have when compared to dissenting local actors, seem obstacles that cannot be overcome by ICC actions. Finally, the exploitation of arrest warrants to justify international military actions is unlikely to mitigate accusations that the Court is only a tool in the hands of powerful Western actors, especially if the latter only support the ICC and its SHoS prosecutions when it suits them. In Libya this has created a quagmire that the Court, and the international community at large, is yet to recover from.

Western policy-makers need to take these concerns, and the existence of the symbolism paradox, seriously. Clinging on an outdated view of humanitarianism is likely to polarise the debate even further and as shown when discussing the recent UNSC deadlock over Syria and Russia, this would ultimately serve to reinforce sovereignty and non-intervention—killing the prospects of a future for SHoS prosecutions. Revising their stance by acknowledging this would allow them to better understand the need to stop dividing the world between good and bad states, and reassert the centrality of dialogue in international politics. This, in the end, is the only way to challenge norms that have been in place for almost four centuries. On the other hand, non-Western policy-makers genuinely interested in promoting more humanitarian norms, need to consider the current standoff not as an ending but as a starting point. The risk of mimicking every humanitarian conception (such as global accountability or humanitarian interventions) as an extension of neo-imperialism, is likely to hamper the quest for more humanitarian norms. In the future there will be space for re-discussing the saliency of sovereignty and non-intervention. A more proactive stance by non-Western actors in proposing future normative trajectories seems the only way for compromise on these thorny issues. The political complexities that the book explored suggest that the idea of holding SHoS accountable for their crimes is indeed revolutionary in international politics and, as akin to any other revolution in history, it is facing formidable opposition.

Index

M. Cacciatori, *The International Criminal Court and the Prosecution of Sitting Heads of State*,
https://doi.org/10.1007/978-3-031-54646-4

The manufacturer's authorised representative in the EU is Springer Nature Customer Service Centre GmbH, Europaplatz 3, 69115 Heidelberg, Germany. If you have any concerns regarding our products, please contact ProductSafety@springernature.com

Printed and bound by CPI Group (UK) Ltd, Croydon, CR0 4YY
01/10/2026
02225903-0004